KU-790-904

Contents

Illustrations

(between pages 128 and 129)

My Mother
My Father
Off for a walk with Nanny, Pretoria Prison in the background
Mom, Poppy and me

Dad, Poppy and me
The New Hospital and our house, seen from the koppie
Pretoria Girls' High Tennis Team

James Stewart at a première – I am the fan on the right
Judge Brinton
John Murray in Cairo

Captain Pixie Benson
Alan Paton
Tshekedi Khama and Michael Scott

Michael Scott

Chief Hosea Kutako
Nelson Mandela at lunch in London, 1962

Chief Albert Lutuli
Walter Sisulu
Bram Fischer

Athol Fugard and Serpent Players
With Pa at Jan Smuts Airport, 1966

Acknowledgements

Once again, thanks to P.R. for her acute criticism and generous encouragement.

Lines from 'Simplify me when I'm dead' from *The Complete Poems of Keith Douglas*, edited by Desmond Graham, reprinted by permission of Oxford University Press.

Lines from *Cry, the Beloved Country* by Alan Paton reprinted by permission of the author.

Lines from *Four Quartets* by T. S. Eliot reprinted by permission of Faber and Faber Ltd.

Lines from *The Life of Galileo* by Bertolt Brecht reprinted by permission of Methuen, London.

An adapted version of the chapter on Bram Fischer was published in *Granta* No. 19 as 'A True Afrikaner', and the chapter on Alan Paton, slightly abridged, appeared in *The Southern African Review of Books*, Summer 1988, as 'Recollecting Alan Paton'.

Glossary

braaivleis	barbecue
brak	mongrel
doek	headscarf
dompas	damned pass
kloof	ravine
krans	cliff
kwela	dance
landdrost	magistrate
lolwapa	yard
pondok	shack
stoep	verandah
takkies	tennis shoes
tsotsis	young delinquent

PART I
Escaping

And the end of all our exploring
Will be to arrive where we started
And know the place for the first time.

T. S. Eliot, *Four Quartets*

I

From Pretoria to Hollywood

At night when a summer storm crashed open our sleep and drove us from our beds on the verandah, my father was in command. Calmly, he let down the blinds against the beating rain while lightning forked and hail began to pound the corrugated-iron roof. Mom and Poppy and I huddled together on the box ottoman. 'Dad, come away from the window!' How reckless he was as he stood there, marking the seconds between flash and boom, with the lightning getting closer.

'Daddy, you'll be struck!' But from his vantage-point he reported, 'The street's become a river. Good lord, the railway compound's flooded. The natives are out! Just look!' Lightning illuminated black bodies, water swirling about their legs.

Next morning the natives were once more invisible behind the compound walls, only the street deep in mud. And we woke to the light of the sun, to a clear blue sky as always. Then I watched my father as he stood at the basin, shaving and singing:

> She told me her age was five-and-twenty,
> Cash in the bank she said she'd plenty,
> I like a fool believed it all,
> 'Cos I was an M U G.
> At Trinity Church I met my doom,
> Now I live in the top back room . . .

Smiling into the mirror as he made pink tracks through the white foam on each side of his Roman nose, telling about Ireland: 'We are descended from one of the kings. Yes, we were the O'Banaghans of Castle Banaghan in County Sligo. More than one of them was hanged.' It was years before I heard the joke about every Irishman being descended from a king. But I believed, for hadn't he frequented the Viceroy's receptions at the 'Cassle', as he pronounced it, in Phoenix Park, 'With the cavalry in full dress, Lancers, Hussars, Dragoons, their spurs jingling. And *Floradora* at the Gaiety!'? Then, with a flourish of hand and voice:

'Once upon a time, when I was a boy at my father's school, I fell from the topmost branch of the old elm tree and broke my arm!'

'Broke your arm!'

'That was before I Knew the Truth.'

The Truth. Perhaps only an Irishman could at the same time be an ardent Christian Scientist *and* Secretary of a hospital. In those early years he'd even converted the matron of the hospital.

Before breakfast he sat with his Bible and *Science and Health with Key to the Scriptures*. Mrs Mary Baker Eddy, I wondered, could she be married to God? Motes of dust danced in the sunlight flooding through the study window. 'Thy kingdom is come.' He sounded confident. 'Thou art ever-present.' Mrs Joubert, who looked like a raisin-eyed Pekinese in black velvet toque and who owned a wireless with morning-glory horn, had actually met Mary Baker Eddy.

The hooter sounding from the railway yards across the street told it was time for breakfast. After bending his close-cropped handsome head for a final silent communing with God, he rose refreshed, tall and smiling. Soon he would choose a rosebud for his buttonhole as he went through the garden to his office. In Pretoria he was known as Mr Benson of the Hospital.

He doted on me, of that there was no doubt, and I on him. In family quarrels he and I ganged up on my mother and Poppy. 'Pix and I, we're such pals!' he liked to say, and I was an eager accomplice, reciting phrases from Mrs Eddy's works for visiting Christian Science lecturers and, when leading ladies from *Queen High* and *No, No, Nanette* were brought home to tea, entertaining them with my cartwheels and backbends.

He played tennis, at which he was a wizard, slicing the ball this way and that and cackling with laughter as his opponents ran hither and thither. My mother played golf. Year after year he drove Poppy and me past the cemetery, through Marabastad, the 'native location', to the West End Golf Club for the final of the annual championship. On the eighteenth green we awaited Mom's approach. A last triumphant putt and, after handing her club to the small black caddy, she acknowledged the applause – always modest, green eyes smiling.

She had been christened Lucy Mary, after one of her 1820 settler ancestors, but my father called her Kit. Her family had a propensity for irrelevant nicknames: though Dad's name was Cyril and he was dark, they called him Sandy; her sister Annie was Sal, her brothers Ernest and Cecil were Sonny and Jim; George was Jack and Ina was Georgie; Ronald was Dick and Robert was Dickie; our cousins Cecil and Campbell were Toetie and Tiny, while Thora and Mabel were Molly and Bobbie. Our favourite cousin, a lovely young woman with a gentle nature, was 'Bully'. As for my sister, Kathleen Ismena, and myself, Dorothy Mary, we'd been nicknamed Poppy and Pixie, giving an impression of affinity, but I, who'd been born when she was five, was a usurper and her teasing was a blight on my sunny days; if she and I touched it was by accident or in combat.

Our small brick house in the hospital grounds stood next door to the jail. Nanny – Mrs Eliza Miles, a Cockney from London, England, starch-aproned, snug-corseted, smelling of Sunlight soap and Reckitt's Blue – took Poppy and me for walks, through the front gate to the sound of loud Zulu gossip from Sam the cook and the 'garden-boy', and up Potgieter Street, past the red-brick turreted wall with its small barred windows from which black faces peered down. Then on we went, past the warders' houses, where black convicts hosed and mowed neat lawns, watched by a white warder who slouched over his rifle, to Magazine Road, where the Boers had stored gunpowder – might it blow up? – and across to the shade of gum trees lining the dusty track leading to the old Boer fort. Around us was the veld, with aloes and suikerbos and, mocking from a branch, a Pietmyvrou.

The prison was part of our everyday landscape. Warders' sons stole peaches from our orchard, a warder's daughter gave me piano lessons, we waited outside its formidable doors for trams into town. Long afterwards I learned that its bleak iron-barred interior contained the gallows, where many hundreds of black men and women, and occasionally whites, were hanged. We were surrounded by symbols of a system that was to become infamous, a system which I was to spend much of my life opposing and of which I was at that time totally oblivious. That small colonial prison has grown to be a vast conglomeration and, at its heart, political prisoners, black and white, are held. The open veld where Nanny took us for walks is now dominated by the Voortrekker Monument. Down Potgieter Street lay Defence Headquarters, where plans have been laid for the destabilizing of Namibia and the Front Line States. A few blocks away was a cream-painted building which by the 1960s had become notorious as COMPOL; behind that colonial façade Security Police tortured political detainees. On the corner where Potgieter Street meets Church Street stood the Dopper Kerk. There, on Sundays, to the tolling of a bell, grim black-clad figures assembled. Opposite was a low-roofed grey house, one-time home of the revered Boer leader Paul Kruger – a stern old rascal, it was said, but he'd give coffee to anyone who came along, serving it on the *stoep*, where two stone lions still keep guard. His grave in the nearby cemetery lies close to that of Verwoerd and other Afrikaner Nationalist leaders in what is known as Heroes' Acre.

In that forbidding corner of Pretoria our garden was an oasis. We looked out on jacarandas; their mauve radiance remains fixed in memory although they blossomed only briefly in October. A time of ignorance, if not of innocence. Photo after photo in the family album recording those early years has the same background: the high walls, the small barred windows of the prison and, in the foreground, our smiling faces. One photo, however, is different: aged about four, I am reaching up to Pumpkin the cat, who is sitting on a branch of a jacaranda tree; in the background is a corrugated-iron shed, Sam the cook's room.

In 1930 we moved to the north of the city, to Pretoria's imposing new General Hospital, which my father had helped design. Our big white house stood at the foot of a koppie. Before a tennis court and garden could be made, terraces must be sliced from the rough grassy slopes. One morning a van from the jail on Potgieter Street drew up outside our gate and barefoot, shaven-headed black men in red-and-white striped vests and khaki shorts clambered out to be ordered into line by a white warder with rifle. A foreman lit a fuse leading to dynamite packed into the hillside, shouted '*Pas op!*' and blew a whistle. Silence, then a flash and boom as rock cracked open.

As soon as the rubble subsided, the convicts, pickaxes against shoulders, trotted to the gash. Watching from the upstairs verandah, I noticed they had a bent-kneed, subservient trot. In unison they began to heave their pickaxes high in the air, to chant, before swinging down to cleave the rock; then they sang a phrase in deep-voiced harmony, heaved up, chanted and swung down. Again and again they repeated the routine, now and then pausing to wipe away sweat and snot, while I, a ten-year-old, observed their labour. This was the first step in transforming the rock-face into a garden, which my mother, aided by Cornelius, the 'garden-boy', filled with a profusion of flowers and shrubs. Soon peaches, figs, nectarines and grapes flourished in the orchard.

Climbing to the crest of the koppie, far on the horizon I could see the massive range of the Magaliesberg, grey in noon's stifling heat, purple at sunset, the intervening landscape bleak with its scattering of houses, mostly 'Poor Whites', here and there a windmill, a cluster of gum trees – a sight that symbolized history lessons in which time and again we had to study the Great Trek. The Voortrekkers, Die Volk. A professor at Pretoria University who dared to portray them honestly in a novel was tarred and feathered by students. The men who led the exodus from the Cape, from British rule – the freeing of slaves, the unfair method of compensation – their names now denoted streets and neighbouring dorps. In history classes they became a dreary litany: Potgieter and Maritz, Trichardt and Pretorius and Retief – Piet Retief, who with his followers was murdered by Dingane and his Zulu warriors.

> Dis donker, donker middernag,
> Nader kruip die Zulumag,
> Kruip swart adders om die laer . . .

(It's dark, dark midnight/Nearer creep the Zulu hordes/Black snakes creeping about the laager.)

That poem, learned at Afrikaans lessons, lodged in the mind. Like the 'Kaffir Wars' of the nineteenth century, which was all we learned about 'natives' at school, it told of something remote and exotic. It had no connection with small neat Alpheus, the new cook, in his starched white uniform, nor Cornelius, big and amiable in hospital uniform of blue blouse and shorts. We never questioned the ludicrousness, let alone the humiliation to them, of calling these men 'boys'. From the time I had learned to write well enough, if the rest of the family was absent, they would come to me: 'Can I have a night pass, please, nonnie?' Then I would spell out on a piece of paper: 'Please pass native Alpheus . . .', with our address, the date and time, and sign my name.

English poetry naturally moved me:

> The curfew tolls the knell of parting day,
> The lowing herd winds slowly o'er the lea . . .

I saw the ploughman plodding his weary way and felt the stillness of that world as it grew dark, a gentle darkness, melancholy.

After sunset on sultry evenings the first star appeared, then, in the sudden dark, the entire magnificent Milky Way silently exploded. I thought I felt the earth's turning, myself a speck on its face and it a fragment in the universe.

Yet I was quite unconscious of being a part of Africa. Perhaps there were whites, or Europeans, as we were called, with that awareness, but not in our small world.

We teenagers played tennis and swam, had picnics and dances, fell in and out of love –

> Heaven, I'm in heaven,
> And the cares that hung around me through the week,
> Seem to vanish like a gambler's lucky streak,
> When we're out together dancing cheek to cheek.

Did any of us know there was a war in Spain? If so, it meant nothing as we drove back from a party in Jo'burg at ninety miles an hour.

But I was determined to escape from a life centred on the Country Club. From the age of fifteen I had been making plans. Half-way up the koppie stood a big rock. There I sat dreaming of a future alive with possibilities. I might fly around the globe like Amelia Earhart, or play tennis at Wimbledon, or be the first girl to explore the South Pole. Above all, I dreamt about

Hollywood, about how I would become a movie star, because bioscope, ever since childhood, had been magical. I remembered going hand in hand with Poppy from the bright sun of Andries Street into the dark of the Grand Theatre, where ringleted Mary Pickford smiled and wept and Douglas Fairbanks leapt from balconies. Then, with the talkies, each Friday night in the two-and-tens at the Plaza, or the Capitol, which had wondrous Roman ruins under a fake starry sky, while the Wurlitzer played the latest hits, a prelude to the film. Films with glamorous stars: Garbo, Gable, Garland; Bette and Joan and Marlene and Mae; James Stewart and Katharine Hepburn; Gary and Cary; Fred and Ginger; Dick and Ruby and their wise-cracking sidekick, Ross Alexander – I cried bitterly when I read that he'd committed suicide.

Perched on the rock I could feel the heat of spotlights, could hear the band play as I burst into song – Noël Coward numbers, sung in clipped off-key imitation, or my *pièce de résistance*,

> Three little words,
> Oh, what I'd give for that wonderful phrase . . .

belting out the syrupy denouement,

> Eight little letters which simply mean
> I love yeeoouu.

While a Hollywood producer appeared over the crest of the koppie, exclaiming, 'You're the one I've been searching for!'

I wrote fan letters galore; the thrill of opening envelopes postmarked Hollywood – that paradise on earth – to find autographed portraits of favourite stars. Childhood's *Tiger Tim* and *Greyfriars* comics had been replaced by monthly movie magazines – that smell of freshly opened pages promising new treats. Dreaming, like so many teenagers; but I did have experience. At eight I'd played the heroine in a musical of Red Riding Hood, at twelve – in borrowed mortar-board and academic gown – I'd been Portia and at fourteen I had uttered almighty cries of horror as Macduff. Now I performed *A Midsummer Night's Dream* and *As You Like It* with paperdolls and flowers from the garden, studied Stanislavski and took elocution lessons: 'No, no, no. Don't you see? Oh, how wooden you are, girl!' Then, with school French, I attempted Sarah Bernhardt's greatest roles, *Phèdre* and *L'Aiglon*. I sent to London for a record of her 'golden' voice, only to be sadly disappointed by the high-pitched crackling rhetoric. After matric, with £8 a month, like other 'socialites' I counted banknotes in the Reserve Bank until I'd saved enough for the fare to Europe. My father, who had backed each stage of my plans, saw me off at Cape Town.

Over London the skies seemed to close in on the enormous, ancient city where unsmiling people passed each other by. One afternoon I arrived in Islington, numb with nerves, at the London Theatre Studio. In the glare of footlights, from an empty stage I recited set speeches from Shakespeare, feeling clumsy, my voice strained. From the gloomy auditorium came a voice, 'Thank you very much.' Michel St Denis's French accent. 'We'll be getting in touch with you.' That would be George Devine. I knew already I had failed. Without the scholarship I could not afford to study at their school. I went through the stage door, back into the real world, and kept on walking, putting distance between myself and my failure, until night fell and I found myself in a street where strangers stared into lighted shop-windows: Oxford Street. Next day I saw three movies.

I stuffed the emptiness with food. Under the African sun my body had been lithe; now suddenly I was gross. To be eighteen years old, weighing 163 pounds, with the name of Pixie! Just another Colonial, seeking Culture. I took in every play, ballet and Continental film, did the museums and galleries, ate at Lyons or ABC cafés and, occasionally, with giggling attempts at vivacity, went to parties or weekends in the country organized for Colonials by Lady Frances Ryder and Miss MacDonald of the Isles from their house in Cadogan Place. But I had a streak of common sense. 'If I fail the audition,' I had written to a friend, 'I do not intend to struggle for years on the stage with no definite hope. I'm determined my life shall be eventful.'

Meanwhile, I took night classes in acting and mime at Miss Pickersgill's London School of Dramatic Art and twice a week, under an elderly, bewigged French instructress, studied fencing, retiring humiliated after breaking my foil against her leather-shielded bosom. Mornings were spent in the humdrum study of shorthand and typing at Pitman's College in Bloomsbury.

Lonely through a snowbound Christmas and New Year, I saw *You Can't Take It with You* five times. In an appreciative letter to its star, James Stewart, I confided that I had written to Admiral Byrd, asking to join his next expedition to the Antarctic. 'Tell me more about the South Pole,' Stewart said in his reply. I needed no encouragement and although the Admiral had ignored my appeal, I swotted up the subject in books bought at Foyles and irrepressibly responded to the actor's urging. The reward was another friendly letter, this time signed 'Jimmy' Stewart.

Before long I was bound for the States in a cargo ship from Liverpool, along with ten French fishermen in great woollen jerseys who were going to Nova Scotia. The captain said it was one of the stormiest voyages he had ever experienced. The fare was £15. A pilgrimage to the Mother Church in Boston, Mass., then across America by Greyhound bus, five days and nights, stopping for meals at drive-ins, changing buses at all hours in anonymous terminals, the continent blanketed in snow. At last we drove through orange groves and arrived in Los Angeles. I roomed with two maiden ladies, Miss Amy and Miss Louisa, in their wood-frame house at 1824 North Cherokee, up the hill from Hollywood Boulevard.

Even I had to admit that Hollywood was no paradise. The shops along Sunset and Wilshire seemed mere façades, like movie sets; the stars' homes in Beverly Hills, Bel Air and Malibu were not much grander than those of the rich in Johannesburg's Houghton. But it was all thrilling. Of course, I could not afford the restaurants I'd read about in movie magazines, the Brown Derby, Romanoffs and the Coconut Grove. I ate at drugstores, served by pretty girls and boys, all no doubt longing to be 'discovered', as once in my daydreams I had longed. Now I was content to be a fan and, perhaps, a writer; in London I had actually interviewed a monocled Rex Harrison and suave Conrad Veidt.

In those days 'I've come from South Africa' was an Open Sesame. That phrase had won a brief but, since I admired her above all other actresses, deeply affecting meeting with the reclusive Katharine Hepburn in Philadelphia, backstage after a performance of *The Philadelphia Story*. In Culver City the publicity department at Warner Brothers invited me to watch

Bette Davis and Miriam Hopkins rehearse a scene for *The Old Maid* and at MGM Woody van Dyke welcomed me – he was directing diminutive Mickey Rooney in an Andy Hardy story. But most memorable was the visit to Columbia, where the director I considered the greatest, Frank Capra – a small man with brilliant dark eyes, humorous and unassuming – had me seated beside him as he directed crowd scenes for *Mr Smith Goes to Washington*.

At night we fans were drawn like moths to the source of searchlights criss-crossing the sky, to throng outside movie houses for premières – Grauman's Chinese Theatre was the most alluring. Like children at the zoo we gawped at Marlene and Joan and Gary, at Norma Shearer, Margaret Sullavan and Errol Flynn, and at Barbara Stanwyck and Robert Taylor, wearing the fashion they had set of 'lookalike' check jackets. 'Dietrich,' I was to write somewhat patronizingly, 'seems the most beautiful now that she has gone "natural". Her suntan makeup and thicker eyebrows have improved her immensely, while her golden hair is glorious.'

It was the time of great comic radio-shows performed in theatres before carefully drilled audiences: Jack Benny with his wife Mary and Rochester, Charlie McCarthy and his ventriloquist, Edgar Bergen, Bob Hope, and Burns and Allen. Fans awaited them and their guest stars at the stage door. Our wants were modest: a smile, a few words from the objects of our worship. The other fans, gum-chewing bobby-soxers and the odd sailor, also wanted autographs, but I preferred to take snaps: of Cary Grant in brown porkpie hat, of Loretta Young, Robert Taylor, Deanna Durbin and the charming Brian Aherne, who interrupted a rehearsal to be photographed by 'the South African'.

When James Stewart approached I was wildly excited. 'Mr Stewart, I'm the South African girl you wrote to.' He had the greenest eyes. 'Yes, well, er – ' So his shyness was genuine. I was elated. Would I phone him on Monday at the studio, he asked. I walked on air.

During the weekend, an apparently nice and respectable man drew alongside me on Wilshire Boulevard and began to chat, drawing me out about myself and my travels. His reaction when I happened to mention James Stewart left me in a state of shock.

Speaking as if he had intimate knowledge, he said the actor had a dreadful reputation with women. After enlarging on the subject, he warned me to be very, very careful. I was far too innocent to see through his perverse teasing and by Monday morning was still dejected when I called the studio and asked for Mr Stewart. After a while a voice said, 'Jimmy Stewart here.' Thinking it a bluff, I angrily retorted, 'Well, it certainly doesn't sound like him!' His mumbled protest convinced me. He made some excuse about being too busy with the film to meet and I realized, hopeless idiot that I was, I had ruined everything.

But I was resilient. The *Outspan*, a weekly magazine published in Bloemfontein, paid £5 for my article. COULDN'T BELIEVE SHE WAS TALKING TO JAMES STEWART, read the headline: 'Amusing experiences of a South African in Hollywood'. Unashamedly I declared that I was a 'born celebrity-hunter'. Among pictures illustrating the article is one of Stewart arriving at a sneak preview, watched by beaming fans roped off to one side, among them myself, in flannel skirt and Prince of Wales check jacket, a replica of the jacket worn by him on that first ill-fated encounter.

Summer 1939. Across the globe the threat of war. I had 'done' Hollywood and set off by Greyhound for New Orleans, and from there by cargo ship down the Atlantic. Table Mountain. Pretoria station. Home again.

Many years later, while lecturing on the history of the African National Congress at the University of California in Los Angeles, I drove along Hollywood Boulevard and, a few blocks beyond Grauman's Chinese Theatre, turned left and up the hill. There the frame house still stood, although dilapidated, the palm trees each side of the front path bigger and darker: 1824 North Cherokee

2

To the War

During 1940 I got a much-coveted secretarial job on the staff of the British High Commissioner. One of its attractions was travelling between the Transvaal and the Cape, as the diplomatic corps accompanied the Government on its annual journeys from the administrative to the parliamentary capital. The war against Hitler's Germany and Mussolini's Italy had broken out and, remote though we were, the girls on the staff felt tremendously patriotic. In Pretoria we joined the Young Allies Club and danced with South Africans who had enlisted to serve in East Africa; in Cape Town we entertained British officers who passed through on their way to the Middle East. I longed to get away from South Africa, to take part in this great adventure. The chance came in August 1941. Women were wanted to relieve men from desk jobs in Middle East headquarters and, together with two friends, I volunteered. Joining the South African Women's Auxiliary Army Service as privates, we were known as WAASIES.

At Defence HQ on Potgieter Street we took an oath of allegiance to King and Country, and an elderly Afrikaner officer said he was very proud of us. For our part we were proud of our red shoulder flashes, which signified willingness to serve 'Up North'. We learned to salute. My friend Ranee, brown-eyed, thin as a lath, mercurial, thought it a contemptibly servile gesture and fled whenever she saw an officer, but I was dead keen and in my fervour even saluted a sergeant. Fitted with gasmasks, our Martian figures shuffled through an evil-smelling gas chamber. After a night in camp, under the command of two WAAS officers we were driven in troop carriers to Pretoria station; a hundred ill-assorted young and not-so-young women heartily singing, 'Ay-ay yippee yippee ay, We're going Middle East when we go . . .' A harrowing farewell of my family and we piled into the train. In Durban we boarded a ship from Britain – lower decks packed with Tommies, baggy shorts drooping over pale knees; upper decks reserved for officers, elegant, narrow-trousered, Oxford-accented cavalrymen and for the suntanned South African girls. From the dock crowds cheered, hands signalled V-for-Victory and a band played as we steamed away in the *Nieuw Amsterdam*, followed by the *Ile de France* and the *Mauretania*, transatlantic liners on the way to war.

Sailing northwards through tropical seas, we could have been in a movie. In a shady corner of the deck, a young lieutenant sat cross-legged at my feet, reciting:

> Remember me when I am dead
> and simplify me when I'm dead.
> As the processes of earth
> strip off the colour and the skin:
> take the brown hair and blue eye . . .*

Keith Douglas, thick hair tumbling over his blue eyes, was my age, twenty-one. Though flattered when he went on to read one of John Donne's love poems to me, I thought him too solemn and shy and had no sense of the complex nature of the youth who would become the war's finest poet.

Each morning we drilled to an audience of grinning cavalry officers. You must not think. If you thought, your arms went *with* your legs. 'No, Benson. NO! *Not* like a chimpanzee!' Deck sports filled the afternoons. At night we danced and flirted – it was sheer delight to be kissed under a starry sky while the blacked-out ship glided through a dark sea where enemy submarines lurked, perhaps.

But pleasure turned to sweating discomfort when we landed at Suez and, under a brassy sky, toiled westwards in an oven-hot train. Damp patches spread across backs and under arms, our wrists ached from waving off greasy flies. At last, silhouetted against the sunset, we saw black kites slowly circling high above palm trees, minarets and domes. We had arrived in Cairo.

* From *The Complete Poems of Keith Douglas*, edited by Desmond Graham, Oxford University Press, 1978.

Searchlights, reminiscent of Hollywood premières, criss-crossed the night sky as we drove through chaotic streets – bedlam pervaded by a spicy stink – to Sharia Champollion and the building requisitioned for our barracks. Past caring, we ate a bully-beef supper and then, four to a room, dropped into bed.

I was ardent, self-willed, full of energy and eager to work hard in the great struggle against the Nazi menace. Too naïve to realize that wars are not only about danger, fear and death, about high courage, self-sacrifice and comradeship, but also about boredom and inefficiency with frequent lapses into farce. 'You're a secretary, Benson? Well, "A" Branch in BTE needs a clerk.' In a small back room of the HQ of British Troops in Egypt, previously the luxurious Hotel Semiramis on the Nile, I addressed and licked envelopes under the watchful eye of a walrus-moustached corporal. Nearby, Ranee worked in 'Deep and Shallow Trench Latrines and Burials': for Other Ranks there was a coffin with a false bottom through which the body slid into the grave so that the coffin could be retrieved for the next incumbent; officers were buried in individual coffins.

We drew strength from each other, enjoying a youthful mockery of officious rules, sharing our bliss and our woes. Experiences that at the time were thoroughly disagreeable became hilarious in retrospect. Once a week in the vast parade ground of Kasr-el-Nil barracks we drilled to commands bellowed by a Scots Guards sergeant-major. He and I were pictured together in a Cairo newspaper: '*Qui est le plus martial?*' the caption asked, and our fame reached Tobruk, where, someone unkindly informed me, we had become a popular pin-up.

A swarm of tenacious street arabs pestered us whenever we emerged from our front door, shrilly demanding to shine our shoes, tugging at our sleeves until we bought their flowering plants, which turned out to be blossoms stuck in earth. As the blinding heat of siesta brought the city to a standstill, with animals asleep in their tracks, those urchins joined the multitude of pedlars and beggars slumped in any patch of shade, while we repaired to the delectable chill of Groppi's Rotunda, where khaki and RAF blue mingled with the fur coats of exotic young women who were escorted by tarbooshed gentlemen.

The novelty of being in uniform soon wore off and we longed to get back into 'civvies', but to be caught wearing evening dress meant several nights CB – confined to barracks. As a gesture of independence, but also out of vanity, I acquired a new uniform in pale-grey gaberdine with shoulder flashes to match my lipstick and blue-green scarf to match my eyes.

A colonel sent by the War Office in London to weed out shirkers toured the headquarters, questioning whether our jobs were really necessary. I was the only one in 'A' Branch to tell the truth: ignoring the Corporal's glare at this betrayal, I declared that mine took two hours a day. The reward was a transfer to GHQ Middle East to be 'shorthand-typiste' – nothing so grand as 'secretary' – to Brigadier Surtees, a thin, small man with brushed-back auburn hair and moustache. He was peppery but kind, and immensely efficient. At last I was doing valuable work, in 'Q' Branch, which organized supplies such as petrol, ammunition, water, food and mail to the army in the Western Desert; the greatest problem was the flimsiness of our 4-gallon petrol tins – the losses of vital fuel were immense.

The 'Cherrypickers', Dragoons and Lancers we'd flirted with were in that interminable desert, under the same bleached sky. They'd spoken almost with veneration of their regiments and the peculiar customs deriving from historic battles. Now, instead of horses, they were mastering tanks and armoured cars. Tradition, however, dies hard and it was said that some blew hunting horns as they drove into action against the enemy. Most of them seemed ridiculously young to be commanding other men. 'Desert Rats', they rolled forward in out-of-date armour to confront Rommel and his formidable Panzerarmee. At HQ there were rumours of battles, uncertain victories, possible defeats.

Whenever the fighting halted, exhausted, strained, sweating men poured into Cairo, wanting to forget what they'd just left, forget that they must soon return. Bathed and shaved, they turned up, boldly or timidly, at our barracks. When we arrived back from work in the evenings we found them waiting there, eager for female company. Even the least attractive among us was invited out night after night. Pretoria and Johannesburg were nothing like this. We were having the time of our lives; how incredibly fortunate we were to be *there*, and not in a boring job back home, or having to endure air-raids and the dreariness of rationing in Britain.

After the gritty oppression and smells of the day, jasmine scented the night air as we clipclopped in gharries down the sharias and around the midans in a city glamorous under the sapphire glow of black-out lamps. Unlikely Cinderellas, WAASIES had to be in barracks by midnight since late passes were limited.

While dining and dancing our partners joked about that other life, not the bloody battles but what lay between – the boredom, the brewing up of endless cups of tea and gyppy tummies from food alive with flies. One told of how, when the tension grew intolerable, they collapsed in hysterics: 'Almost wetting ourselves laughing,' as he graphically put it, 'only to be driven to despair at some cock-up in orders!' Remarks casually dropped in the conversation disclosed acts of reckless heroism. And when the brief respite ended, troop-carriers could be heard rumbling through city streets, transporting them back to the desert, back into battle.

In face of all they were enduring, it seemed unpardonable to frustrate their desire for sex, but I resolutely preserved my virginity. James, a lieutenant in the Indian Army, took me to lunch at the (White) Russian Club and afterwards, seated at an old piano in the sitting-room, played the *Appassionata Sonata*, only to find it was Beethoven rather than he himself who captivated me. Henry, a Master of Fox Hounds, whinnied feverishly when I said No. While Andrew, beguilingly sophisticated Hussar, left me speechless by his taunt: 'All you're fit for is a frigid clergyman!'

John Murray, bony and olive-skinned, handsome, was deputed to take pictures for the Army Film Unit of 'two Waasies in Cairo' and I was one. He photographed us in the Muski, in the great mosque of Sultan Hassan in the Citadel and over tea at Shepheards. Not only were we the same age, twenty-two, but he also was mad about movies. Dining at Mena House or waiting for the moon to cast silver light over the Pyramids, he was fun to be with, companionable. On leave he took a room in a *pension* and during siesta I could escape there, change into a dress and wash my hair, while we talked of our lives and ideas, books, the future – the films he was going to make when the war ended.

To him, as to Ranee, I confided my belief that I had fallen in love with a staff officer who from time to time had passed me by in the corridors of the headquarters. Probably in his early thirties, he was, I thought, wildly attractive, very tall and strongly built yet moving with a lazy grace. But he seemed to regard me with an amused detachment that was exasperating. I wondered obsessively how I could get to meet this stranger.

On John's last afternoon before rejoining the Army Film Unit in the desert, we found relief from the burning sun in a cool bookshop. Browsing among the shelves of poetry, we chose gifts for each other: he gave me a collection of Yeats's poems and I gave him the *Rubaiyat*. We kissed and he promised, 'See you on my next leave.'

A day or two later, walking away from the headquarters at lunchtime, the stranger suddenly appeared at my side. Would I mind if he accompanied me? He was intrigued to notice that I was carrying a copy of Yeats's poems. He recited something about swans wheeling on clamorous wings and my acute self-consciousness was rapidly dispelled by his warmth. With Ranee and a friend of his, we dined at Les Pigeons on the Nile. The following night we dined alone. It was not a question of losing my virginity; with Gavin I ecstatically abandoned it, but I was nevertheless astonished by the thought that I was his mistress. I had been brought up to expect that when 'Mr Right' came along, we would be engaged, then married. Gavin was already married. I tried not to think about his wife or the risk of becoming pregnant – the ultimate disgrace, which meant expulsion to South Africa.

The days took on a pattern: siesta together in the small hotel where he lived and then, after the evening's work, dining and dancing at the Continental, at the Auberge des Pyramides or the Hôtel des Roses. Sunday afternoon had its own ritual: leaving the barracks wearing an army overcoat to disguise my dress, I joined Gavin in a taxi; by the time we reached the exclusive Gezira Sporting Club – Out-of-Bounds to Other Ranks – I'd shed the coat and, as a civilian, could watch cricket with him and his friends, reclining on long chairs in the shade of flamboyant trees. He had a ribald sense of humour. I loved the sound of his laughter and watching him, dark head bent in concentration, as he drew witty sketches of who or whatever took his fancy. At dusk we drove back to the city along a Nile shimmering through rising mist, felucca sails drifting by like great wings.

June 1942. Suddenly the streets emptied of troops. Terrible battles were fought that summer. Rommel routed our forces, capturing Tobruk. Tens of thousands were killed or taken prisoner. Survivors beaten back to the Alamein line were strafed by the Luftwaffe as they retreated. Those who arrived for a day's leave were haggard and quiet; many seemed to be on the verge of tears. There was no word of John. When I visited wounded men in hospital, a South African had news of another friend, Brewer – tall, blond and cheerful. After killing four Italians as he single-handedly captured a machine-gun post, he had been badly wounded, his leg would have to be amputated; he'd just sat there, *laughing*, until he was captured by the Italians.

In the streets soldiers were spat on by Arabs. However, not all were hostile to the occupying forces at this moment when our defeat seemed imminent. Ranee and another WAAS who had been studying Arabic were suddenly visited at the barracks by their teacher, a dull little man who now moved them by his offer of refuge in his home should the Germans invade the city.

The Afrika Korps radio jubilantly warned the ladies of Alexandria and Cairo to get out their party dresses. The nights echoed with the wail of air-raid sirens. In a khamsin thick as a London fog, the enemy swept forward to within forty miles of Alexandria, 120 miles from Cairo.

At HQ we burnt secret files, code books and maps; a pall of smoke hung over the buildings. Yet it all seemed bizarrely unreal as, after siesta, Gavin and I continued to have tea in the garden of the YWCA before returning to our offices. Until, late on the night of 1 July, the WAAS were ordered to 'Stand by with full equipment!' All women were to be evacuated. There was just time to warn Gavin, who arrived as we were about to climb into troop-carriers, bound for a 'secret destination'. I ran towards him in the dark street, but even as we embraced an officer shouted at me to get on board.

A train waited at a railway siding. We were packed into third-class carriages already occupied by British nurses and, strangers propped against strangers, we travelled through the night. I woke repeatedly to wonder what was happening to Gavin, to pray that the enemy would not bomb Cairo. And where on earth were we headed? Dreading that it might be South Africa and that I would never see him again. It was early next morning, as the train halted at a siding for us to wash in horse-troughs, that a girl I hardly knew approached me with the words: 'I'm so sorry about your friend John.' She had heard from someone in the Army Film Unit that he had been blown up by a mine.

John dead. But he was so young, he had so much living to do. As the train rattled on under the unrelenting sun, his dying gave immediacy to all those thousands of senseless shattering deaths which before had seemed remote. I desperately wanted Gavin. He knew how fond I was of John, he would understand and would comfort me. During a stop for coffee I ran from carriage to carriage searching for Ranee, and, moving into her compartment, wept long and hopelessly against her shoulder for that lost youth.

In Aswan's Cataract Hotel, closed for the summer, mattresses were dragged from storage and laid on bedroom floors. There was nothing to do but stare at the dam below. I thought of Gavin and I thought of John – tall, lean, brown-skinned, gentle and generous. Of his ambition to make a great movie. Of his loving gaze that day in the bookshop, from which I had deliberately turned away. He had copied lines from my gift to him on the flyleaf of the Yeats, lines that had become unbearably appropriate:

> There was a Door to which I had no key:
> There was a Veil past which I could not see:
> Some little Talk awhile of Me and Thee
> There seem'd – and then no more of Thee and Me.

Within a day the Brigadier urgently recalled me from Aswan. Gavin and I were reunited. Lover and friend, he gave consolation, but all too briefly. He was transferred to Baghdad. His letters, illustrated by enchanting sketches, brought him a little closer.

The work became more demanding as Brig Q was elevated to Major-General and I, his Personal Assistant, to Lieutenant. It was thrilling to be part of the team – under a new commander, General Alexander – which backed up the Eighth Army's great counter-attack on Rommel's forces. Fresh equipment with

American tanks poured in, as did freshly trained men. Morale soared. On the night of 23 October 1942 the artillery of a thousand guns fired – an awesome sight in newsreels seen long after. Tanks and infantry fought their way slowly forward. The casualties were massive. Two weeks later came the break-through. Now it was the turn of the Allies to capture thousands of prisoners as the enemy was forced back through Cyrenaica, then through Tripolitania.

As an officer I was free of the constraints and the abnormal life of barracks, free to live in a flat on Gezira Island and to play tennis at the club. Among new friends was a droll commodore with a lively resemblance to Punch. I was showered with attention by top brass, they were sweet and avuncular. It all went to my head. Even Ranee lost patience at my capriciousness.

Gavin suggested meeting for Christmas in the Lebanon. I agreed. It seemed a wonderful idea. But as the moment approached, enthusiasm waned. Without the rapture of his presence, my own passion grew uncertain and guilt and fear of pregnancy were reawakened. At the last moment I telephoned him in Baghdad with a lame excuse. He did not write again.

I threw myself into superficial flirtations and my erratic behaviour culminated in a crisis when I overstayed a weekend's leave. General Surtees grimly pointed out the seriousness of going AWOL, especially during a war. He had no alternative, he said, but to order my return to South Africa. Shocked, I could think of nothing to say. Quietly but devastatingly he described a series of lapses in my conduct. With tears of contrition I appealed for another chance. Generously he relented.

The battle moved on to Tunisia. As the atmosphere calmed down, there was time for friendships to flourish. One was special and did much to restore self-respect.

'If you go to Alexandria, you must meet my father,' said an American I'd encountered in Cairo. And so, having arrived at a hotel in Alex, I telephoned 'Mr Brinton', who promptly turned up – a slight, unassuming man in his sixties, casually dressed in battered straw hat and plimsolls. 'I thought we might bum around,' he said, 'and go sailing.' He had a dinghy in the harbour. Only later did I discover that he was Judge Jasper Yeates Brinton, President of the Mixed Courts of Egypt – a great international institution embracing fourteen nations – and that he and his wife, Geneva, were renowned for their hospitality, especially to badly wounded men, who convalesced at their spacious house in Ramleh.

Whenever possible I took a train to Alexandria to stay with them. Even at midnight, the Judge would be waiting at Sidi Gaber station with a welcoming, 'Grand that you made it!' After raiding the larder for fruit cake and tea, we repaired to the library – in winter sitting by the fire – to catch up on each other's activities. When not translating Homer, he worked on a 'little edition of Horace for gentlemen'. The quiet library became a haven as he introduced me to splendid books, from Pater's *Marius the Epicurean* to moderns like Thomas Wolfe and Scott Fitzgerald. He allowed me to take books back to Cairo and, when I returned them, said, 'If I love to lend books, I confess to a weak joy at seeing them come back.' And he added that my high credit was higher than ever. Despite his shyness he had a great feeling for friendship: the ideal, he remarked on one occasion, was, 'To speak with one's real self to everyone, and with one's heart, fearlessly, to a few.'

Although physically and temperamentally a patrician, he shared a sense of fun with his wife, but she was more gregarious, a large woman, beautiful, with elegant hands. Irrepressible curiosity kept him young; he had a way of walking, fast and leaning slightly forward, as if eagerly heading for new adventures. Only recently he had been one of a team patrolling the entrance to the harbour at night in search of marauding Italian mini-submarines.

I was eager to move on and the Brintons, though 'very glum' at the thought, agreed: 'You should leave Egypt now,' said the Judge. 'The tide is flowing west.' It was painful saying goodbye to them when I succeeded in getting a transfer to the Anglo-American HQ in Algiers. Ever encouraging, he sent a touching farewell note: 'God bless you, girl. Keep up with your brave curiosity, with your gentle fearless daring.' He had two somewhat conflicting ambitions for me: to become a true writer and to play at Wimbledon.

Arriving in Algiers, I found the tide had already shifted to the north; soon I was on my way again, this time to Europe.

★

In Cairo I had met Brian Robertson when he was with the Eighth Army. He was a superb administrator whose medal ribbons testified also to great courage in action during the First World War. Tall and slim, with a fair moustache and shaggy eyebrows, he was regarded by many as stern, but I enjoyed his tart sense of humour.

When he sent for me during the summer of 1944 to join his staff under General Alexander in Italy, I witnessed for the first time war's wholesale destruction, the bombed cities and villages. In Africa one *knew* of the ghastly deaths of men killed in battle – the horrifying waste – but there had been little evidence of the additional havoc wrought among civilians, who in Europe struggled to survive among the ruins.

Physically, however, we were cocooned. Our HQ in Rome was established in the fascist ostentation of Mussolini's Air Ministry, where General Robertson sat enthroned across a slippery expanse of marble floor – he could not entirely suppress the sly expectation that whoever entered might abruptly skid into his presence. An Italian phrase embossed on the wall facing my typewriter enigmatically proclaimed OLTRE IL DESTINO – Beyond Destiny. Mussolini's Villa Torlonia had been taken over for our officers' mess and on occasion the General travelled in the dictator's luxuriously equipped private train. Our military presence imposed our alien language and customs. All the more memorable, then, was a moment of shared excitement at the opera, when Tito Gobbi's glorious singing of *Rigoletto* brought everyone, Italians and military alike, to our feet to shout for an encore.

As the armies inched their way northwards up Italy's difficult terrain, Alexander's HQ moved to the shores of Lake Trasimeno. The supporting staff, now also proudly wearing the sleeve badge of the Eighth Army, left the city in September. Together, Robertson and I were driven through a ravishing tapestry of vineyards and olive groves which throbbed with cicada. Gradually his alert features relaxed and as, dead tired, he dozed, I suddenly saw how vulnerable this commanding man was.

We settled into our new HQ in Siena, where I was billeted with British women in the seventeenth-century Palazzo Ravizza.

The General and his senior staff had a villa in the Tuscan hills, but he was usually with Alexander at the camp by the lake.

I had looked forward to the increasing responsibilities the job seemed to promise, but soon found that important subjects were dealt with by Robertson's Military Assistant. Searching for an outlet for my insatiable energy, a frivolous idea took hold of me. Brian Aherne and the great American actress Katharine Cornell had arrived in Naples with a production of *The Barretts of Wimpole Street*. Could I bring them to Siena? Robertson found the thought of my becoming an impresario quite comic. I promptly made the arrangements.

The day before company and scenery were due, the heavens opened. All aircraft, including the Dakotas I had organized to bring them, were grounded in mud. Somehow cars and trucks were found to transport them, and Flush the spaniel, from Rome. A drenched Miss Cornell, with her husband, Guthrie McClintic, was delivered at the theatre. When I introduced myself, she looked startled, then, laughing, explained. The invitation from a 'Captain Pixie Benson' had reminded her of receiving a letter from South Africa – 'What strange names parents give their sons', had been her reaction – and here I was, a young woman. It took me back to that letter asking for her advice, and to those early ambitions. Naturally, when Brian Aherne appeared, I reminded him of the South African who had once photographed him in Hollywood.

Over dinner the stars were getting on famously with a group of generals, but I was still out in the rain, trying to trace the car bringing two young actresses and, most important, Flush. It was discovered, in Pisa. Eventually, after what seemed an infinite series of mishaps, British troops in and around Siena were able to see and cheer this great production before the company set off to perform for the American Fifth Army in Florence.

Those rains bogged down Allies and enemy alike. With aircraft useless and trucks lurching as wheels revolved impotently in the heavy mud, supplies were drastically delayed. The Eighth Army had already been dangerously weakened by Churchill's insistence that seven divisions be transferred for the invasion of southern France. He spoke of Italy as the 'soft underbelly of the Axis', but the appalling conditions as our armies struggled northwards up that mountainous terrain made it one of the cruellest campaigns of the war. 300,000 men were killed.

Among them was Christopher Cramb – 'P.T.' Very tall, thin, with thick light-brown hair and greenish eyes, he was witty, sensitive, potentially brilliant. He remains forever young. I can hear his voice, see his gestures, his teasing grin – even from that distant past he has a marvellous capacity to make me laugh. Of all those friends from the thirties in Pretoria he was the one most likely to break from the mould in which we had been cast.

'You South Africans always think the grass in the next field is greener.' That was Brian Robertson's immediate reaction when I asked for a transfer to Athens since there was not enough work for me on his staff. By chance I had met a Brigadier about to organize desperately needed relief for the Greeks who was seeking a secretary. Robertson wished me well.

On a freezing winter's day in December 1944 I flew from Naples to Athens airport, only to be greeted by the sight of puffs of shellfire and the racket of machine-guns. To my disgust, a furious O. C. Aerodrome ordered me to return immediately to Italy, indicating as he did so two armoured cars waiting on the tarmac – Field Marshal Alexander and Harold Macmillan were about to climb into one. That, he said, was the only safe way of driving to the city, where British soldiers were fighting ELAS, the Greek liberation army. It was a controversial bloody little war, but I knew nothing of Greek history and politics or the anger aroused by Churchill's attempts to force the return of an exiled King who was widely despised.

I flew back a few weeks later to find the grass *was* greener; the five months in Greece were among the happiest of my life. The personality of my boss, Reggie Palmer, was written clear across his pugilist's face: he was tough but sunny and immensely energetic. From our pleasant HQ with a balcony looking across rooftops to the distant Parthenon, we worked long hours on the huge task of reconstruction, a task signified on our sleeve badges by a Phoenix rising from the ashes. German demolition of docks, railways, rolling stock and transport, the blocking of the Corinth canal and the mining of main roads, had not only brought industry to a standstill but prevented food from reaching people throughout the devastated country. As for inflation, one cigarette cost 100 billion drachmae.

From Lavrion in the east to Salonika in the north and Patras in the south, I accompanied Brigadier Palmer on his tours of inspection. Tough he might be, but he too was moved by the hope visibly stirring in managers and workers alike as he discussed plans for revival of wrecked factories. And it was exhilarating to drive to distant villages with Howard, an American friend who had sailed between islands in a small boat, rescuing Greeks at the time of the German invasion. He spoke fluent Greek. We took food to famished people with worn faces who emerged from whitewashed houses to welcome us. Each village seemed to have an inhabitant eager to tell us how he'd once lived in America. In Markopoloun everyone crowded into Harry Orphanos's small house for the unexpected banquet of turkey. As the retsina flowed they sang rousing Greek songs, to which we responded with a spirited rendering of a ballad Howard had just taught me: 'Cocaine Bill and Morphine Sue, walkin' up Fifth Avenue, two by two, Hi hi baby, have a little sniff on me . . .'

Parades brought excitement and colour to drab streets and in Athens one magnificent procession also inspired hope in the faithful. Escorted by Evzones and gorgeously brocaded clergy, Archbishop Damaskinos, the Regent, bore aloft a sacred icon from the island of Tinos. Its fabled powers promised a cure for the prevailing social and economic ills – ills which seemed not to affect the wealthy, who had somehow contrived to prosper. At lavish parties for officers of the Royal Navy, wives now danced with Liberators, while husbands sat like wallflowers, as no doubt they had when the Occupiers were their honoured guests.

Gradually the country began to recover. It was tremendously satisfying to be involved in such work after years of war's destruction. And there was Paul. When first we met – he had the office next door to mine – I thought him a shy, rather conventional man, certainly good-looking and able. In the evenings we joined others chatting in the bar of the King George Hotel, where we all lived. I discovered he had a sense of the ridiculous, unusually appealing in a man who was obviously as upright in nature as in posture. It was equally obvious that we were falling in love.

We became inseparable so far as that was possible and happiness seemed the natural state. We ate our lunch-hour sandwiches on the steps of the Parthenon, which glowed in the spring sunshine. We gazed across the blue-green sea to row on row of distant islands, purple on the horizon, and realized why people spoke in special tones of the Greek light, indescribably clear. We slept one night under olive trees on the great plain below Delphi. Whenever we reached the coast, we swam in a transparent sea.

But Paul was married. His wife was a Roman Catholic, which meant that divorce was out of the question. Besides, he was devoted to his small children. In letters home he tried to keep up the pretence of being a good husband. For someone essentially honest, it was doubly painful, the lies as well as the dread of hurting them. And I could not entirely suppress pangs of jealousy, however fiercely he insisted that, somehow, we would be married, somehow it *would* work out! While he, in his own moments of jealousy, could not forgive Gavin for 'seducing' me. But anguish, as it broke surface, was always suppressed by the intensity of our passion.

Easter and the scent of lemon blossom. In the Byzantine church where we stood, a mass of icons glittered in the candlelight and at midnight austere chants proclaimed '*Christos anesti*' – Christ is risen!

In May the war in Europe ended. We all joined the vast crowds celebrating in Constitution Square.

The Greeks, aided by UNRRA, were to carry on our work. A last day in Athens, a last lunch under a tree in the Royal Gardens. While Paul and I ate our sandwiches, a bird flew to a nearby branch and sang, more sweetly than I'd ever heard a bird sing before.

We were intrigued by what lay ahead. Under Reggie Palmer we were to be part of the first attempt at four-powered military government of a foreign city: Russians, Americans, French and British cooperating in the reconstruction of Vienna. That was the intention. The Russians had already made their presence felt: after conquering the city, they gained control of the zone immediately to the west and proceeded to obstruct our arrival. The village where we waited lay in the foothills of the Venetian Alps and when work was done Paul and I could swim in the clear waters of the Tagliamento. But one morning in my mail I found an unstamped letter, an anonymous letter. I felt the nausea, the horror of being spied on. At meals in the inn where we all messed I searched faces, wondering, was it you . . .? Paul and I no longer dared meet in the suspect privacy of our rooms.

It came as a relief when at last the Russians gave us the go-ahead and we could escape from that contaminated atmosphere. To our surprise their guards greeted our convoy warmly at the final road-block. Surely, this augured well? Interpreting for us was the Brigadier's deputy, Colonel Gordon-Smith, a delight-fully eccentric man who bore an uncanny resemblance to the White Knight in *Alice in Wonderland*. He had insisted, rather tactlessly, we thought, on sporting a decoration presented to him by the Tsar. With unconcealed mirth he told us it had been much admired by one of the guards. And so, in high good humour, we drove on into Vienna, Paul and I standing together in an open-roofed car, waving to people lining the pavements, resolute in our romantic idea of showing erstwhile enemies that the war was over. We had come to help renew a city which only recently had been shelled by the departing Germans.

We lived in what had been Richard Strauss's home. Paul shared the composer's spacious bedroom with another colonel, while I shared Frau Strauss's room with a young Englishwoman. It had been given to Strauss by a grateful Vienna in 1925, when the grounds on which it stood had been part of Belvedere Palace. It was probably there that he composed *Metamorphosen*, an 'elegy for the destruction of German culture', after American bombing had left the Opera House a burnt-out shell. From the garden we could see the ruined palace, the pattern of its formal gardens distorted by bomb craters and the litter of tanks.

Despite the summer sun the heavily Baroque city presented a sinister aspect – the blitzed streets piled high with rubble, at its heart Stefansdom Cathedral, charred and roofless. The Prater's big wheel, soon to be immortalized in *The Third Man*, stood motionless and silent where once shrieks of panic and laughter had mingled with the music of a carousel. The Danube was disconcertingly dun-coloured. Only from Leopoldsberg, high in the Vienna Woods, could one glimpse the city of Mozart and Beethoven in spires and coppery-green domes rising from thin mist. Through those woods hungry people dragged carts in search of fuel and food. Unlike the equally destitute Greeks, they proved reluctant to help clear streets or unload supplies from Allied trains.

Our team covered a wide field: from rationing to medical, legal, policing and religious matters, as well as art. Each of the four powers took it in turn to run the city for a month, working through its Mayor and Council. We got along tolerably with the Americans; the French were courteous; while the Russians kept us guessing – they could be aggravating, disarming, comic, baffling or, as we had already experienced, obstructive. No sooner had we settled in than they blockaded our rations. We were reduced to limited quantities of tinned M & V, an insipid stew of meat and veg.

Every day convoys of lumbering carts transported their troops through the city. In parades where each Commander in turn took the salute, they marched like high-stepping manikins along a street defaced by huge effigies of Stalin, Lenin and Marx. As for the classless society, officers treated the men like serfs. From Austrians we heard rumours of widespread raping. Their looting was all too evident: soldier after soldier flaunted half-a-dozen watches on each arm. We were more circumspect in pocketing enemy property: from my office I guiltily stole a lacquered Chinese inkwell.

But a discreetly amiable sergeant showed that individuals could be friendly whatever the political differences. He was interpreter to General Blagodatov, a plump man, watchful through pince-nez, heavily scented. At our regular four-power meetings I sat between Brigadier Palmer and this sergeant, who, on discovering how hungry I was, smuggled honeycakes to me under the table while our bosses engaged in discussion. I later shared these with the others in our mess. Encountering me on the stairs one day and making sure no one could overhear, he confided, 'If only you were Russian, I would have liked to marry you.'

Nor shall I forget the wife of a Russian from a different era, a pale, desperate woman who came into the office to beg for food, not for herself, she explained, but for her husband, who was ill. She was Romola Nijinsky. The Brigadier was too busy to see her. I had to explain to her that aid must go through city institutions, that there was no way in which we could help individuals. I had to watch while she struggled to conceal distress at my humiliating rejection. I'd read about Nijinsky, I'd worshipped that image which was given a semblance of actuality by André Eglevsky's performances in *Schéhérazade* and *Le Spectre de la Rose* in Pretoria's Opera House. Only after she had left did it occur to me that I could have smuggled something to her from our meagre rations. But I had not asked for her address.

The exquisite Kinsky Palace became an officers' club, where Paul and I could find relief from the austerity of our head-quarters. In a small circular ballroom lit by chandeliers, we waltzed hectically to the violins of a Viennese orchestra. But as our times alone together diminished, sexual frustration goaded me when he uttered those words that had become an article of faith:

'But somehow it will work out, we *will* be married.'

'Yes,' I now said impatiently, 'When you get a divorce.'

And so our moods, like those of the city, swung between despair and happiness. One Sunday morning while we were having coffee – a bitter brew of acorns – in one of Vienna's famed coffee-houses, we noticed crowds gathering in the street. For a military parade? we wondered, joining the throng. But no music sounded, nor marching feet. Suddenly from around a corner a brightly clad bicyclist flashed, followed by another and another – a bicycle race. As we too cheered and applauded, we marvelled at this sign of vitality when rations were pathetically low and food, even on the Black Market, so scarce that people could barely struggle through the day.

By autumn rations had been increased, trams ran again and repairs to the cathedral were begun, as well as to the Schönbrunn Palace and other historic buildings. The opera and ballet had already opened in the Theater an der Wien, where *Fidelio* had first been performed during Napoleon's invasion.

Meanwhile, an expedition set out from our mess, led by Colonel Gordon-Smith in an old Mercedes – our intrepid White Knight was hunting not for bees and mice but crayfish from the clear streams of the Vienna Woods, now glowing with colour.

Having trapped the creatures in jam-jars, we brought them back triumphantly to Strauss's garden. Under the colonel's supervision, a fine tree had been chopped down and, in its place, an oblong concrete pool had been constructed, specifically for the crayfish. Next day, the Commander-in-Chief himself, while visiting the mess, came to inspect our catch. Not a crayfish to be seen, not even a corpse. But the perfectly hideous pool survived, a memorial to British Military Government's brief reign.

The first light snow had fallen. Early one morning Brigadier Palmer called me into his office. As soon as I saw the expression on his usually cheerful face I knew something terrible had happened. Trying to be gentle, he told me that Paul had been ordered to return home on compassionate grounds. His wife had come to know about our affair and was ill.

The next day Paul climbed into the car that was to drive him to the British zone. Struggling to smile, we gabbled empty phrases about 'taking care', then, as the door closed on him, he leaned out to repeat those words which never lost their freshness: 'I'll love you always.'

'Yes, always . . .'

Affirmations left echoing on the frosty air as the car drove away.

From a snowbound Vienna I returned to South Africa's mid-summer heat in December 1945. The old life in Pretoria was ended, not simply because my family now lived in Johannesburg but because friends had been killed in action in the Western Desert, over the Mediterranean, in Italy. I did not yet know about the other role white South Africans had played in the war: the activities of pro-Nazi Afrikaner extremists, among them a man who would one day be Prime Minister, J. B. Vorster.

Once again I was determined to leave. I wanted to be near Paul. As soon as I'd earned the fare, I sailed for England.

Our first meeting took place in Paddington Station. Living outside London, he could risk a mere half-hour between trains. His wife must not suspect; he must not cause more pain. As we hurried towards each other, I thought idiotically how strange it was to see him in an ordinary suit. We kissed and sat side by side on a bench. 'I think of you all the time, all my happiness depends on memories of you,' he said. Hands clinging as once

40

our bodies had clung, we were silent, aware only of the joy and agony of stifled desire.

He had written to say he was trying to prove to his wife and to himself that he still loved her, and in an attempt to break away I had lied that I was going to be married.

We met again, in a park, again sitting on a bench, hand in hand, invoking that article of faith in face of desolation. When he left, I watched his tall, upright form hurrying away, his final wave, and heard again the echo: 'I'll love you always.'

In utter misery I set about finding a job that might distract and absorb me. The first attempt brought the discovery that I could still laugh at myself – it was my salvation. An old friend, General Dick Lewis, had become a director of UNRRA and readily agreed to see me. Wanting to impress, I dressed in my best suit, a bold pink and blue checked tweed. The jacket, with heavily padded shoulders, had been made by a men's tailor in Johannesburg and the skirt, with a tendency to slant at the hem, by my mother. In his office in Portland Place, General Lewis, a thin, acerbic little man, rose from his desk to greet me, but as I approached, he staggered back as if he were about to be attacked. Supporting himself against the mantelpiece, he gasped a greeting. Then, in wonderment, he asked, 'Is that a South African outfit?' When we had recovered from our laughter, he offered me a job in Germany.

In a country scarred by bombed cities, people existed like rats in skeletal ruins. From the pleasant town of Iserlohn our HQ administered centres for Displaced Persons throughout Westphalia and the industrial Ruhr. DPs: men and women, remnants from concentration camps and forced-labour units deported by the Nazis to Germany from Poland, Latvia, Lithuania, Estonia, the Ukraine and Czechoslovakia. And children, war orphans and those suitably Aryan who had been torn from parents to be adopted by Germans to augment the Master Race. It had been assumed that most refugees would gladly return home when they could, but when peace came, millions chose to wait and see. Only a lucky few succeeded in emigrating to the Americas and other remote havens. The rest, human flotsam, survivors of unimaginable horrors, were crowded into barracks or hutted camps.

We in UNRRA were an odd lot, a mix of nationalities as well

41

as a handful of British who had evaded military service and now were cashing in on the perks. My job was to liaise with Voluntary Societies attempting to fulfil the DP's cultural and spiritual needs. I was billeted with a handsome German family in their Buddenbrooks house near a small lake surrounded by woods.

Letters home recounted my activities and I am amazed, looking back, at the temerity with which I tackled problems: on a Monday in Lippstadt settling a dispute between a voluble, gesticulating couple – Mr Pan, a Pole, and Lieutenant Krawczyk, a Czech; on a Tuesday inspecting Polish Red Cross billets needing stoves; on a Wednesday attending an international YMCA/YWCA conference at Möhne See at which I was guest of honour, sitting enveloped in blankets to keep out the cold; on a Thursday arranging medical treatment for tubercular Polish prisoners. We were constantly racing along the autobahns, through the rubble of flattened Cologne, its two bridges a twisted mess in the Rhine, the cathedral a black shell, through Bonn and Bad Godesberg and across the Rhine by ferry to Königswinter and on north up the Ruhr.

But life went on and, paradoxically, there were occasional parties, a point-to-point with friends in cavalry units stationed in the British Zone, a dance in one of the DP camps, its pathos somehow accentuating the indomitability of the human spirit.

The sight of emaciated figures toiling along roads and up hills naturally distressed me, as it had in Greece and Vienna. I asked a Belgian driver whether he ever gave lifts to Germans. 'Never!' was his gruff reply. Even such 'fraternizing' was forbidden, but occasionally when alone I did so.

All the while the steady pain of wanting Paul, the guilt for what his wife must have endured, the jealousy, intensified now that she was pregnant. A letter arrived one lunchtime telling me the baby had been born. Paul added sadly that there was some defect. I found refuge in the woods and lay sobbing until tears dried in a bone-aching emptiness. And then I went back to the office, to the routine of other people's suffering. I could not shake off the conviction that the baby's defect was partly my fault. That night I wrote a letter that would end the hopes and fantasies, a final letter.

A railway station on the outskirts of a wrecked town, a

banner inscribed in Polish suspended across the entrance, red and white flags fluttering in the bitter wind. Drawn up at the platform, a train, branches of greenery stuck into window frames. Shabbily dressed DPs of all ages line up for soup or fuss over an assortment of suitcases, boxes and blanketed bundles held together with string, while khaki-uniformed UNRRA officials bustle about. A DP band, their uniforms a brave attempt at smartness, with white forage caps like something out of a Christmas cracker, plays furiously. Loudspeakers order the crowd into the train, where they pack every window. The band plays 'God Save the King', followed by the Polish national anthem; a whistle blows and, waved off by us from UNRRA, cheered by the Polish staff, away they go, mothers waggling babies' arms in farewell, young men saluting, many in tears, a few smiling.

This was but one of the weekly repatriation trains. Their destination – countries which had fallen under Russian domination. After those months in Vienna I wondered: to what have we encouraged them to return?

'I am trying to get on top of intense depression over Germany and Europe and suffering in general,' I wrote to my family. I decided to resign from UNRRA. 'Each day,' I explained to them, 'I meet a dozen people who have lost their home, their parents or a wife, in the most terrible manner, or simply haven't heard from them for years, and I feel so sort of inadequate, so ineffectual.'

Resign? Colleagues in UNRRA urged me to think of what I was giving up. Certainly, I was well paid – about £50 a month. But I felt I had reached a turning-point. Since I loved Paul, there could be no prospect of marriage. I must find a career.

I had no interest in going back to South Africa. While working for UNRRA it never occurred to me that millions of my fellow-citizens were treated like Displaced Persons in the country of their birth. When it came to racial prejudice I remained a typical white South African, little changed from my nineteen-year-old self travelling by Greyhound bus from Kansas City to Albuquerque and furious when a Negro had the 'cheek' to sit beside me. Or the twenty-year-old in Cape Town disgusted by the sight of Maori officers dancing with white girls.

Preparing to return to England, I considered the Judge's

abiding expectation – perhaps I should again try writing. I sent him an article I was rather proud of. With typical candour, he replied: 'It was good to have written on the atomic bomb – just to find out what *not* to write about. What have you got to do with the atomic bomb? You have never seen one. But what *are* you seeing, and whom, and what are they saying, and how goes your life? These are the things the world is waiting – unbeknownst to you – to hear!' But I was not convinced.

Perhaps, then, I should aim at a job in films – not acting, of course, but something that might lead to work on the technical side. I was still an unabashed fan, but also – despite the Judge's entreaty to be sure and have some fun – I was animated by an idea that films could help create better understanding between nations.

Brief Encounter was showing in the local cinema for British troops. Its echoes of my relationship with Paul gave added poignancy to a deeply moving film. And it was superbly directed. As soon as I had arrived in London, I wrote to David Lean to ask if he needed a secretary. He did, and within days I had the job.

PART II
Learning

3

Alan Paton

'There is a lovely road that runs from Ixopo into the hills. These hills are grass-covered and rolling, and they are beyond any singing of it.'

I read those words one momentous day in 1948. They still strike at my heart. Exile gives them added poignancy. Through its revelation of South Africa, the landscape, the people – the black people – *Cry, the Beloved Country* crashed open the mould in which my white consciousness had been formed. This complex and marvellous country was *my* country. The place I had found boring and kept running away from was my heritage.

One passage could have been about myself:

I was . . . brought up by honourable parents, given all that a child could need or desire. They were upright and kind and law-abiding; they taught me my prayers and took me regularly to church; they had no trouble with servants. From them I learned all that a child should learn of honour and charity and generosity. But of South Africa I learned nothing at all.[*]

The little I knew of the author came from the dust cover: born in 1903, he was married with two sons and for twelve years had been Principal of a reformatory for delinquent African boys. From London I wrote to tell him of the profound emotion his book had stirred in me, how I'd been unable to put it down – fortunately, part of my job in films was to read new novels. He must have received hundreds of similar letters and perhaps the clue to his response and the easy way our friendship developed lay in my mentioning that my favourite scene was the return of Kumalo to his village, Ndotsheni. 'You are right,'

[*] *Cry, the Beloved Country* by Alan Paton, Cape, 1948.

Paton replied. 'When I wrote it I knew it was the best, and as you yourself can see, it evoked the best and deepest language of the book.'

He relished sharing the news of its ever-widening success: a bestseller in America, where Princeton was using it for the History course, Yale for Sociology and Bryn Mawr for English; unanimous praise from critics in South Africa as in Britain. 'The plum I keep to the last,' he added. 'The *Manchester Evening News* says "Genius tells story of Negro". Isn't that nice, now? So you see, I had to tell you myself . . . That's enough, but I feel relieved, strangely enough for your sake as well as my own. For I think you would have felt sorry and uncomfortable for me, had it been otherwise.'

He mentioned that Maxwell Anderson was dramatizing the story for a Broadway musical with Kurt Weill, the composer. When he added that it was also to be made into a movie, I was in my element. Enthusiastically, I replied that I'd been convinced it would make a great movie but, alas, the man I was working for, David Lean, was not interested in such subjects – he was looking for a love story for Ann Todd. The perfect director would be Roberto Rossellini, whom I had recently met, and I had been telling Claude Rains about the book and thought he would be excellent as Mr Jarvis. Flamboyantly, I rounded off this flow of name-dropping and gratuitous advice: 'I once thought I'd have loved to have written *War and Peace* but now I think your book is finer and more worth having done than any other.'

Alexander Korda had the film rights, came the reply, and had sent a cable 'couched in the rather extravagant language you use yourself, though he didn't go so far as *War and Peace*! I agree with you about Rossellini – I had the same idea myself. And that's not bad, seeing that I am totally ignorant of films.'

In response I told him about a dinner Korda had given at Claridges for movie directors and producers, members of the newly formed British Film Academy. I explained that as David Lean was its chairman, I acted as secretary of the Academy and, to my delight, had sat beside Korda, a 'wonderfully amusing man'. Over sole with Liebfraumilch – except for Korda, who drank soda-water – they'd discussed actors, Carol Reed telling of the remarkable Irish players he'd worked with in *Odd Man*

Out and Korda declaring that Hollywood had spoilt Charles Laughton – 'I lost it!' Laughton had said of himself. And when the dessert appeared, Omelette Surprise, a cloud-like froth of hot whipped egg-white containing ice cream, Korda said it reminded him of Russian women, their warm exterior that was so deceptive . . .

So from thousands of miles apart, Paton and I wrote to each other, imagined presences, he from his house at Diepkloof Reformatory in the Transvaal, I from an attic in Kensington. Of course, I was flattered and excited by his letters and I wanted to know all about his life. Originally a teacher, he had gone on to run a reformatory, and he described how, on arrival there, he'd found 'a prison . . . well equipped with gates and barbed wire and bars and locks and sentry bars. Punishment was the great weapon. It was a hard and unlovely place; it contained about 600 native boys, among them some of the hardest and unhappiest of human beings.' Step by step he had introduced reforms. 'But it was a very dangerous place, for it is quite wrong to suppose that warped and wild creatures turn naturally towards light and freedom.' Piece by piece the barbed wire was taken away, then the bars and locks, and, as education advanced, violence, resentment and insolence declined until, 'Last year 800 leaves were granted for boys to visit their homes; of these two failed to return, and two tried to fail to return, and two got into trouble.'

Now he was throwing away all other activities to write, 'not without fear'. Of course, it would be painful to leave the reformatory, but he was also glad to retire to a life where he hoped never again to command any human being. In July 1948 he moved with his family to a cottage on the Natal coast. We had spent holidays there and I could picture him at his desk at a window overlooking the Indian Ocean; it would be hot and steamy in January while in London we froze, struggling to make do with rationed food and clothes.

A gloomy winter in which, very early each morning, I travelled to Pinewood Studios with David Lean in his hired Rolls. As an individual and as a director he was quite fascinating and could be immensely stimulating. Having sat in on his sessions with the producer, Stanley Haynes, as they wrote the script of *Oliver Twist*, I was enthralled to witness each stage of the film's production, from the first morning's shoot, when actors, director and technicians were reduced to tears of laughter by Alec Guinness's comic choreography of Fagan's lesson in the art of picking pockets. One legacy of those months was new friends, among them Arnold Bax, who composed music for the film, a touchingly sensitive man who hated growing old.

Paton, settling in to his life on the coast, *was*, so he reported, writing, but not a novel. In fact, he said, he hadn't a single idea for a book. Now that I myself know all too well the emptiness, the sense of foolishness, the awful failure in confidence of a writer's block, I can better sense the panic underlying his joking anticipation of becoming 'a beach-comber of the more respectable kind, finding that a trip to the post office and the store took all the time between breakfast and eleven, and a bathe all the time between eleven and lunch, and a nap all the time between lunch and four, and a walk all the time between four and dinner. After dinner it would be an effort to send off some cheques, and perhaps one could postpone such a small duty, and settle down to Graham Greene (for one must study novels now) till one was tired out and ready for bed. And where would the great writing come in, the great host of living words that were going to tumble out the moment one was free?' But he had written two 'rather Whitmanesque' poems, and one for myself. 'Tear it up into a thousand pieces,' he enjoined. It was called 'Sanna'.

> The village lies in Sabbath heat
> The dog lies in the sun
> But hot or cold the elders go
> They pass me one by one.
>
> The alien traffic swirls and blows
> The dust about the street
> But resolute the elders go
> In rain or dust or heat.
>
> And idle words are spoken
> By loafers of the place
> But stern and strict the elders go
> To hear the words of grace.

And stern and strict the Sabbath clothes
And stern the face above
And stern and strict the elders go
To hear the words of love.

And Sanna follows all demure
And plays her little part
The child of love moves in her womb
And terror in her heart.

I passed on the advice I'd heard somewhere that the way to write was to apply the seat of one's pants to the seat of one's chair, but this, he retorted, was precisely what he was doing in order to write reams of letters occasioned by 'that confounded book'. As he continued to read novels, we swopped views of the great Russians as well as recent bestsellers. From childhood I had been peculiarly influenced by books: although Peter Pan's ability to fly like a bird did not have me leaping off the roof, it undoubtedly led to my choice of a tenth birthday present, a glorious flight in an Avro-Avian two-seater biplane; and *The Constant Nymph* sent me on a solitary pilgrimage to the Austrian Tyrol in 1938 in hope of finding an exotic Bohemian family like the Sangers, although I could never quite reconcile my idea of a fragile Tessa with Michelangelo's ample Delphic Sibyl to whom the author compared her.

To Paton I sent a copy of the latest novel to enthral me, R. C. Hutchinson's *Testament*, a monumental saga about the Russian revolution. After the destruction and suffering in Europe, I was inspired by the central character, and surely he was relevant (I now see prophetic) to South Africa: Anton Scheffler, a lawyer, who uncompromisingly resisted injustice whether under Tsar or under Bolsheviks. Imprisoned, then tortured, before being brought to face a firing-squad he had written to his wife:

I thought that all I had tried to do was wasted, I thought that every battle was lost and no voice left against the driving power of evil. And now I see that the seed you plant stays in the ground while the grass above it shrivels and burns, and the fire can't touch it, and the soil made up of all dead things will keep it alive and ready to give new life . . . And the

51

vision stays, and keeps me in its warmth, and wherever I go I cannot lose it.★

'It's not like my book that you finish in an hour or two,' Paton wrote in thanking me. 'You look forward to your hour with it, you are quite bereft when it is finished.'

Much of his next letter was taken up in quoting from one he had just received:

You will have received very many letters thanking you for *Cry, the Beloved Country* but I cannot resist adding one more to the number. Perhaps it is superfluous, now, to speak of the book's nobility. But because I do some writing myself I am perhaps better able than some other readers to appreciate the skill with which so much reasoning on large and complex issues has been forged into the form of a story, and a style of such apparent simplicity made to echo with music. I humbly offer my congratulation on a work of art of major beauty; the spirit of Christ has not often, I think, shone so powerfully in a modern work of fiction.

Jubilantly Paton asked, 'And why should I trouble to tell you about it? Don't I get thousands, almost millions of letters, saying that I am equal to Shakespeare, Dante and Ella Wheeler Wilcox all in one? Didn't one person, while not comparing me with Tolstoy, say that she would rather have written my book than his? Well, this letter comes from R. C. Hutchinson.'

For quite a while we addressed each other formally and then it seemed natural to use first names – he made no comment about mine being 'Pixie'. I decided he must be a good listener: he considered what one wrote and actually replied to it. I told him I was fed up with my job. After the pleasure of being a tiny cog in the production of *Oliver Twist*, it had been frankly dispiriting to work on Lean's next film, *The Passionate Friends*, based on a banal novel by H. G. Wells. I had neither the gifts nor the drive to aim at becoming a director or even an editor, and clearly my hope that films might transform international relations was no more than a pipe-dream.

★ *Testament* by R. C. Hutchinson, Cassell, 1938.

'I want to have lived for some "purpose"!' I cried out to Alan. Not for nothing did close friends find me too serious. 'And above all,' I added, 'I suddenly feel acutely homesick.'

'*Don't* come back to South Africa unless it becomes a compulsion,' he warned. 'I know quite well what you mean by saying that you want to have lived for some purpose. But you've got to get the purpose first.'

He seemed a contented person who had himself lived with a purpose. That was only partly true, he replied, and purpose could cramp and confine. 'If you know Freud, you will remember that life is a compromise between reality and desire . . . mine was a compromise between desire and desire. What I did, I did honestly and dutifully; but that other part of me that wrote the book was in chains.'

I was still hopelessly ignorant about Africans and wondered how I could meet them; at a party in South Africa House I'd seen a solitary black man, but been too shy to approach him. 'You're right,' Alan commented. 'Don't go "out of your way" to meet Africans.' He suggested that there must be clubs where one could meet naturally, but the idea didn't appeal to me.

Early in 1949 – autumn for him, spring for me – we were both in the dumps. Should I leave my job with Lean? And if so, to do what? In response to my floundering he rose from 'a bed of pain to administer a shot or two of confidence . . . And that is *noble*, because I'm depressed myself (about ever writing another word, of course). Shake out of yourself, woman.' The best possible tonic was his announcement that he would be coming to London on his way to New York for the production of the musical.

Curiosity had me asking how he pictured me. 'I have tried to,' he replied, 'but without success. Is my creative inspiration failing? Or am I an old realist, knowing that it saves time and thought to wait and see anyway? But I know something about your mind even if I know so little about your appearance. One thing, you can't be ugly, or you'd never dream of asking such a question, and that's a comfort! Are you vain, perhaps? I might under pressure concede that I am a trifle curious about your appearance. As for mine, it is entirely undistinguished, of medium height, too thin in the face, uninterested in clothes, not a brilliant talker, sometimes won't talk at all.'

That self-portrait was not wholly accurate, as I discovered when he turned up for dinner on his first evening in London. Since the attic was hardly suitable for this great occasion, I borrowed a friend's flat in St John's Wood and fretted all day about my cooking and my conversation. He arrived with a signed copy of his novel and a box of chocolates, a spiky man, shorter and a good deal older than I. Yes, he was undistinguished, with glued-down hair and pale-blue eyes that peered at me over his spectacles, and yes, his off-the-peg double-breasted grey suit showed a certain failure in interest, but when he began to talk he was immensely entertaining – his eyes sparkled, his lemon-sour mouth curled around witticisms that were engagingly accompanied by chuckles. We talked non-stop until he left at midnight and next day he returned for lunch before a visit to the Tate Gallery, dinner and a movie, Graham Greene's *The Third Man*.

In those October days we discussed his ideas for novels. One theme had Christ coming to Johannesburg, but for that he would have to undergo an 'experience', as he had done before writing *Cry, the Beloved Country*. Another was about a young white policeman obsessed by desire for a black woman.

We hardly touched on politics, yet the previous year the Afrikaner Nationalists had come to power in South Africa, vaunting their policy of apartheid. I remained ignorant and Alan remarked that he himself was not 'political', not like the priest who had exposed slave-labour conditions on farms in the Transvaal – a brave and single-minded man but controversial. His name, Michael Scott, meant nothing to me.

Alan set off for America, where he was fêted. In years to come, he would grow accustomed to being a celebrity, but then it was a fabulous experience for this unsophisticated man, especially after long months in a remote coastal village, struggling to prove that he was, indeed, a novelist. With innocent gusto, he continued to share the nuggets of praise when we met again in New York. At the first night of the Anderson/Weill musical, *Lost In the Stars*, I wept as I'd wept while reading the novel, but the critics thought it did not do justice to the book. Alan went on to lecture in six cities, ending up in a small, warm log cabin among California's redwoods. 'There is a place to eat a hundred yards away,' he reported. 'I have cigarettes and a bottle of whiskey and two packs of cards. An anthology of verse, an English and a Zulu bible, an Afrikaans New Testament, Jeffers's poems, Henry Green's *Loving*, Thoreau's *Walden*, paper, pen, ink. You'd think that would be enough but the compulsion to write has not yet descended upon the cabin.' He continued to write poems.

I had eventually resigned my job and was staying with Frances and Claude Rains on their tranquil farm in Pennsylvania, where I was ambitiously attempting to write a screenplay of *Testament*, with Alec Guinness in mind for Scheffler. And I brooded. Perhaps I could be useful in Harlem? Visiting Manhattan, I went uptown to a Catholic Welfare Center, determined to scrub out a rat-ridden apartment for some poor black family, only to be given a stack of copy-typing, which promptly deflated my zeal. An encounter downtown was to have a more lasting effect. Through Judge Brinton I met Henry Seidel Canby, eminent editor of the *Saturday Review of Literature*. In reporting back to the Judge, Canby remarked on the peculiarity of a mature woman being called Pixie. Its cuteness had occasionally bothered me, not that I felt mature but rather because of my height, and after Canby's provocation I decided to use one of my proper names. I didn't care for Dorothy, my name at school, apt to be turned into Dotty; I would henceforth be Mary.

Should I return to South Africa and if so, what should I do there? 'Why don't you join the multi-racial TB community in Natal?' Alan repeated a suggestion he'd made in New York. 'Over my dead body!' declared Claude. Their patience was inexhaustible. Alan knew about my affair with Paul and my hope, my longing, somehow to combine love and a normal sexual relationship with that elusive 'purpose' in life. 'I feel sure,' he wrote, 'that your inability to reach a decision is because you feel that you are shutting a door on life, which you fear will never open again . . . the door on marriage, love, children, home, security and so forth . . . I feel for you very much. It is not my wish to stand on the bank and watch you struggling in the water, but you've got to struggle in the water. Once I reach down and pull you out, there you are on the bank with me, but that's the last place you must be if you want to "make your mark in life and so justify living". You told me I didn't need to comment on you and your cares. Well, I couldn't just leave them so to speak unnoticed. I worry about them. But I know that they are yours, and that the solution of them is something that has to be worked out in your own time and way.'

Rereading those words as I write, I realize how generous was Paton's attentiveness – I must have been a fearful bore. His New Year wishes for 1950 hoped I would find fulfilment. 'If what you want is marriage, I wish you all fortune; but if it's something else, I don't think you realize yet that you'll have to pay for it.'

Just as warmly, I wished he would finally break through to the novel he was striving to write. But he would have to wait another year, and then, by chance, he would stay in the hotel in London where I happened to be working. Finally gripped by the idea he'd mentioned of the Afrikaner policeman, he wrote his prophetic novel *Too Late the Phalarope*.

4

Michael Scott

Shortly before the Christmas of 1949, while still in America, I was spellbound by a profile in the London *Observer* which told the dramatic story of an Anglican priest in South Africa. In Johannesburg he'd lived among Africans in the dangerous squalor of a shantytown called Tobruk and been arrested for trespass; in Durban he'd joined Indian passive resisters and with them gone to jail; in the Transvaal, after exposing near-slavery conditions on farms, he'd been threatened with lynching by angry farmers.

Of course, this was the man Alan Paton had spoken of whose name had meant nothing to me at the time, Michael Scott. Something else Paton said was borne out by the article. Increasingly, as Scott's reputation for fearless championship of the Africans spread, his name became associated with trouble, and white South Africans regarded him as a dangerous crank, a misinformed fanatic. Those who knew him best spoke of his diffidence and reserve, yet where principles of justice and humanity were involved, he was totally uncompromising. Aged forty-two, despite ill-health he was in appearance 'still youthful, with a strikingly handsome face', as the article expressed it, 'which had something about it of the saint and something of the rebel'.

He was virtually penniless; tribesmen and a handful of Indian friends had collected money for him to fly to the United Nations in New York. There he represented the tribes of South-West Africa, who were protesting against the South African government's attempt to incorporate this mandated territory. With no organization to back him, after a three-year struggle he had made a spectacular breakthrough and had testified on their behalf. He had also appealed for the policy of apartheid to be referred to the Security Council as 'a threat to peace and racial harmony'.

I still have a copy of that profile, yellowing and slightly tattered, so predictably a part of my destiny, and of an article from the *News Chronicle* in which Stanley Burch vividly described Scott's testimony:

> The angry mutter of Africa has broken through the crust of the United Nations . . . To some of the delegations – Britain among them – a 'very dangerous precedent' has been established. To others the United Nations have found their soul . . . Black tribesmen of South-West Africa, who for decades have been dumb under the white man's rule, have smashed through the cleverest opposition on earth and have presented their petition for redress to the UN Assembly. By one of history's ironies their cry for help has been presented by a white man.

I wrote to Scott at the UN to say I was planning to return to South Africa and could he suggest how I could 'work with Natives'? A reply came from Dr Ralph Bunche, Assistant Secretary-General: Scott had already left the States; one of his supporters, Sartell Prentice, might know his whereabouts. Sartell was only too delighted to talk about Scott, who had stayed with him and would soon be in London, where he was due to work on an autobiography. The Judge had just given me $500 and Howard, now at Princeton, had bought me a $25 typewriter; what if I put off my return to South Africa, I suggested to Sartell, and offered to help Scott? His enthusiasm matched my own.

On a February afternoon in 1950 an expectant group waited in a viewing-room of the British Film Institute in London, journalists, a film director and myself included. Scott arrived, accompanied by the committee who had invited us: three Quakers and an Anglican priest. Very tall, almost gaunt, he was sunburnt after attending a conference of Gandhi's followers in India and was wearing an ankle-length coat of yellowish tweed, no doubt from the ashram. He was not strictly handsome. Perhaps his face revealed the two sides to his nature, one austere, the other mischievous, but he radiated spiritual strength and the overriding impression was one of beauty. (R. C. Hutchinson, author of *Testament*, would one day remark, 'Surely Father Scott is the finest-looking priest in the Church of England.') He had a steady, penetrating gaze, but I found his handshake disconcertingly limp. Clearly, he was extremely shy.

The amateurishness of the documentary film he showed us heightened its effect. The locations and shanties around South African cities where people lived in slum conditions retained an unimagined vitality. Black miners – migrant labourers – streamed from a compound. Small boys danced to the sound of a pennywhistle and white-garmented members of the Zionist Church pranced along dusty paths. He gave a commentary, telling about the pass laws, tens of thousands of arrests, the colour bar and denial of human rights.

The scene switched to South-West Africa. Tall, black men in nondescript uniforms marched in slow motion. The Hereros, he explained, were performing the annual ceremony at the graves of their ancestors slain by the Kaiser's Germans. Following the men came elegant women, wearing turbans and high-waisted long floral dresses, skirts swaying to the rhythm of their movements. The Germans, he added, in their war of decimation early in the century had reduced the Herero people from 80,000 to 15,000 and had robbed them of their lands. The young man who had led those survivors, Chief Hosea Kutako, was now very old; it was he who had initiated the protests against South African rule and whose petitions Scott had read to the UN.

As the film came to an end, Scott repeated the last words of a prayer Chief Hosea had spoken that day beside the ancestral graves: 'O Lord, help us who roam about. Help us who have been placed in Africa and have no dwelling place of our own. Give us back a dwelling place. O God, all power is yours in Heaven and Earth.'

Though Scott had spoken quietly and as a mere witness, the shocking facts brought his life and work into sharp focus; the knowledge of all he had endured, of harassment by the police, gave resonance to his words.

The revelations which in Paton's book had opened heart and mind were now there before my eyes and I tried to catch up on long years of ignorance by reading all the relevant books and articles I could find. Meanwhile, I was vetted by the self-styled

'Michael Scott Committee', which had come into existence to support his work. John Fletcher, an elderly bearded Quaker, responded approvingly to a remark that I had been influenced by Schweitzer's *Reverence for Life*; George Norton, a Friar Tuck of a missionary on leave from Zululand, was charmed to find that I, like himself, came from the Transvaal; and Esther Muirhead, impressed by my background and experience, invited me to tea with Scott and herself at the Friends' International Centre in Bloomsbury.

I went there after lunching with movie actors. It didn't occur to me that in a Quaker setting my appearance in a New Look black coat, with broad shoulders and small waist, might seem rather startling. At all events, although this and other encounters with Scott did not differ remarkably from those between any employer and an eager prospective employee, the committee suddenly became alarmed. Each in turn uttered a grave warning, a warning which I found difficult to take seriously, so solemn were their expressions, as in almost identical terms they spoke about the special nature of this uniquely dedicated man: how disastrous it would be for Michael and for 'The Cause' if he were to be regarded as an ordinary mortal. Long afterwards, a friend surmised that a possible explanation of their attempts to protect him from my apparently predatory intrusion was that we looked as if we were 'made for each other'.

Then I discovered that they suspected me of being a spy. An energetic, highly qualified secretary offering to work without pay and a South African at that! But my efficiency in sorting and cataloguing box after box of boring documents brought by Scott from the UN finally convinced them that I was genuine and the episode ended in relieved hilarity. Scott and I were to work together for the next seven years.

It meant a great deal to him that I was South African, politically naïve but a keen and responsive student, coming to share his dedication to the work. Looking back from a distance of twenty-five years, he was to recall: 'Halcyon days when things were happy and simple and straightforward', days which began when he was at a retreat house in Sussex and I eagerly joined him to collect pages of the autobiography for typing. I learned that he was the son of a clergyman and that both his brothers were also in the church. As a youth, because of ill-health, instead of studying at Cambridge he'd gone to South Africa and there worked in a leper colony before being ordained. Experience as curate to a bishop in India had drawn him to Gandhi's philosophy. During the war he'd been accepted, then rejected, by the Royal Air Force on medical grounds. It was on medical grounds that he had returned to South Africa in 1943.

A sense of shared interests was reinforced when he discovered that I had read the *Bhagavad Gita*. Would I get him the Isherwood translation? he asked; he wanted to compare it with one by Arnold. And could I translate, just roughly, *Le Royaume de Dieu*?

After those agonizing years of uncertainty, I rapturously informed Alan that I had found my purpose in life, to which he, always concerned to keep my feet on the ground, replied, 'You've clearly been bitten by the bug of holiness, one of the most powerful diseases imaginable.'

Back in London Michael stayed at the Friends' International Centre as the guest of Fred and Dorothy Irvine, the hospitable wardens. The house bustled with students of all nationalities. He worked in his bedroom overlooking Tavistock Square, while I typed in a small kitchen next door, breaking off to make him cups of strong, sweet tea, a welcome diversion from speeches and sermons he was writing in response to invitations from all over the country. Much though he longed to return to South Africa, he had postponed his departure in order to campaign in the hope that if the British people were aroused, they could in time shift the Labour Government from its shameful support for South Africa at the UN.

The campaign opened with a packed meeting in Westminster's Central Hall, organized by Christian Action. An overflow crowd massed in the foyer, listening via loudspeakers. Scott was not an eloquent speaker – he tended to ramble – but he seemed to impart to his audience a sense of actually hearing those voiceless Africans whose cause he represented. His very quietness was magnetic and, beneath the arid exposition of facts and figures which were always a part of his speeches, was a prophetic fire.

Along with Ritchie Calder, the influential scientist, he addressed a national conference on reconstruction in Africa. At

61

the UN his call for a Pan African Conference on the economic and social future of the continent had gone unheeded, as had his warning of the danger ahead unless there was regional development. (Today, when death from famine is a horrifying commonplace, experts suggest that such disasters might be survived if Africa would 'dare' to think regionally.) Another theme was that only by black and white cooperation in resistance to both commercial and nationalist pressures could racial conflict be avoided and the land be saved from widespread erosion.

The Second World War had only recently ended. The early fifties was a time of optimism: despite the hardships of continuing rationing, there was a prospect of creating a better world; in Britain a Labour government promised massive social reform. And what more obvious injustice was there than apartheid in South Africa, still a member of the Commonwealth and profiting from ever-multiplying British business interests? Scott's solitary and uncompromising stand was both a challenge and an appeal to his fellow-countrymen.

He toured the country, returning worn out, pale and plagued by insomnia. Occasionally, glad to be away from the hectic activity of the Centre, he stayed in the attic which I shared with a friend. He was clearly relieved to be in a relaxed domestic atmosphere and welcomed my affectionate attention. I tidied him up and, when his back was turned, gave his ankle-length coat to charity. But I discovered he had a penchant for bright colours, particularly yellow – sisters at a convent where he was giving Mass were startled, each time he genuflected, to see a flash of canary-yellow socks. On another occasion, on the way to a formal appointment with the Pakistani High Commissioner, he stopped to buy a decent pair of shoes at a sale – 'such a bargain!' Their conspicuously yellow colour pleased him until he found the High Commissioner transfixed by the sight. 'It made me feel,' recounted Michael quaintly, 'an utter bounder!'

Meanwhile, Alan was in London, working on the screenplay of *Cry, the Beloved Country*. I helped with the typing and he sometimes came to a meal in the attic. After lunch one Sunday he preached at evensong in St Paul's Cathedral, a fine sermon, his wisdom and faith spiced with wry wit. The *Observer* described him as the 'literary Michael Scott'. 'I take it,' commented Alan, 'that that makes Michael the political Alan Paton.' But, of course, Michael had dared to break the law.

Three months later Michael preached in the cathedral. That he was in demand as a preacher had special meaning for him: he'd come to expect little sympathy from his church in South Africa, let alone active backing. A congregation of 3,000 awaited him in St Paul's, 300 of them robed clergy. I had starched and ironed his cotter, a chore which both amused me, coming as I did from an alien tradition, and made me proud as I watched his distinguished figure go by in a long procession of bishops and missionaries. From the great pulpit he expressed his revolutionary concept of the faith signified by Christ on the Cross: faith must destroy man-made laws when those laws contradicted divine justice; faith must construct a new way of life out of the ruins of hatred and humiliation, a new system of law and of human relationships. Life had drained from Socialism; the salt must be resavoured. 'We must learn from the lowly,' he urged, 'for it is with them that the solution will lie.'

Abruptly changing course, he expounded a plan which seemed somewhat inappropriate to the occasion but which, in his thinking, was entirely logical: in Bechuanaland, he correctly informed the congregation, the Okavango River flowed into the desert at 15,000 'cusecs'; drain those swamps, eradicate the tsetse fly and communal agricultural projects could be set up under a system of regional development.

As always when preaching, he ended the service with Chief Hosea Kutako's prayer.

We seemed a perfect team. So evident was his dependence on me, his sharing of intimate anxieties and of profound thoughts, that I brushed off his warnings that he could not have anything 'personal' in his life. I could not help assuming that his feelings in time would respond to the physical attraction I felt for him, just as he had come to look forward to and to collect the brief letters I tucked into his pockets whenever he was feeling unwell or depressed. When I compared him to other men, Michael was without doubt more fascinating. He had a wide intelligence and probing mind which delved into the spiritual yet mocked respectability: 'If we prefer our religion in a morning coat,' he remarked, 'let us not pretend to the Africans that we have put on the whole armour of God.'

Gandhi's *satyagraha* – soul force – inspired him. The great dividing line of his life had been his decision to break the law by joining Indians in passive resistance in Durban. In our quiet discussions, he spoke of the necessity of going on from where Gandhi had left off. But Orwell, I reminded him, had questioned Gandhi's advocacy of passive resistance as a universal force. 'What about the Jews under Hitler?' Orwell had asked. And an American writer, Louis Fischer, said Gandhi was a tribute to Britain: that Stalin would have used a Gandhi to cut timber in Siberia until he died of hunger and if he fasted, so much the quicker. Both men, said Michael, approached the problem from the wrong end: 'It is not a question of finding peace, of ending war, but of man loving God. It is not a question of how to combat Stalinism, but of how Jesus' teachings can become vital and dynamic. His teaching has been emasculated: rather than "passive" resistance, it should be Christ's "positive" resistance.'

He was often surprisingly comic. Recalling his days as a young curate in a Kensington parish, a broad grin spread over his face: he'd just remembered taking his first funeral service. The grin turned to chuckles, then suddenly he was convulsed with laughter. At last he managed to continue. In pouring rain, the genteel mourners hunched under umbrellas as they gathered about the grave, while he prepared to commit the body to the ground. He had reached the words 'In the midst of life we are in death . . .' when he felt the muddy earth give way beneath him and found himself capsized on top of the coffin. Utterly humiliated, he eagerly grasped the helping hand of an undertaker only to find this man in turn sliding into the grave on top of him, while outraged mourners watched accusingly.

He inspired his assistants, even when we also were exhausted. With volunteers, I was happy to perform humble chores, driving around London late at night, surreptitiously sticking up posters to advertise meetings. We shared Michael's confidence that we were getting somewhere in putting the facts about South Africa on the map. If ever we verged on reverence, believing his vision and actions could transform society and infuse it with new life, he would bring us down to earth: 'The sad, the bad and the mad, that's what we are,' he reminded us, emphasizing the self-mockery by telling of a speech he'd made at Dartmoor Prison: opening his mouth to address the captive audience and before he could utter a word, a donkey's braying

64

filled the air. It was a long while before the prisoners could control their mirth.

He exerted great natural charm but nothing exasperated him more than the suggestion that it might be his own person which attracted people. Among those who made a point of seeking him out early in 1950, none was to be a more loyal friend and ally than David Astor, editor of the *Observer*. Three or four years earlier an article describing Scott's involvement with the squatters of Tobruk shantytown had lodged in Astor's memory and it was he who had commissioned the profile of Scott I had read. But he never expected to encounter this 'awkward clergyman', whom he thought of as 'a hero of our time'. He himself, encouraged by his friend George Orwell, was already interested in Africa, believing that Britain had an opportunity to avoid there the mistakes made in Asia. When the Afrikaner Nationalists had come to power in 1948 he had written an editorial comparing the racism of apartheid to Nazism.

For all the glamour of Astor's family name, he was almost as shy as Scott, but over a series of lunches and meetings their friendship grew. Astor, son of an immensely wealthy father and Nancy, *enfant terrible* of the House of Commons, had been brought up in the palatial surroundings of Cliveden. Scott's father had been vicar of a slum parish in Southampton, where it was a struggle to make ends meet. Both men had had a religious upbringing, but Astor's was Christian Science, with its negation of suffering, while Scott's was Anglo-Catholic, glorifying the Cross.

What mattered to Scott was Astor's understanding and his readiness, as editor of the *Observer*, for the newspaper to campaign on African issues – a lonely campaign which provoked sharp criticism, even ridicule. He also valued Astor's readiness to draw potentially influential people into the work. Astor asked me how could Scott not be solely identified with those who had hitherto supported him, with their tendency to be 'chronically oppositional' and 'crankish'? I agreed a change must be faced, but pointed out how much these 'good people' had done for Scott, particularly when he'd first arrived in Britain and others had given him no help and little sympathy. John Fletcher, for instance, was tireless – perhaps his over-zealous treatment of Scott was born of his own vitality – though I had to admit he was also a stubborn man, who met protests about overtaxing Scott with the airy rebuttal: 'But dear Michael is sustained by the grace of God.'

Michael himself was eager to set up an organization in Britain to carry on the work when he returned to South Africa. I wrote to explain to my family that I could not yet come home. It had been a shock for them, my joining this man who to most whites was a notorious agitator, but they had been generous with encouragement. I sugared the pill by such assurances as: 'M is being warmly regarded by some bishops and statesmen, which is nice. David Astor, the young editor of the best Sunday paper, whose parents go to Ninth Church, has been most kind.' When they expressed concern at the £5 a week which was the most the committee could afford to pay me, I reminded them of the lilies of the field and assured them that, unlike Scott, I'd not yet had to apply to the Poor Clergy Relief since friends had given me clothes, and also lipsticks, which wouldn't be on clerical shelves anyway.

To Alan, back in his cottage on the Natal coast, I solemnly confided that I was committed to the work and believed that even without Michael, I would still go on. 'I guess you are rapidly rising heavenwards,' he replied. 'I guess when you come out here you'll die soon. I shall long outlive you.'

There was no question of going there, nor any question of setting up an organization, since for all John Fletcher's confidence in God's grace, Michael was desperately ill. He had long suffered from an excruciating and often humiliating intestinal illness – Crohn's Disease – and now, weakened by the heavy routine of meetings and stressful discussions on South-West Africa at the International Court of Justice, he was forced to have yet another operation to remove part of the intestine.

Then and on many occasions when he again fell ill, Michael tried to mask pain, but even his extreme self-control could not always check an agonized gasp, a constriction of his pale features. His anguish was not only physical. Day and night he fretted at failing those whose cause he had made his own. In mid-October, defying doctors and friends who pleaded with him, he flew to New York to lobby delegates before the UN debate on South-West Africa. Following by boat, I found him in hospital, surrounded by patients whose radios were going full-blast in a small public ward. He struggled weakly to throw off the bedclothes. He must get out of this infernal bedlam! Helplessly I tried to soothe him, but I had no resources and was commuting by subway from Brooklyn. That night he escaped, after persuading an American friend to take him by taxi to a modest hotel.

But funds were low and David Astor's sudden arrival on his way to Washington was a godsend. He arranged for Michael to move into the luxurious Carlton House Hotel, where delegates visited him, among them Nehru's sister, Madam Pandit, head of the Indian delegation.

Supporters from previous years rallied round. Michael could rely on invaluable practical advice from members of the UN Secretariat, especially Jack Harris, the American anthropologist, whose distinguished career in the UN was subsequently destroyed by the McCarthy purge and ended in ostracism and self-exile. Some eager volunteers, on the other hand, however much they admired Michael, were inclined to use his platform for haranguing delegates with their own passionately held convictions. Weightier support came from Quakers such as Agatha Harrison, a British associate of Gandhi's, a deeply spiritual woman who was an old hand at mediation and negotiation. Michael, however, thought placatory tactics singularly inappropriate when dealing with the South African Government, which, whether under Smuts or under Malan, the present Prime Minister, defied moral and juridical pressure.

South-West Africa was so remote; the reality of the lives of the Africans there was unimaginable to these Asians and Europeans and Americans – and, indeed, to me, whose only experience had been of servants or glimpses of the inhabitants of Marabastad as we drove through their location. Patiently Michael explained and argued and discussed tactics. He had an air of quiet authority. I began to understand the subtlety of his political instincts. Clearly he was respected not only for his integrity but for his acumen in preparing for the pitfalls and devious transactions that lay ahead.

The UN was in its infancy. The only African members were Egypt, Ethiopia and Liberia. To an organization still taken up with the problems of a newly divided Europe and decolonized Asia, what could a few small and distant African tribes matter?

The colonial powers, Britain and France, along with the United States, had supported the South African government in rejecting UN supervision over its administration of South-West Africa; they had opposed giving Scott a hearing. Only with the vital support of India, and after nearly three years of relentless lobbying of small Latin American countries, had he won the necessary majority enabling him to testify. At the core of his argument lay the fact that South-West Africa had been made a Mandated Territory by the old League of Nations; that the British government, entrusted with its administration after the defeat of Germany in the First World War, had passed on this responsibility to South Africa. Under the Mandate, that government was obliged to 'promote to the utmost the material and moral well-being and the social progress of the inhabitants'. The territory must now be placed under UN Trusteeship, as was happening to other former German colonies which had been made Mandated Territories, such as Tanganyika.

Michael churned out memoranda through strenuous, claustrophobic days, while the city baked in a Fall heatwave. A welcome diversion was the regular arrival of impeccable waiters wheeling in trolleys of delicious food, served in gleaming dishes with freshly starched linen – after England's rationing it all felt like a Hollywood movie. His appetite picked up.

But I, meanwhile, had grown restless. I felt burdened by Michael's illness and was only too ready to escape to the company of new friends. David Astor had introduced me to Arthur Koestler, whose novels I greatly admired. I had expected to be intimidated by his powerful intellect. Instead, I was entranced to find that this short, intense man, with heavy Hungarian accent, was witty and affectionate – so long as you kept out of range of his unpredictable temper. Through Arthur I met Louis Fischer, whose biography of Gandhi had just been published to great acclaim. Old friends – both, as disillusioned Communists, had contributed to *The God That Failed* – they were also fierce rivals, especially when it came to women. I was flattered by their invitations to lunches or dinners, at times *à deux*, sometimes the three of us together. Louis's relaxed charm concealed immense energy, an energy that warmed his gaze as he devoted himself wholly to his companion of the moment. They teased me, but fondly. Arthur argued that self-sacrifice was no life for me, even Communists knew you must be properly paid and live in comfort if you were to function effectively – the continual racketing by subway from Brooklyn, the life among 'cabbages' in Tavistock Square, would soon wear me down. While Louis maintained that Michael's 'stage' was a regrettably small one, to which I hotly retorted that the race question would become more important than the East-West conflict, that Michael was prophetic and that I was committed to the work.

At last, one bright day the doctor declared Michael fit to go for a walk in Central Park. We strolled through the zoo, where seals leapt in great sleek arcs to catch fish tossed by their keeper, diving into the water and emerging from the depths again to grunt for more. As we watched together, Michael's laughter was a celebration.

South-West Africa was not yet listed but the annual debate on the Treatment of Indians in South Africa was due. A package arrived from Johannesburg, the manuscript of a pamphlet sent to Scott by the Indian Congress, with whom he had worked in the forties. Somehow a printer willing to do a rush job was found and by the morning of the debate we were able to infiltrate copies into the UN Press Section. *South Africa Behind Bars* was the title; the cover depicted caged Africans arrested under the pass laws.

Though still weak, Michael made the journey to Lake Success on Long Island, where the UN was housed in a converted war factory. From the public gallery of the Political Committee's conference room we sat watching the South African delegation. A commotion heralded the delivery of 'our' pamphlet by one of the staff. As they skimmed through it, angrily reacting to its attack on apartheid, the discomfiture of the delegation gave us absurd gratification.

Through four days of debate they remained impervious to appeals for their government to extend freedom in South Africa. The American delegate went so far as to quote extracts from the great religions: neither Greek nor Jew but all one in Christ Jesus; the stranger shall be as one born among you, love him as thyself; the heathen is thy brother, to wrong him is to sin; men are equal like the fingers of a hand. Britain and Australia remained silent.

'We are unique,' retorted the South African delegate; no one could say the 'natives' did not have fundamental rights and freedoms, the same rights as 'Europeans'.

Although the debates were ostensibly confined to the treatment of Indians, delegates used them to express abhorrence of the whole range of repressive racial policies. It paved the way for the subject of apartheid to be formally included in the UN's agenda two years later.

A violent storm broke the heatwave and there were alarmist fears that the new UN headquarters, being built on the East River, might topple. With South-West Africa at last on the list to be debated, Michael wrote to Dr Dönges, South Africa's Minister of the Interior, who was leading that delegation, to ask for an informal talk. The request was ignored and when he chanced to encounter Dönges in the lobby, the Minister did an abrupt about-turn. It gave cause for laughter at the time, but later Michael confided that he had been hurt by the rebuff – only those close to him knew how vulnerable a man he was. And for all I had learned, for all my growing commitment, I was finding it painful to hear my country castigated from every side.

Until the last moment Michael argued with neutral or hostile delegations. All he was asking was support for the International Court's advisory opinion which required the South African government to submit annual reports on South-West Africa to the UN and to forward petitions from the inhabitants. He never knew whether representatives of small countries would resist the blandishments or deals proffered by powerful nations, bargaining that turned the UN's lounges and corridors into a political marketplace.

On 29 November the debate opened. Dr Dönges appealed to the UN to be 'truly great' and admit its past errors over South-West Africa. Britain and America both urged postponement of action. India riposted that for five years South Africa had ignored UN resolutions – that was enough! South-West Africa was an international trust; a commission should now be set up to receive reports and petitions in accordance with the Court's advice. Several Latin American countries supported this. Days of argument followed, with Michael beavering away at reluctant delegations, but only a feeble compromise was adopted: the UN was to form a committee to confer with the South Africans on how to implement the Court's advice. At least, he reasoned, clutching at a straw, this kept the case firmly in the international arena.

The British Labour government's continuing support for South Africa was a cruel disappointment, as was the American's. Year after year after year, Michael returned to the UN and listened to speeches from their delegates which condemned apartheid with increasing fervour, knowing that when it came to the vote, abstention was the most that could be hoped for. In a letter from New York in 1958 he was to say: 'This year it has been a battle unlike any other . . . it was all very controversial. At one stage in the voting we had the spectacle of the US and the UK – the only two – voting against a paragraph merely expressing "deep concern" at the policies being practised in SWA.' After his first reaction of acute depression, he would rally. On one occasion he went on to write: 'Am feeling a bit spent tho' a bit restored by hearing Pablo Casals this afternoon at UN day concert, Bach's Cantata No. 2.'

But how to explain the behaviour of these great powers to the people in South-West Africa. Shortly before leaving New York, we received a letter from Chief Hosea. It was addressed to me, since his correspondence with 'Father Michael' had been inter-fered with by the authorities. One letter from Michael which reached him was promptly confiscated. He had not yet heard the outcome of the debate. 'We wish,' he said, happily ignorant of the obstructive role they had played, 'that both the British and American governments will assist us in this case.'

Towards the end of 1951 I flew home to be with my father, who was very ill with pernicious anaemia. That year the UN session was in Paris. It was hard to leave Michael, fragile as ever, to cope virtually alone, but at least the daily papers kept me in touch. South-West Africa was front-page news. Very early each morning, the moment I heard the *Rand Daily Mail* land with a smack on the verandah of our small house in Pretoria, I hurried to read it. After Michael's years of lobbying for the tribal leaders to put their own case, the UN finally cabled an invitation to the chiefs to appear before the Assembly in Paris. The South African government was called upon to 'facilitate' their 'prompt travel' – whereupon its delegate promptly walked out of the UN committee. And even in this well-known liberal newspaper, Michael Scott was referred to as 'a hostile foreigner'. Britain was among the minority to vote against the invitation – because 'correct procedure' had not been followed.

'I've been thinking of you a great deal,' wrote Alan Paton from his home in Natal, 'especially as I can hardly open the paper without seeing something about Scott, Dönges, or "those nasty dagoes" who have it in for us! Do you now feel that you are responsible for South Africa walking out? If so, you needn't; great forces are at work and this is a mere crack in the roof of the world. I know just how you feel, and why you feel it, and where you feel it, and when you feel it. You have been marching along, a musket bearer, and suddenly the opposition put a light on you; you feel naked and exposed. Will you ever get used to it? Will I? Is Michael used to it now?'

Actually I didn't yet feel naked or exposed. Michael had not thought I was likely to become involved. Now, however, as the government ignored the UN's request and there was no sign of the chiefs' applying for the necessary permits to go to the UN, letters and cables from Paris and London poured into our house. My father, who was steadily recovering, seemed unperturbed. He automatically supported whatever I did. It was more complicated for my mother, who came from a Settler background in the Eastern Cape. Two of her nephews were officials in the Bantu Administration Department and her eldest brother – my favourite uncle – had been a Senator for 'Native Interests' and head of the 'Non-European' Army. He told her that I must be prepared to be very unpopular, advice which provoked a biblical riposte from my father: 'As long as you can say, "Father, not my will but Thine be done", you haven't got to worry.' One day, this Uncle 'Sonny' turned up and delighted us all when he expressed admiration for Michael's courage. Then, with a customary, affectionate slap on my back, he commended my 'devotion to the cause of easing some of the problems that beset this benighted country of ours'. But he could not resist a parting shot: 'Of course, I don't agree with a lot of what Scott does.'

For our sakes, Michael sometimes used a code name, and for some reason he chose 'James'. Using this name, he had communicated with a liberal Member of Parliament in Cape Town, requesting assistance. 'I do not know what "James" expects us to do,' the MP protested to me. 'Obviously the impossible!!! That never worries "James" nor possibly you, but sometimes me!'

At the MP's suggestion, I found the courage to approach the head of the Department of the Interior. All he could or would tell me was that no applications for permits had been received, that the government had made no decision and that it was a delicate matter. Scott, he added, had just been made a prohibited immigrant.

Michael had already written to Chief Hosea Kutako, urging him to go to Paris. 'I did once speak for you, but now is the time for you yourself to speak. And the UN wants to know the whole truth. No one must fear the truth, either to tell it or to hear it. You will tell all that you have known and experienced in your own life. You are an old man and it is right that you tell all this to those who want to help your people in the future.' Of course, he explained, an interpreter should also go, and the fares would be covered by a fund collected in New York.

More than two weeks had passed and there was no sign of action by the chiefs. Clearly someone must go on the long and possibly hazardous journey to Windhoek to assist them. The South African Council of Churches felt that as a South African body they could not intervene in South-West Africa; also, they did not want to prejudice overtures they were making to the Dutch Reformed Churches. So I approached the head of the Institute of Race Relations, Dr Rheinallt Jones, who himself had made a study of South-West Africa, but it turned out that he had already tried for two years without success to get the Institute to move on the matter. All but one member of their action committee, and he was black – Barney Ngakane – believed the UN had acted illegally in inviting the chiefs.

There had been no question that I should act politically on the spot. Michael, for my safety's sake, was definitely against my going. He had been followed by police on his last visit. But obviously there was no one else. In London I had often thought how easy it was to criticize the South African government from outside. Now, facing a reality I had never before experienced, I wondered what it would be like actually confronting the South African authorities in Africa. 'Do you think it's wrong to want to test oneself?' I asked Michael – I'd caught his habit of using the impersonal 'one'. His answer had a compelling significance for me: 'One must not go out of one's way, either towards suffering or towards comfort, but follow one's aim. Your strongest asset is your freedom and lack of material roots. And your possibilities are great provided you do things not for the Africans, nor for me, but because you were born in South Africa, of your parents, at a particular time. As a result you have a certain responsibility.'

Surely, this was an occasion when I should take responsibility? A letter from him sent me off in pouring rain to Sunday service in the local Anglican church. 'I know and hope you will follow your conscience,' he had written. 'No one else's advice can ever take the place of that, certainly not mine.' The vicar, a former commander in the Royal Navy, gave a sermon on the breaking of bread. Many great men had to be broken before they could be used: Nelson had gone into the Navy for his health and was seasick all his life, while Abraham Lincoln was continually on the verge of mental breakdown. Never averse to identifying myself with the great and famous, it struck me as singularly appropriate and, emerging exalted, I raced home and telephoned the airline. A seat was available on next morning's flight to Windhoek, due to a fortuitous cancellation.

I was surprised and enchanted by my mother's sensitive anticipation of events. She had returned from town one morning looking flushed and pleased; she had emptied her savings account to lend me £100. Now, wearing her familiar blue dressing-gown, she ironed my dresses and helped me pack. We talked easily and intimately. I told her how much I loved Michael, how he was one of those rare individuals who, in one's moments of despair, restored faith in human beings. Embracing her comfortable body as we said goodnight, I felt closer to her than ever before.

Overnight in Johannesburg, I found Alan Paton and his wife, Dorrie, staying in the same hotel. It was a relief to be with them and frankly admit that I was frightened of going into an unknown territory where Michael was the political *bête noire*. Dorrie, whom I had not met before, proved to be a pleasant, straightforward woman with a dry sense of humour.

A five-hour flight via Bloemfontein, hot and bumpy. 'In South-West you can pick diamonds from the sand,' said a proud old Afrikaner sitting beside me as I looked down on the vast barren wastes. 'And at night you can put up your hands and pluck a star from the sky.'

Scrub-dotted hills surrounded a wide valley and Windhoek lay at its centre, a small town with domestic castles topping its hills. 'Our showplace!' and the old man pointed to a patch of dark green trees. 'The cemetery! You must be sure and go there.'

At the airport I climbed into a car advertising the Continental, which proved to be a big, brash and expensive hotel. I hoped to be anonymous there.

Bob Stimson, a friend in the BBC, had given me an introduction to Frank Dixon, an architect reputedly the only liberal in town. At a party in his attractive house we ate stinging hot curry. My explanation that I'd come to South-West Africa on behalf of a missionary body – a slight gloss on the truth – to assist the tribal leaders, precipitated an onslaught on the UN and on Scott for 'meddling' in something he knew nothing about. You had to live here for years to understand the problem! Precisely, I agreed. That was a good reason to let the tribesmen go to Paris to speak for themselves. 'What. The natives? Ridiculous!'

Away in the darkness, dim lights flickered, dogs barked, voices shouted. The 'native location'. I wondered if Chief Hosea Kutako was there.

Next morning the wife of an Anglican priest drove me along the main *strasse* of the picturesque Germanic town to the mission school on the outskirts of Windhoek. One of the teachers was sent for, a tall, bright young African who ran to shake my hand. 'You have come from Father Michael!' He was Berthold Himumuine. He acted as the Chief's interpreter and would arrange a meeting that afternoon at St George's Cathedral.

In the hall attached to the tiny cathedral, Berthold waited with three other men. One was tall and grave and very old. He was dressed in a worn grey suit and Homburg hat and the aristocratic distinction of his features was already familiar to me from Scott's film: Chief Hosea Kutako. The embodiment of his people's history. As a young man, he had wanted to become a minister of religion; instead, he had found himself chosen to lead back across the desert the refugees who had survived the

German massacre. From them, the present tribe was descended; under him the Herero people had been re-created.

He took both my hands in his. Berthold interpreted: 'We usually have elderly grey-haired gentlemen coming to see us. It is a great pleasure to see you.' And he added: 'I had to tie the other men to a tree to keep them from coming too!' His laughter set us all off.

I had brought an article about Michael from *Picture Post*, showing him testifying at the UN in 1949. 'Michael Scott! Michael Scott!' The Chief excitedly showed the picture to the others. They had not seen him since 1948, when, refused a permit to visit them, he had camped near the location in a dry river bed.

We discussed the question of permits to go to the UN. Chief Hosea, with the Chief of the Namas, had indeed written to the Administrator some weeks before and, although ill, he had then journeyed from his home in Gobabis to await the reply in Windhoek. He was still ill, he said, and had only been able to come this afternoon because he was eager to see me. They understood the need for their representatives to apply for passports and have the necessary inoculations so that, should the government grant permission, they would be ready to fly to Paris. And Chief Hosea assured me that he realized they would probably not be given that permission.

I told him that 'Father Michael' would go on working for him and his people to the last breath, that he constantly held them in thought and prayer. 'No, you did not need to tell us that,' he replied. 'The whole tribe has him in their hearts.' And Lukas Kandjii, the councillor accompanying him, remarked, 'Father Michael is like a mirror to every Herero.'

The Chief was obviously very tired, but he wanted to pray before we parted. Berthold interpreted. 'O Lord who art the Great God invincible. Thou who our mouths cannot describe. We thank you for sending us our young lady friend who was eager to see us, as we were eager to see her. Thou only art God above all gods. No man is wise without Thy help. Let it be that we shall laugh again and that our sorrows will be overcome. We can do nothing without Thee.'

Again he took my hands in his. They drove off in an old

truck. I sat in the cathedral, noting down the words of his prayer. I felt lonely and sad and small.

Next day, the Chief Native Commissioner, Mr Neser, a brisk, bespectacled man, received me courteously. When I asked why the Secretary for the Interior had told me that no application to go to the UN had been received from the chiefs, when in fact they had applied, he corrected me. No application for *passports* had been received. He added that the 'natives' going to the UN would do far more harm than good and they would be 'spoiled' – apart from Kutako, he hastened to add, of whom he had a very high opinion. He was equally frank in expressing aversion to 'meddlers' like me. As for Scott, his appeals to the UN had hardened opinion against the Hereros.

The sullen Afrikaner taxidriver made no bones about his attitude when I asked to be taken to the location. We drove along a track, dipping and twisting to avoid dusty crevasses covered in dry grass and thorn trees, until we reached tin shanties and hovels and small, low houses. For the first time I saw a location with unblinkered eyes. We passed stately Herero women like those in Michael's film. They wore long floral dresses, high-waisted and matched by great turbans which set off their Hamitic features.

Berthold had given me directions and as we approached a whitewashed house I stopped the driver. Accepting the fare, but otherwise disgusted, he drove off.

On the *stoep* a row of men waited, all in grey or khaki, most of them wearing hats. Chief Hosea was absent. He was not well, but would join us shortly. Meanwhile, Berthold introduced Herero and Nama headmen from Gobabis and Waterberg, the reserves to which Africans were restricted in the 'Police Zone' (as the white-occupied area of South-West Africa was called), while the Ovambo lived to the north in their traditional lands and provided a vast reservoir of cheap labour for white farmers and the mines. Two or three spoke English; some had a smattering of Afrikaans or German.

The Chief emerged to greet me as an old friend. After apologizing for the surroundings, he made a remark which was met with loud laughter. Berthold translated: 'The Chief says he told you yesterday that he had to tie some of them to a tree to stop them coming to see you. Now here they all are.'

I reported on my meeting with the official, Neser. The Chief said the administration had refused to send his reply to the UN because the invitation had been cabled direct to him and not through the 'correct channels' of the government. When I went on to suggest that, if convenient for the Chief, the Airways doctor could examine him to see if he was fit enough to fly, a hot debate began. Berthold explained that they all felt the Chief was too ill to undertake the journey. He had been under medical treatment for some months with no improvement. 'I fear I myself cannot go,' Hosea confirmed. I was shocked by the irony – he had waited so long for that invitation – but he was very old, probably in his eighties, and clearly very frail. Lukas Kandjii would go in his stead and, since Scott could pay for only two fares, they agreed to collect funds for representatives of the Namas and Berg Damaras. Again I warned how unlikely it was that they would get permission. They murmured their agreement.

Michael, who was finding the UN 'inexpressibly tiring', had just written to say the debates on South-West Africa were taking place against a background of 'mounting antagonism and seemingly unbridgeable cleavages between East and West on disarmament. Almost everything of importance seemed to be regarded as grist for the mill of propaganda or counter propaganda.' I tried to explain to the men that their case was affected by conflicts between the great powers. But how could they possibly imagine the stultifying impact of the Cold War? In a forlorn attempt at reassurance, I said that even if nothing much was accomplished in their lifetime, people would go on trying to help and their case would continue to be discussed.

I dreaded reporting the voting record of the country in which they had most confidence, Britain, and when I asked Berthold to explain that unfortunately Britain had voted against their being invited to the UN, he remained silent. 'No,' he said at last, turning to me with tears in his eyes, 'I cannot tell the Chief that.'

Chief Hosea was watching and even as I insisted, I knew that the information would add to the burden he had borne all the years of his life. 'He should know where the British government stands,' I said. 'That Britain argued that the invitation did not follow the correct rules.' Berthold translated.

'Do rules like that mean more than justice?' the Chief demanded. 'How is it that if the people of Britain sympathize with us, their government can vote against us?'

Desperately I changed the subject to ask what their principal aims were. 'We want the international status of the country to be maintained,' the Chief declared. Moreover, the Hereros, divided between eight reserves and with part of the tribe still living in exile in Bechuanaland, wanted to be reunited. Also they wanted Michael Scott to be allowed to return.

The following day, in scorching heat, I accompanied Lukas Kandjii, his interpreter, Theophilus, and another representative to the Airways doctor's surgery, where they were inoculated. Next we strode along Kaiserstrasse to a photographer for passport pictures. At the administration building, the magistrate witnessed their passport applications, which we then delivered to Neser's secretary. Back in town at the lunch hour, we encountered men and women pouring from shops and offices, a stream of whites who stared at the unusual, perhaps shocking, sight of three Herero men walking with a white woman. I felt those stares hotter than the sun on my spine, shrivelling my courage. Abruptly I explained that I had to be back at the hotel. Hurriedly I shook their hands and walked off.

But I had lied and was left with a sense of betrayal of those men. I can still feel the shame of being seen with them and the desolation of having abandoned them. Although I had 'abandoned' them only momentarily, and only after we had completed our tasks, I felt that I had nevertheless abandoned them spiritually, and that is how it will always feel.

In the hotel restaurant, I thought about the Chief and the others waiting in the location. Their faith was extraordinary; they were sure that they would one day achieve their freedom. My thoughts were interrupted by harsh voices speaking Afrikaans and German. Around me were men who might well have picked diamonds from the sand; their coarseness was exaggerated in my mind by comparison with the dignity of Chief Hosea, condemned by the colour of his skin to live in that sordid location.

The local white press reported that opinion was unanimously indignant at UN interference. Hoping to find someone to give practical assistance to the African leaders, I tracked down a lawyer said to be fairly liberal, but he was categorically opposed to Michael's action in bringing the case before the UN. However, the editor of the local English-language newspaper thought the government should permit the tribal spokesmen to go to the UN. But he had never met Chief Hosea Kutako until I introduced him.

I made a last visit to the location to say goodbye. The old Chief held my hands for a long while and blessed me.

Back in Pretoria I wrote to Michael, expressing misgivings as to Lukas Kandjii's ability to represent his people's case before the UN. Not that I had heard him speak much, but it was a forbidding prospect – men accustomed to tribal gatherings with little if any education appearing in that international forum. 'I don't think you need worry too much about their competence,' Michael replied. 'They are not trained advocates, of course, or preachers! But there are among them men quite capable of giving a good account of themselves. In any case, it is not flights of oratory that are wanted but a living account of how they feel themselves, their own experiences, hopes, fears . . .'

Ralph Bunche's voice, over the radio from Paris one morning, announced that since the tribal representatives had not yet arrived, Scott had been asked to address the Fourth Committee. As Michael's testimony was barely reported in the local press, I quoted from it in a letter published by the Johannesburg *Star*:

Nothing that I could say could possibly take the place of the actual presence of these Africans and the expression of their own views regarding the future of their land and people. But what is sought here is not an occasion for venting petty grievances and complaints against any particular government or administration. It is really the story of the whole impact of our civilization upon that part of Africa from the latter part of the last century until now . . . These old people are waiting in Windhoek for their voices, which are the voices of history, to be heard by you because to them the United Nations represents a hope for their people and their future . . . Before the older men all die it is appropriate that they should be heard, and that the United Nations with all its resources should apply itself to repairing the ravages of the past . . .

Chief Hosea and the inoculated, photographed representatives waited on in the location. The UN adjourned for Christmas.

In the New Year of 1952, the Chief sent me a statement for publication, written after Neser had told them they must continue to wait. 'We think we are delayed purposely so that the case can be discussed during our absence. We thought that the biggest world organization, UNO, will free us and restore happiness and brotherhood to South-West African tribes, by placing us under International Trusteeship . . .' He concluded: 'My last prayer is – Should we wait for God to come and free us? Is the Almighty God to wipe off our tears, our blood and our misery?'

Early in January, the UN Fourth Committee, by forty votes to none, with nine abstentions, expressed regret that the tribal representatives had been prevented from coming.

On 9 January came a cable from Hosea Kutako: 'Passports refused.'

'The winter honeysuckle is out and even a few willow buds are visible,' Michael wrote. I was still in Pretoria and he was recuperating in David Astor's country house, where his doctor had ordered him to remain in bed. 'All in short is much as you would remember no matter what windy wordy warfare shakes the world outside.'

As I would remember . . . Yes. The year before, staying in the vicarage up the road from the manor, aconites, crocuses and snowdrops were just coming into bloom. I'd walked into his room one morning to find him crouched over a typewriter, his face grey and creased with pain as he struggled to write an article. I began to scold – his doctor had repeatedly enjoined me to ensure that he did no work – and suddenly pent-up emotion found an outlet in furious castigation, followed by painful remorse. No reproach came from him. Instead he insisted that he needed my companionship, he wanted me always at his side. He believed we could create an ideal relationship together and he could not imagine the future without me. 'You can have no idea what your coming into my life meant,' he added.

My memory clung to such assurances, just as his pockets bulged with the lightly teasing love letters I wrote him even when we were seeing each other every day. But from the start there had been the warning that there could be nothing 'personal' in his life.

He wrote of his loneliness and I of how much I was missing him, his depressed and solemn and untidy self, as well as his dreamy and funny self. He could not yet afford my return fare; he was still in debt for the emergency flight out.

Meanwhile, in Pretoria and Johannesburg, I continued to move in a world of conflicting perceptions. Three years of apartheid had visibly widened the gulf between black and white, but family friends assured me that 'natives' were now regarded as human beings and were better paid than ever before. Ludicrous assertions – 'Why, look at the way they all carry umbrellas!' – were interlaced with the old clichés about servants who lied, stole or were ungrateful. Endless arguments with those who claimed long experience of the 'native mentality' made caricatures of us all, and both sides remained unconvinced.

Only a handful of whites expressed unqualified support for Scott's work, among them Julius and Eleanor Lewin and Professor Wellington, a geographer.

The Torch Commando of veterans of the Second World War had been formed in protest against government attacks on the constitution. Sailor Malan, the airforce ace who spearheaded the movement, wished Scott well in his 'essential' work, but explained that they were unable to take on anything to do with 'Non-Europeans'.

Disappointment inevitably followed approaches made to other political figures who might favourably influence English-speaking whites. It was with something like relief that I set off for a destination I had not visited before in a bus marked EUROPEANS ONLY, travelling past the Country Club where I had dined and danced the previous week, to the terminus in a suburb where indigent whites lived. A short walk across a stony no-man's-land and I had arrived at the suburb where comparatively well-off blacks lived. As I strode along streets pulsing with noisy activity, black youths teased, 'Mind we don't steal your purse, lady!' The deeper in you got, the more chaotic became the shacks and lean-to's cramming the yards between houses in that unique, volatile world of Sophiatown.

Overlooking it from a hill was St Joseph's Home, the Coloured orphanage, where I spent the weekend. Sister Jessica, a humorous Englishwoman, had a fund of 'Father Michael' stories from the time when he'd been their chaplain. Graphically she recalled his knocking on the door at all hours, accompanied by derelict human beings he'd found in the road, insisting that they be given food and a bed for the night.

A few blocks away at the Community of the Resurrection's house was Father Trevor Huddleston. Like Scott, tall, fine-looking and ascetically spare, but with none of Scott's diffidence, he radiated warm friendliness – this was ironic really, since he had chosen the discipline of a monastic order while Scott had opted for 'freedom'. They had clashed in the past; Michael felt Huddleston had failed him during the Tobruk crisis, and indeed Huddleston spoke of how long it had taken him to 'wake up'. He described sombrely the government's threat to demolish Sophiatown: under the Group Areas Act not just the shacks but the whole vital neighbourhood would be wiped out, kindergarten and school as well, and he led me across the road to Ekutuleni, where black children ran to welcome him, face after face lighting with eagerness.

I found that just as my association with Michael aroused misgivings or hostility in the old familiar South Africa, in my 'new' world it meant spontaneous trust. So it was that Walter Sisulu, Secretary-General of the African National Congress, warmly welcomed me. He was a calm, homely man, wearing heavy-rimmed spectacles. The office in Johannesburg's business section was small, rather dark and dilapidated, reflecting a paucity of funds. I knew little about the organization and was not therefore able to realize the significance of this unassuming man whose generosity and wisdom would contribute to his great leadership.

He whole-heartedly supported Scott's work; indeed, he suggested that Michael should represent the ANC in London. Their confidence in him would be greatly appreciated, I said, but Michael thought it important and urgent for them to have their own, *African*, representatives there – to which I added the advice that to have any influence with Western governments, they should not seem too left-wing. Sisulu explained that there was no question of being able to send their own people abroad at this time. The ANC was wholly preoccupied in organizing a campaign to defy apartheid laws. It was to be non-violent and would be launched in three months' time. He wanted me to meet leaders of the Indian Congress involved in that organizing. We walked along busy streets to a balconied row of shops and offices, Diagonal Street, where we found Dr Yusuf Dadoo and Yusuf Cachalia in their office. They were all tremendously optimistic about the Defiance Campaign; the Indian Congress was about to hold its annual conference, when plans would be discussed, and they invited me to attend. The story of their pamphlet, *South Africa behind Bars*, and the consternation it had caused at the UN was greatly enjoyed.

The conference, when it took place in Johannesburg's City Hall, was packed with Africans as well as Indians. On the platform I recognized Yusuf Cachalia and Dr Silas Molema, whom I had met on a visit to Mafeking. The atmosphere was tense. To judge from the vehemence of some Indian delegates, there was considerable doubt about whether Africans were capable of sustaining non-violence. One of them opined that it would be a disaster for untutored people to attempt such disciplined resistance. Dr Molema effectively dealt with such misgivings and the conference moved on to practical considerations. From where I sat at the back, I could see only one other European – a dark-haired, striking young woman, clearly Jewish and a journalist. This was Ruth First, who, when I met her much later, would become a valued friend. A speaker praised Michael Scott as 'one of a brave breed of men and women who championed the fight against oppression'. At that moment Sisulu arrived and on his way to the platform greeted me. Shortly after, Dr Naicker, the Indian leader from Natal, announced that the Rev. Michael Scott's secretary was seated at the back and every head turned. As applause broke out, Cachalia asked me to join them on the platform. Although I knew this welcome was for Michael's representative, I felt painfully self-conscious: nothing like it had ever happened to me before, but worse was still to come when I was asked to say a few words. Stunned, I stood with empty brain until eventually I blurted out that I was sure people overseas were glad that Africans and Indians were working together in planning the Defiance Campaign and would feel much hope for their success. I added that the Indian Congress had communicated with us, but that

84

sympathizers overseas were also eager to hear from the Africans. Ingloriously, I sat down with a bump.

During the tea-break the Indian who had referred to 'untutored people' introduced himself: he was Gandhi's son, Manilal. (How wrong he would prove to be: before the end of the year 8,500 men and women would court imprisonment, the great majority of them African.)

No whites had protested at Scott being prohibited from returning to the country but now the Indian Congress did so, and passed a resolution acclaiming his 'magnificent untiring and heroic labours' in putting before the UN the case of the African people in South-West Africa, as well as the 'oppression and injustice perpetrated by Malan's government'.

At 5.45 I left for a party in my other world. At 6.00 police raided the conference, arresting ten people, among them Dadoo and Cachalia.

One day my mother asked to come with me to Johannesburg, where a friend of Father Huddleston's was to take me to a child-feeding scheme at Newclare. How would she cope? I wondered. The family had never met Africans socially and the simple gesture of shaking hands was, for many whites, unthinkable. I should not have doubted. When an African woman came forward to welcome us, Mom quite naturally took the out-stretched black hand in hers.

My last visit was to Wilberforce mission school in the Transvaal, where a tall black priest passionately expressed the feelings of his people: 'The whites forget we are men. We are *men*! And we have our feelings. I have one dream,' he confided, 'I long to see a black man as the captain of a ship.'

My mind seethed with such impressions. The Lewins and others urged me to remain and work in South Africa. But I felt my place was beside Michael. Yet how disturbing was Alan Paton's advice: 'If you want to fight against race prejudice, fear, discrimination in South Africa, you can do it *most powerfully* and *more comfortably* outside the country . . . Understand, I'm not sneering. There's a fight to be fought *outside* South Africa, but it's a much easier one than the one here.'

Valuable and moving though the work *inside* might be, it was steadily undermined by government enactment of one apartheid law after another; all the more reason, I reassured Michael, why we should continue to attack the whole system and pave the way for black self-help. Besides, Britain's house must be put in order, both at home and in the colonies. The colour bar in Northern Rhodesia and Nyasaland was no less abhorrent than in South Africa, and the hypocrisy of Britain's vaunted policy of 'partnership' between white and black was transparent.

My own reassurances were emotionally belied by a final note to him: 'I now have some understanding of how awful it is for you to be away from Africa, from South Africa – wrong, wrong, wrong for you to be living that life in England!'

As I flew off, back to London, far below my mother was writing to me: 'You're on board the plane – oh goodness, if it was only bringing you *to* us. There was so much we wanted to do, a game of golf and some tennis, but I suppose these things don't count for much and we did the important ones, at least *you* did. Going out now to watch for the plane and then to iron away my sadness.'

While I experienced, for the first time, a sense of being South African.

A year later, in May 1953, as a former captain in the South African Defence Force, I was selected to be part of a small contingent of WAASIES taking part in the coronation of the young Princess Elizabeth. We were to stand on the island at Hyde Park Corner and I was to carry the flag. The idea of Michael Scott's assistant playing this role greatly amused me. I had my campaign medals professionally polished and was ready to display them on the bosom of the new Horrocks dress I'd bought for the occasion.

On the day before the coronation came a cable from my father: Mom was desperately ill. Doctors had previously said it could be lumbago, but now X-rays revealed extensive cancer of the bone marrow. That night I flew to South Africa. Next morning I walked into the small flat in Pretoria where they lived and took her in my arms. Her body was shockingly frail through the cloth of the old blue dressing-gown which had become far too large.

'Now I'll get better,' she said joyfully, 'now that you've come home!'

With my father in town – he was Clerk of the church – and

Poppy at her job all day, my mother and I warmed ourselves in the winter sunlight flooding the verandah. Tucked into an armchair, her face lifted to the sun, she enjoyed it when I brushed her hair and added a touch of rouge to her ashen cheeks. As I adjusted a cushion in an attempt to ease her pain, she suddenly said, 'I think I've got what poor King George had.' Her voice low, tentative. 'I'd like to go quickly if that isn't a selfish thought, only I'm needed by Dad and Pop and you.'

I wanted to say, yes, you are dying. I longed to hold her very tight and share her dread. But because my father and the Christian Science practitioners who came daily, as well as the doctor, all insisted we must keep up a pretence, instead I took her neat hand in mine and protested that God loved her and was with her. 'Why,' I teased, hating myself, 'you're only just sixty-five – you've got a good twenty years ahead!'

Friends from her church fondly assured her she was looking better. As I accompanied them to the door they gave routine exhortation to 'Hold the Right Thought!' It was her golfing friends who made her laugh, with their stories of small triumphs – the birdie at the ninth and the truly extraordinary drive at the fifteenth. Not once did she complain; the only time she wept was at the flowers which poured into the flat. 'All that love!' she exclaimed.

Just two weeks after my return we waited for an ambulance. My father had decided we should not tell her she was going to hospital. 'Our' hospital.

On a stretcher, swathed in blankets, she was wheeled through the corridors while he and I hurried alongside, holding her hands. Above the blankets her eyes, petrified, watched all that was happening.

In the years that have passed I have been unable to assuage details of her agonized dying; the resonance of her last coherent, aching words: 'There's no knowing, no there's no knowing, nothing there's nothing.'

Michael wrote, 'I wish I could be with you to try and help. One feels that anything one says is so ineffectual and nothing can really mitigate the cruelty and inhumanity of such an ending to a life given to other people . . . Nor do I think we should want to try and mitigate it. These conflicts between birth and death, creation and disintegration, reason and unreason, are part of the life we know and have to reckon with; any faith or philosophy that doesn't recognize that, or obscures the reality of this ceaseless conflict, always seems to produce a mocking echo when it makes utterances in such circumstances as yours and your family's.'

Immediately, I had a job to do in Nyasaland – a welcome distraction – then on to London, where a backlog of work awaited. The organization which Michael had long planned had finally been established as the Africa Bureau in March 1952, together with trust funds to assist a multi-racial farm in Rhodesia and to provide scholarships for young Africans. The Bureau's committee included members of the Labour and Liberal parties, while our Chairman, Lord Hemingford, was a Conservative with long experience in Africa. Michael was determined that its potential influence should not be politically restricted. A young Englishwoman, Jane Symonds, assisted in the office.

Michael was less than satisfactory as a member of the committee. If others disagreed with his point of view, he did not argue and might even nod sympathetically. Not unnaturally, they assumed that his silence signified assent, but often, no sooner were we back in the office than he followed the course on which he had originally decided.

Our work ranged from his annual pursuit of the South-West African case at the UN to backing desperate protests in South Africa against the Sophiatown removals and against the imposition of Bantu Education. Early in 1956, at a meeting arranged in the House of Lords, Trevor Huddleston and Michael initiated a British protest against apartheid in sport and the arts. Among the distinguished writers to attend was R. C. Hutchinson.

But much of the work was taken up with British colonial policies. Travelling between Britain and Africa, we aided the people of Nyasaland and Northern Rhodesia in their opposition to Federation in Central Africa. We lobbied for urgent political, economic and educational reforms in the colonies and in the three High Commission Territories: Basutoland, the Bechuanaland Protectorate and Swaziland – Britain's 'shop window' in southern Africa, as we euphemistically called them. Our small staff seemed always to be battling against actions which showed lamentable disregard for the wishes of the African people. The 'man on the spot' on whom the British government relied was invariably a local white official or settler. We attempted to educate the British people in the facts of life in Africa through meetings and through our publications.

Meanwhile, I had been finding it increasingly painful to type. Rheumatoid arthritis was diagnosed but each drug prescribed gave only temporary relief.

'Michael Scott is of no fixed abode.' The South African government had once made the point in attempted derogation, and as he moved from the Friends' Centre to a series of small hotels and bedsitters, I too became increasingly aware of this handicap. Since he wanted my companionship, a nomadic round of restaurants, cafés and cinemas was the background to our times together. Loving him as I did, I grew rebellious at this lack of privacy. There was one solution that could bring an end to the enervating routine: that we should marry.

And marriage became the theme of obsessive nagging on my part, but Michael simply continued to reiterate that there could be nothing personal in his life. But what could be more 'personal' than the confidences we shared? And clearly he *did* care. The very word 'personal' drove me to a frenzy of frustration which left him drained and bewildered, while I felt sickened at dragging this good man down into a banal desire for marriage, for sex – a word never uttered between us. 'Can't you see,' asked David Astor, who was close to both of us, 'that for Michael marriage is an impossibility?' I could not and would not see. David believed that renunciation of self and therefore of the 'personal' had in part contributed to Michael's greatness and specialness. My own belief was that my love could liberate him from his inhibitions and help him to be yet more effective in his work.

Michael's ideal relationship, 'new and wonderful' without marriage or sex, seemed to me repellent. And when he read to me from the mystics, I was ever more irritated that human sexuality coloured the terms in which God and Christ were addressed when this was precisely what was prohibited from the ideal love he visualized.

Suddenly there would be days luminous with shared happiness. We stayed on the Suffolk coast in a house near the sea. We ambled through reedy marshes, hardly talking but listening to larks and gulls, smelling salt on the breeze, until we came to a pebbly beach and plunged into the delectably cold sea. He was well, sunburnt and proud of the weight he'd put on. We laughed a lot, though I can't recall at what. On such occasions I was enchanted and awed by him. I never ceased to be aware of his uniqueness.

'There is nothing sentimental about his universal love,' I wrote in an article. 'It is a revolutionary power, austere and enduring, yet deep down very emotional, fighting for truth and justice for the weak and dispossessed.' But I felt dry and exhausted from days and nights of work and at times was losing sight of his vision. And whereas once I had patiently tried to dispel his depressions, now I observed with alarm a growing element of paranoia. The conflict provoked by the situation began seriously to affect our work.

One afternoon early in 1955 I announced my intention of going home in the summer. We had just lunched together near our office in Westminster and were walking along Victoria Street. 'What?' he said coldly. But he had heard and he had understood. He gestured dismissively, angrily. 'I'm serious,' I insisted. He stopped dead. He looked dazed. 'How can you take possession, then throw it all away?' he murmured. Those words were to remain imprinted on my mind. Possession? Ownership? And would I 'throw' it all away? Not just our relationship, but the work? The Africa Bureau, which I'd helped to create? Could I?

He turned into a stationer's shop. I followed. He stood, bemused, for a long while. At last, without purpose, he picked up a small diary, paid for it and walked out.

In a side street we came to a small church and he went in. Following, I knelt beside him. When we left, he strode off alone.

It was unbearable to hurt such a man. I wanted to take him in my arms and comfort him. That I could not was equally unbearable.

Not long after, he was confined to hospital, under observation and no visitors permitted.

'Try not to lose hold of any of the things that we have learned and shared together,' he wrote. 'I have gone down very low and it's going to take a little while and a lot of effort to climb up again. I am beginning to feel a gleam of hope of becoming more unified and whole and able to face things.' He sent some lines from Tennyson's 'In Memoriam':

> I can but trust that good shall fall
> At last – far off – at last to all
> And every winter change to spring.

There was no way I could leave him at this time.

I was myself extremely ill. At night the weight of a sheet caused intolerable pain. As a last resort, I went into psychoanalysis and for nearly a year listened to my own voice monotonously uttering as much as my brain did not censor – a boring monologue which shocked me into the knowledge that survival depended on my making a final break from Michael. A decision was reinforced by my doctor, who ordered a long rest, preferably overseas.

Even then I don't suppose I could have carried it through if Michael had been in London, but that winter of 1956 he was at the UN. Not yet comprehending, and assuming that I was planning a convalescent trip, he wrote offering to explore possibilities in Haiti, where, he explained, there had just been a 'rather interesting revolution'. Clearly, he had no sense of the absurdity of his suggestion. 'Take care of your precious self,' he added, urging, 'Don't despair.'

Father Huddleston wrote from Johannesburg suggesting it would be valuable if I came there. It could relieve my personal problem, which he knew of, and I would be able to see the present situation at first-hand. The Treason Trial of 156 men and women had just begun.

Yes, I would go home. I felt a great desire to make a new life.

Michael wanted me to tell our story truthfully; there was no point unless the whole truth was told, and I have tried to do so. But at the time he said this, he himself had not been able to share with any other human being an intimate and painful element: that still could not be revealed. It remained the nightmare that could not be uttered in the light of day; that it could not, was a measure of the damage he had suffered.

David Astor argued that my 'choice' of a man whom he regarded as obviously celibate signified a powerful neurotic drive. I understood his words but my anguish was without choice. Only long after did I read Jung's Brunnhilde theory, which struck me as comically apt: she was spellbound by a father's love; no mortal man could be worthy of her; she was condemned to the need for idols or heroes. Once, Hollywood stars had animated my fantasies. Now, under that same spell, I had found a hero who was handsome, good and pure.

Not until he was dying of cancer did Michael write of his personal torment in a note left among a mass of pages recording the ideas and issues that possessed him to the end. The mystery revealed was the only too familiar story of devastation of the fragile sensitivity of a small boy at school: the sado-masochism of a headmaster who alternated beatings of his favourite pupil with drooling, fondling reconciliations. More grotesque was this 'teacher's' religious fanaticism, ordering the boy to kneel with him and pray for forgiveness. The boy Michael was held in silent bondage by his terror and shame: how could he tell his profoundly religious parents, who admired and respected the headmaster? And so his whole natural development was distorted by a deep loathing and revulsion for any true physical intimacy, let alone sex.

'In every way Mary and I were suited to one another and the work. The whole thing was a real tragedy.' Some twenty years after we'd parted, Michael was speaking of our relationship to a friend. 'Even now,' he added, 'I go and read her letters. How one looks back to halcyon days when things were happy and simple and straightforward.'

We worked together for seven years and that is what mattered; all we shared, all I learned from him, enriched and influenced the rest of my life.

Michael Scott's breakthrough at the UN in 1949 and his subsequent campaigning in the West have been called a crusade to save a people. He dedicated his whole life to them and to people in other parts of Africa and beyond. Seemingly unrelated causes – the struggle for independence of the Nagas from India and the Eritreans from Ethiopia, and the anti-nuclear campaign – were integral to his nature. He died in 1983 without seeing his hopes and aims, all he had worked for, achieved in Namibia, as South-West Africa came to be called.

In a letter from the UN Michael wrote: 'It has been such a long grind – up hill all the way without any chance to rest and survey the direction of one's coming and going. But what we have been trying to do had to be done and few people know what it has all cost us – but once start counting the cost and one is forced back into a little puny world of one's own egocentricity and that way lies some form of madness for one can't combine two sets of values, two ways of life in one existence.'

During the early months of our partnership I came into his room in the Friends' Centre and found him gazing out on the trees in Tavistock Square. He murmured some lines from a poem. 'What is it?' I asked. 'From Eliot's *Quartets*,' he said:

And so each venture is a new beginning
A raid on the inarticulate
With shabby equipment always deteriorating
In the general mess of imprecision of feeling.
And what there is to conquer
By strength and submission, has already been discovered
Once or twice, or several times, by men whom one cannot
   hope
To emulate – but there is no competition –
There is only the fight to recover what has been lost
And found and lost again and again: and now, under
   conditions
That seem unpropitious. But perhaps neither gain nor loss.
For us, there is only the trying. The rest is not our business.*

* From *Four Quartets* by T. S. Eliot, Faber and Faber, 1944.

5

Tshekedi Khama

Thickset, with a bull-like quality to his powerful, fine head, he plunged through a swarm of photographers and journalists and strode towards the official from the Commonwealth Office who had come to welcome him at Victoria Station. His fierce energy belied his forty-six years. When I approached he regarded me with a suspicious wrinkling of the brow, which relaxed as soon as he realized I'd come with a message from Michael Scott, who was convalescing in the country.

That was my introduction to Tshekedi Khama on his arrival in London early in 1951. He was the first African I came to know; working for him gave me a great leap forward in experience – both human and political – and seven years later it was through him that I became a writer.

Tshekedi had been Regent of the Bangwato in Bechuanaland while his nephew, Seretse, was being educated and prepared for chieftainship. The young man's sudden marriage to an English girl, Ruth Williams, provoked widening controversy. Tshekedi bitterly disapproved of this flaunting of tribal tradition, while the South African and Rhodesian governments – horrified by the idea of a mixed marriage just across their borders – put pressure on Britain's Labour government, which exiled Seretse from the Protectorate. Soon after, Tshekedi was also exiled, not from the entire Protectorate but from his tribal area. Actions which predictably turned controversy into chaos among the Bangwato.

In coming to Britain to negotiate or, if necessary, campaign for his return home, Tshekedi naturally sought assistance from two old friends. One was Scott, the other was Margery Perham, Oxford academic and a distinguished authority on Africa, who had first encountered a furious young Tshekedi in the High Commissioner's office in Cape Town in 1930 – after a quarrel with a senior official, he had nearly knocked her over as he rushed down the stairs. Now there were intense consultations with her at David Astor's country house near Oxford before Tshekedi and Scott moved to London.

Early every morning they set out from our makeshift office in the Friends' Centre – the short, heavy-shouldered African and the Englishman, very tall and thin and pale, both carrying bulky briefcases, striding through Tavistock Square as they headed for Whitehall or Westminster or Fleet Street. They were a great team, discussing and arguing by the hour: Tshekedi the strategist and Scott the lobbyist. Though mulishly obstinate, Tshekedi valued intelligent advice. Putting his case to the Secretary of State for Commonwealth Relations, he used arguments as a general deploys troops. Meanwhile, he flooded the Ministry with long and complex memoranda. When eventually negotiations broke down he rallied his forces for a brilliant campaign.

As his secretary, I found those five months enormously exciting. I succumbed to his magnetism and was stimulated by a curious combination of tension and a sense of his unassailable authority. His laughter was infectious, starting deep down, breaking out, then rippling on in shoulder-heaving titters; not only an expression of amusement but of irony, or a disguise for anger. Taking dictation or typing until my fingers swelled ominously and I drooped with exhaustion, I also had first-hand experience of his slave-driving propensity. Only the humblest of us, a typist hired for odd jobs, was shown consideration. Anyone else who'd shown they were on his side, or rather that of his people, was driven to the last breath, including Michael, who had forbidden me to speak of his illness. Watching him grow paler by the day until I could no longer contain my fury, I challenged Tshekedi with insensitivity, with making impossible demands on his friend. He, however, remained unabashed, while Michael himself reproached me, gently but firmly: 'Now is a crucial time. When I try to do the few things I can, I find I have to battle against my friends, so part of the small amount of energy I have has to be spent in resisting these well-meaning efforts.'

Yet Tshekedi was vulnerable, as I discovered one afternoon when a friendly journalist called at the hotel to report on the Secretary of State's latest press conference. The Minister, clearly disturbed by Tshekedi's achievement in winning support for his case, had told the press that this wealthy, self-seeking autocrat did not deserve sympathy. Several journalists, the friend added, were impressed by this argument. Tshekedi, after listening gravely, suddenly excused himself and left the lounge where we were sitting. Shortly after, I had to fetch a document from his room. I found him there, praying, and quietly withdrew. He soon rejoined us, joking, and robustly began to plan a counter-attack.

Within a few weeks, *The Times* carried four editorials on the case as well as long letters from him. Debates were due in both Houses of Parliament. Accompanied by Scott, who was haggard but calm, Tshekedi entered the House of Commons with a smile, like a brave flag flying. Liberals and Conservatives paid tribute to his record of constructive work for the Bangwato. One compared his case to that of Dreyfus. The Minister answered each attack by reiterating the insistence of the 'men on the spot' that the return of the autocratic Tshekedi would gravely endanger the peace of the tribe. Several left-wing Labour Members had assured us they would abstain, but when it came to a vote of confidence in government policy, none did so. The Conservative Churchill, passing one of them on the way to vote, murmured with a grin, 'We're both going in the wrong direction.' The government won by 300 to 279.

In the lobby a Labour MP jovially slapped Tshekedi on the back. 'Anyway,' he boomed, 'you've seen something of our institutions!' Tshekedi laughed long and loud.

'The government's treatment of Tshekedi is one of the blackest spots in the history of the treatment of the African people!' Lord Harlech, former High Commissioner for the Bechuanaland Protectorate, spoke passionately in the House of Lords. 'I speak with feeling,' he added. 'I have worked with Tshekedi. I have the greatest admiration for him.'

It took another year's struggle and a change of government in Britain before Tshekedi achieved his objective. His return to Bangwato territory did not endanger the peace of the tribe. Not for the first time he'd proved the 'man on the spot' wrong – the white official, whose advice was religiously followed by the British government in preference to that of the equally 'on the spot' black inhabitants. In Bechuanaland he was able to add pressure for the return of his nephew. Their cases were an object lesson in the failure of political parties to fulfil enlightened electoral promises once they have acquired power, and they were yet one more example of British subservience to the South African government. Tshekedi had long and intimate experience of this: during one of his earlier clashes the *News Chronicle* had commented, 'Tshekedi has opened all our eyes, and it was fully time. He has reminded us that Africa is awakening.' That was in 1933.

The story of the Khamas is reminiscent of Shakespeare's royal families. Khama the Great not only had a cruel father and jealous younger brothers but fourteen half-brothers and, by his first wife, a son, Sekgoma, who plotted against him. Khama, after banishing Sekgoma, went on to rule until, at the age of ninety-three, he died. Sekgoma succeeded to the chieftainship, but descendants of those half-brothers – the Ratshosas – were already conspiring to seize power. When Sekgoma died two years later, his son, Seretse, was an infant and Tshekedi, son of Khama's third marriage, was therefore appointed Regent. A nervous twenty-one-year-old with a stammer, he unwillingly but dutifully left his studies at Fort Hare College in the Eastern Cape to undertake this heavy task. Whereupon one of the Ratshosas, infuriated at again being thwarted, attempted to assassinate him.

If the royal feuds were Shakespearian, Gilbert and Sullivan would have relished the conflict between one particular official and Tshekedi, except that, as I see it, the consequences were dire. Colonel Charles Rey became Resident Commissioner soon after Tshekedi was made Regent. A wiry, energetic man with bristling moustache, he cared passionately about the Empire and, as a new broom, thought he knew best how to run and develop the Protectorate. Indeed, he had some excellent ideas, but he was defeated by temperament and attitude. In his previous posting to Abyssinia he'd been pro-Italian; now he thought it amusing when his wife called their Tswana chauffeur 'Orang'. But his opinions were not simply activated by racial prejudice: he regarded most human beings as 'utter fools' who inspired him with contempt or dislike.

Accompanied by councillors, Tshekedi paid Rey a formal visit, welcoming him in a short speech – by dogged determination he had by this time conquered his stammer. In response,

Rey made what he evidently thought a rather good joke. Comparing his own name to the Tswana word for father, Rre, he said it was clear he'd been intended to be a father to the young chief and his people. Casually he added, 'As long as you are good boys and do what I tell you.'

That set the tone for their relationship. Rey, who alternately regarded the proud young aristocrat as a 'cunning, slippery devil' and a 'rabbit', was particularly incensed when Tshekedi, egged on by a 'poisonous toad' of a missionary, repeatedly ignored protocol. Not only did he go over Rey's head to the High Commissioner himself; on occasion he appealed directly to the Secretary of State, as Rey discovered when eagerly propagating a plan to grant mining concessions in Bangwato territory to the British South Africa Company.

When it came to mining development, Tshekedi and his people were well aware of what had happened in the Transvaal: exploitation by the company, domination by white miners, the loss of land and breakdown in family life. His prolonged resistance to the plan eventually took him to London, where he won support from the press and from distinguished public figures. To Rey's fury, he also argued successfully with the Minister. The feud reached a climax in 1933.

'Join the Royal Navy and see the Kalahari!' one newspaper mocked. It all began when Phinehas McIntosh, a dissolute young white man, repeatedly assaulted both the African girl he lived with in Serowe and the men who tried to protect her. Chief Tshekedi's complaints to the British Magistrate met with the retort that it was *his* responsibility to look after the woman. McIntosh – not for the first time – was then brought before Tshekedi and the tribal court. He was given the usual sentence for such offences, a flogging, although during a moment of confusion the actual flogging was not carried out. The Magistrate promptly reported the incident to the Resident Commissioner, who in turn reported to the Acting-High Commissioner. He happened to be Admiral Evans of the Broke. (The Admiral had definite views: he thought the Batswana 'nasty' and the Negro a 'great liar, naturally lazy, understanding rough justice'.)* He and Colonel Rey agreed on action: Tshekedi was

* *Adventurous Life* by Admiral Lord Mountevans, Hutchinson, 1946.

placed under arrest. Naval units and marines from warships off the Cape were entrained for the thousand-mile journey to Bechuanaland. They were followed by the press, who had been alerted by officials to expect alarms and excursions.

Tshekedi was joined by Douglas Buchanan, KC, his legal adviser from Cape Town, who found him 'full of beans'. 'The world will know of the Bangwato now!' he declared, and he was right. As steel-helmeted marines toiled to drag howitzers through the heavy sands between Palapye station and Serowe, the scene was set for a historic farce.

In open ground at Serowe the tribesmen assembled, while the white residents – virtually all sympathetic to Tshekedi – grouped together. Rey appeared in khaki uniform to receive Evans in full Admiral's regalia.

'Tell me,' the Admiral asked, 'is it war or peace?'

'Trembling on the brink, sir,' was the reputed reply.

Surrounded by officials and senior police officers, they mounted a makeshift platform under a lopsided awning. Tshekedi, bareheaded in a dark suit, stood before them, accompanied by three senior councillors and a police guard. The howitzers fired a salute. With one accord the tribesmen threw themselves flat on their faces. Officials furiously signalled to them to stand up. The Admiral pronounced sentence: Tshekedi was guilty of unlawfully inflicting corporal punishment on a white man; he was suspended from the chieftainship and banished to Francistown, in the north of the Protectorate. There was a murmur of disapproval from the tribesmen, while the whites, including McIntosh's parents, each in turn shook Tshekedi's hand and said they hoped he would soon be reinstated.

The case was headline news throughout South Africa and Britain and continued to be so until a telegram from the King announced that, as Tshekedi had abandoned any claim to the right to try a European and had expressed regret for what had occurred, His Majesty was pleased to announce the termination of the suspension and banishment. Rey regarded it as 'a huge triumph' and believed Tshekedi was 'flattened out for all time, or at all events, for a long time to come'.

Conflicting emotions were aroused in editorial writers: a black man had put a white man on trial and, to make it worse for some, the black was able, hard-working, clean-living and honourable. Lord Northcliffe's Bristol *Evening World* (19 September, 1933) insisted that, 'British administrators must at all times be regarded as the dominant race', while the *Yorkshire Evening News* asked what other course an enlightened chief could have taken.

Admiral Evans declared the outcry by the press had been mainly fomented by missionaries and by 'Negrophiles' in South Africa. He was heartened by appreciation from his friend, Oswald Pirow, South Africa's Minister of Defence – a man who would soon declare himself a staunch admirer of Hitler's.

Perhaps the last word should go to Simon Ratshosa, who had once tried to kill Tshekedi. Now he wrote of Tshekedi's dignity and bulldog pertinacity, his generosity to rich and poor alike, his good nature but strong will, adding that although impatient of opposition, he was the most acute and enlightened politician of modern chiefs. However, Ratshosa's castigation of Europeans met with this reproof from Tshekedi: 'It would be doing serious injustice to the British people if you were to take as an instance of their character in dealing with Natives our local officials. One has to sympathize with the latter, because they have often not been trained for the position which they have filled.'

Magnanimous words, but I see it as tragic that Tshekedi, so early in his chieftainship, should have encountered Rey. Their conflicts meant a dreadful waste of energy and time that should have been devoted to the constructive projects Tshekedi continually generated – not that Rey was by any means the only official incapable of recognizing that Bechuanaland was the Batswana's country and not British property.

Among the exceptions was Rey's successor, Charles Arden Clarke, who had worked in Nigeria and therefore had experience of more advanced policies and was not continually looking over his shoulder at South Africa. He had the calibre and vision to face Tshekedi man to man. They worked together to reform tribal treasuries and courts, in planning economic development and evolving a system of tribal granaries to ensure people would be fed through lean years of drought. Arden Clarke even invited Tshekedi and the other chiefs and their wives to tea.

As Regent, Tshekedi continued to face almost insurmountable obstacles: huge distances, prolonged droughts, outbreaks of foot-and-mouth disease and poverty – the Protectorate was known as the Cinderella of the British Empire. Meanwhile, he was repeatedly distracted by the South African government's threat to incorporate the Protectorate and the other two High Commission Territories, Basutoland and Swaziland. For three decades he played a unique and historic role in organizing effective opposition, exposing the injustice of South Africa's system, its colour bar and degrading pass laws. It was he who initiated Michael Scott's original journey to Hosea Kutako. He personally organized protests against South Africa's threatened incorporation of South-West Africa, protests not just from fellow-chiefs in Bechuanaland but from black intellectuals such as Dr A. B. Xuma and Professor Z. K. Matthews, who were leaders of the African National Congress in South Africa.

In June 1957 I visited Tshekedi and his wife, Ella. A shy woman yet full of fun, she was obviously devoted – and only too happy to be dominated – by him. In Pilikwe, the village he had created during exile, they lived in a modest bungalow with a corrugated-iron roof, its ugliness relieved by a garden of roses and fruit trees. Spread out at the foot of densely wooded hills, the square thatched Tswana houses had impeccable yards – *lolwapa* – surrounded by low walls. School and clinic, football and basketball fields and a small store were the only visible amenities. In his thatched office, Tshekedi had a well-stocked library – classics, Shakespeare and Dickens, modern novels and works on law and colonial legislatures, history and economics, horse and cattle breeding, irrigation and education, as well as do-it-yourself instruction on mechanics, fruit-growing and football.

Very early each morning he attended to a stream of tribesmen seeking advice or assistance. Then, ensuring that I had cushions to ease my arthritic joints, he drove me along terrifyingly rough and winding tracks through the vast, austere country to see the schools he'd built, the cattle he'd bred – splendid beasts with wide-spread horns. Everywhere there were goats, nosing for berries in the sand, tearing at bushes, bleating in confusion as our truck approached. Staying in a hut on the lands which were supervised by his sister, Bonyerile, I watched men laboriously hack a clearing in deep-rooted bush to provide fields for crops and vegetables, while women threshed beans. At night, well wrapped against the winter wind and seated around a great wood fire, we had our meal under the stars.

Back in Pilikwe, at sunset, under a pale lemon sky, the children living in Ella's *lolwapa* joined a handful of adults singing 'Take me up to Heaven'. As their clear trebles faded on the cold air, a cicada shrilled. In rapidly gathering darkness, the singers returned to their huts. One ancient, nearly blind, cheerful woman in layers of garments, *takkies* on her feet, a torn white cloth for a *doek*, struggled to rise from the ground and eventually hobbled away to her hut. For much of each day she sat leaning against the low wall, crocheting, and from the white thread deftly hooked in and out by her wrinkled fingers, an intricate pattern was spun into lacy table-mats. She had been taught as a child by Tshekedi's mother, Queen Semane, and the pattern book she used had been brought from London by Khama the Great after his visit to Queen Victoria.

Visiting Serowe, the Bangwato capital, meeting councillors and teachers and members of the royal family, I learned more about Tshekedi's manifold activities and came to see him as a high-powered engine relentlessly driving the old-fashioned vehicle of the tribe through an arid tough wilderness towards a productive, more prosperous and enlightened future.

Within months of that visit, I had to go into hospital in Pretoria. Afterwards, while convalescing in Cape Town, I was asked to write a biography of Tshekedi Khama. With a small publisher's advance, supplemented by an annual grant generously provided by David Astor, I began interviewing officials.

'A book about Tshekedi!' exclaimed a senior member of the British High Commission in Pretoria. 'The perennially angry young man of the Bangwato, grossly overrated! Preposterous that the insignificant Bangwato should have been the centre of more publicity over the years than any other people in Africa!' It struck me that little had changed since I'd been a secretary in that office, twenty years earlier: during interviews for the job, no one had questioned my attitude toward Africans; if I'd met Chief Tshekedi Khama in the corridor, I would have treated him like a 'native'.

Towards the end of May 1959, in the company of 'Jeff' Clark, the official who had met Tshekedi at Victoria Station eight years earlier, I awaited his arrival at London airport. I felt frightened. An ambulance brought him and Ella from the plane and he was carried out, no longer that familiar dynamic figure but limp and shrunken. Ella tried to smile confidently. Once installed in bed in the London Clinic, surrounded by flowers sent by friends, he came to life, teasing Clark: 'Just wait till I'm out of here! I'll be down at the office to worry you all about the abattoir.' His shoulders heaved and out poured the old laughter, rippling on.

He had nephritis. Doctors in Rhodesia had sent him to London in an attempt to save his life. He was fifty-four years old. The disease had struck suddenly, just as objectives he'd persistently worked for were about to be achieved: reforms to the legislature and in education, as well as promising mining developments.

Early one morning Ella telephoned me to come at once to the Clinic. I fould Tshekedi, face stained from a bleeding nose, eyes bunged up.

'What do I look like?' he demanded.

'As if you've been in a prize-fight.'

I tried to make a joke of it. Michael arrived just then and Tshekedi told him of our exchange. 'I believe I've won that prize-fight,' he said.

Later that day he seemed so much stronger that we were sure the worst had passed, but the specialist told Michael and David Astor that there was no hope. Seretse Khama was sent for and the news was cabled to Bonyerile, Tshekedi's sister, who was leading the women of Serowe in prayer. Tshekedi wished he could see all those who had been his opponents, to show he bore no resentment.

Two weeks from the time he'd arrived, he sent for Astor and Scott. Speaking with difficulty he told them what he wanted for his sons' education – the two elder boys had come to London from Ireland, where they were at school. Suddenly he remarked sternly: 'Astor is a fanatic.' David was startled but assumed this was delirium coming on. Then Tshekedi said: 'Scott is a fanatic.' David found this more comprehensible. Tshekedi went on in a voice crackling with glee: 'There are three fanatics in this room!'

But he was infinitely tired, like a giant slowly, slowly drowning in a sea of coma. Yet when Seretse walked in he surfaced with a smile of welcome.

Soon after, he murmured, 'I have made peace with my Maker. What is keeping me?'

Repeatedly next day he insisted on being helped to stand and, the third time, declared, 'I have won a victory!' And asked quietly, 'Where is *thy* victory, where is thy sting?'

Late that evening we found him sitting up in buoyant mood, which had infected Ella as well. 'I think,' he announced, 'it would be a good position if we all had a cup of tea.' It was so comic we burst out laughing, he too. His voice but a crackle, he joined Ella in singing a fragment of his favourite hymn, 'Thy way, not mine, O Lord, However dark it be . . .'

An hour or two afterwards he collapsed. Oxygen was rushed to him. Together we watched him slowly die. Outside a turbulent wind blew as though his spirit was at large.

He was buried on the rocky height above Serowe, beside the grave of his father, Khama the Great.

A few months later I climbed that hill and from the graves looked down on tidy homesteads fenced by sticks or bright green hedges, each built near a shade tree. Goats nibbled at leaves. Cocks crowed, children called out, a cow bellowed, people shouted greetings to each other. A small boy in loincloth half-walked, half-danced down a path. Women in bright dresses, carrying buckets of water on their heads, passed between the huts. Men gathered round a herd of cattle. Someone began to sing. The red earth was bleached almost white by the sun and from Serowe's twin hills a line of undulating hillocks ran through scrub to the horizon. This was the land, these the people Tshekedi loved.

PART III
Returning

6

Treason? A Sacred Trust?

Under a tropical sun the Natal coast was just as I remembered from my youth: the smell of damp earth in the belt of jungle, where chattering monkeys cavorted and lizards darted back and forth across the path leading to white sands and the dazzling expanse of the Indian Ocean. But instead of breaking into a trot at the first sight of the sea, I limped creakily and, far from plunging into the surf, cautiously lowered myself into a pool carved in the rocks. Lazy days on the beach, which at seventeen had seemed bliss and were precisely what the doctor had ordered, at thirty-seven bored me. Yet as I breathed, gazed, listened and touched, senses long atrophied were reanimated in moments of pure happiness. And at night, when the Milky Way filled the sky, I discerned that familiar modest constellation, the Southern Cross. I had come home.

After sailing from Southampton early in January 1957, the ship had made its customary brief stop at each port in turn. In Cape Town I caught haunting glimpses of the mountains and vineyards, all too brief between intense encounters with dissident politicians, academics and writers. These encounters eased the trauma of breaking away from Michael Scott and left me restless at the thought of 'convalescence'.

I met Alex Hepple and his wife, Girlie, for coffee. A Member of Parliament and leader of the Labour Party, he spoke excitedly about the Treason Trial, which had recently opened in Johannesburg. The 156 men and women who had been arrested had shown tremendous spirit and, in a remarkable show of unity, liberal and left-wing whites had come together with the African National Congress and the Indian Congress to rally support for their defence. Rich and poor alike had provided bail and the Bishop of Johannesburg, Ambrose Reeves, chaired the Defence Fund committee. Leading the defendants, the ANC's president,

Chief Lutuli, exuded confidence and calm. The trial, Alex emphasized, would be *the* issue for a long time to come. Girlie interrupted: 'And what about the police shooting!' On the opening day of the trial, she explained, huge crowds had gathered in the street outside the court to show support for the defendants. They had been peaceful and good-humoured until police took fright and fired. Then the Bishop and her husband, 'These two small men, so brave!', had angrily intervened with the officer in charge, before going into the thick of the crowd to calm people.

From the Hepples I went on to a boarding house to visit Aunt Annie – very old, but spirited as ever. 'How do I look, my baby?' she asked, with a familiar gesture of dabbing at her softly piled hair as she blatantly awaited a compliment. I was very fond of her. It was she who had brought Mom up, after their mother's early death. Now, keeping to safe ground, I reminded her how they used to gossip about the old days in the Eastern Cape. There always seemed to be some admirer who 'fancied' her. 'A nice specimen, he is!' she would say. And Mom used to exclaim, 'What, that old rattletrap!' or 'That reprobate!' She chuckled at the memory, and I at the language. Although they'd been poor, their life sounded like a continual round of picnics and parties. But there was a dark side to their lives. 'If you knew the suffering drink causes!' Mom would say, and with a sigh leave the horror floating in the air.

Aunt Annie was staying with her son, Tiny, and his loyal wife. They well knew that suffering. During the First World War, as a sixteen-year-old, Tiny had joined the Royal Flying Corps. It was the time of his life. When everything afterwards proved a disappointment, he found relief in alcohol. Recently he'd got a humble job in the Bantu Administration Department – he thought himself fortunate to have such security and would have been hurt and insulted by my perception of him as a petty bureaucrat juggling with lives under the Group Areas Act. His section organized the 'endorsing out' – a euphemism for forced removal – of 'Bantu' from the Western Cape to remote reserves in the Transkei and Ciskei. Since those poverty-stricken areas offered few jobs, the displaced persons in despair returned to the city, risking imprisonment, to reconstruct demolished shacks. 'Reserves', 'black spots', 'locations' – white South Africans were adept at coining words which expunged humanity and turned families into ciphers which could be scattered at the stroke of a pen.

Small, vain, vulnerable, with red-gold wavy hair artistically brushed back, Cousin Tiny dutifully carried out Pretoria's departmental instructions by day. In the evening, returning to the boarding house, he settled down at the piano in the lounge and lost himself in the music of Chopin and Debussy. His playing was a part of childhood in the house by the koppie: Poulenc's *Mouvement Perpétuel* never fails to evoke sun-filled mornings with Cousin Tiny at the upright piano in our living-room, smilingly obeying my command to play it once more.

At the next port of call, the industrial centre of Port Elizabeth, in a sunlit house Christopher Gell was propped up in bed, his emaciated body just visible above the sheets, his whole being concentrated in a thin amused face and sparkling bespectacled eyes. From the moment we shook hands there was a sense of mutual trust and affection. Nearby was the iron lung to which he had been confined for much of each day ever since, as a young man in the Indian Civil Service, he had contracted polio. His wife, Norah, turned out to be an old friend of mine from high school. Now a physiotherapist, her untiring care was an essential element in his survival and in his unique role in South Africa as a sophisticated essayist. He wrote regular articles which powerfully challenged the state and ironically analysed each new apartheid law. And he carried on a running battle with those white liberals who urged blacks to compromise or saw reds under the beds of black leaders. Of course, his telephone was tapped. Norah warned that he must return to the lung within forty-five minutes. Since he could only breathe by using neck muscles and had to speak from his throat, he wasted no time on the frills of social exchange. He was an honorary member of the African National Congress and expressed the firm belief that an integrated state was possible. Unfortunately, he added, most whites were incapable of realizing that Africans didn't have to be literate to understand about politics, incapable of understanding that whereas they themselves had everything laid on from the start, blacks had 'one long problem from birth to death'. Among his friends living in New Brighton, the militant Xhosa township on the outskirts of Port Elizabeth, were defendants in the Treason Trial and a distinguished political journalist, Govan Mbeki. I was to meet them before long in Johannesburg, remarkable men who spoke of the inspiration and counsel they derived from Gell.

He told me: 'What we are fighting for is far bigger than any of us. And none of us – none at all – is indispensable.' ('None of us is indispensable.' It was not true. When he died a year later at the age of forty-one, there was no one to fill the gap, no writer with quite that combination of authority, precision and passionate irony.) He had continued: 'The campaign will be won, however many battles are lost on the way and however many fall by the wayside. I think you will realize all this more fully and surely from the sum of your impressions while you are in this country.'

Impression crowded on impression: New Brighton – the city's 'prize' township – proved to be row on row of matchbox houses ranged about a barren hill; unlike a similarly depressing panorama in Johannesburg's Orlando Township, which I had visited a few years earlier, the match boxes were many-coloured. As always, there was the attachment of a 'site and service' area, marked by concrete lavatories standing like sentry boxes among a jumble of tin and hessian shanties – deliberate over-crowding in a country of vast spaces.

Space which, in Zululand's lovely hills and valleys, was ominously scarred by erosion. At Nqutu two doctors, Anthony and Maggie Barker, with limitless energy and good-humour, had dedicated their lives to working in an area of poverty and malnutrition. Despite increasing government pressure, they continued to attract a multi-racial staff and to expand the mission hospital. During my short visit I helped sort a backlog of filing. Many of their patients were victims of the government's policy of eradicating 'black spots', and the Barkers, like Cousin Tiny, who implemented it, found relief in music. One evening, leaving them listening to Vivaldi on their stereo, I went for a walk across Zulu fields, straight into a scene from *Cry, the Beloved Country*. Children were rounding up cattle and goats and, as they made for their kraals, they cried out to each other. Through the gathering dusk their unearthly high calls echoed across the valley.

The Barkers hoped I would join their staff, but I was not yet sure what I wanted to do. The Treason Trial kept cropping up, even in the unlikely surroundings of the small railway station at Glencoe, where I waited for a train to Pretoria to visit my father. The Afrikaner who ran the refreshment room raised the subject while I was having a remarkably good meal. We'd talked about his family, then about the 'native problem' and he'd expressed the view that if people were educated, it was only natural they should want political rights. That led on to his confiding that at first he'd thought the trial a serious matter of treason, but before long he'd come to the conclusion that the arrests were a political move by the government, and he was unhappy that people like himself, in the Civil Service, were afraid to speak their minds. Before leaving I tipped the black waiter – an extraordinary event to judge from his excessive gratitude and his boss's explanation that 'the madam' was not an Afrikaner but from England.

As the train journeyed north towards the Transvaal, I wondered how many other lonely Afrikaners in small dorps harboured his heretical views. And I wondered whether he would have been so forthcoming had he realized that I was not English but South African.

'The Treason Trial's Defence Fund urgently needs a secretary,' wrote Ambrose Reeves. 'Can you start at once?' Knowing of my physical problems, he assured me that typing assistance would be provided; the pay would be £35 a month and I could stay with him and his family until I'd found a permanent place. The appeal was irresistible. Within days I had settled into his lively household and the busy Defence Fund office at the Labour Party's headquarters.

Chaired by the Bishop, the Working Committee of academics, politicians and professional men and women met regularly and proved true to its title, raising funds for legal defence, organizing welfare and publicity, liaising with a defendants' committee and generally assisting Remus, the African clerk, and myself in attending to defendants' needs. The Anglican Archbishop, a Roman Catholic bishop and Alan Paton were among presidents of the Fund, while counsel for the defence included distinguished advocates.

During my first lunch-hour, somewhat nervous at the prospect of encountering 156 'traitors', even though I already knew several of them, I set off by tram for the Drill Hall. A colonial, iron-roofed barn of a hall, it had been crudely converted into a court for the preliminary hearings. High Treason? The atmosphere was startlingly informal. Even the armed police seemed phlegmatic and at the back of the hall defendants were playing darts, while another group lustily rehearsed freedom songs. I found Professor Z. K. Matthews queuing for a hot meal served by Indian women. We had met in 1952 at the United Nations, when he had been Visiting Professor of Theology in a New York seminary. With him was a dignified, immensely impressive man with greying hair, Chief Albert Lutuli, who studied me attentively before giving me a warm welcome which dissipated my nervousness. Walter Sisulu reinforced the welcome, as did the quietly spoken, reflective lawyer Oliver Tambo and his partner, Nelson Mandela, whom I had met four years earlier: a young giant with a striking air of authority, debonair in a three-piece suit. Close friends, the three men were a unique political partnership which had vitally influenced the ANC since the early forties.

I met Ruth First and her husband, Joe Slovo, a lawyer; their friendliness did not dispel my unease at being with Communists, unease which *was* dispelled as I came to know them. Soon I had personal experience of the generosity with which they and other Communists supported the fund, getting no credit and asking for none, and learned of their courage and readiness for self-sacrifice over long years of struggle. Ruth had shown exceptional daring as an investigative reporter. A teenager in 1947, she had driven Michael Scott and Henry Nxumalo – known as 'Mr Drum' for the exposures he'd written for that magazine – to Bethal in the Eastern Transvaal. There they had interviewed farm labourers held captive by farmers in atrocious conditions. Now she introduced me to another defendant, a big, vigorous, slow-speaking man, Gert Sibande, who had taken them into the compounds at great risk, since he was himself a farm labourer in that area.

In twenty years of protest against the ill-treatment of his fellows, Sibande had been dubbed the 'lion of the East'. A widower with ten children, not only had he been banished from Bethal but he was repeatedly arrested and banned from political activity. He and Annie Silinga, a huge, jolly matriarch from the Cape who also had been regularly imprisoned, for refusing to carry a pass, symbolized the majority of the African and Indian defendants. Peasants and workers with little if any formal education, they were often important local organizers for the Congresses. Humorous and tough, often wise, with only an occasional complainer, they were cut off from families, out of jobs, their needs usually desperate. I saw a good deal of them when it came to dispensing food and clothing coupons, persuading shopkeepers not to foreclose on unpaid hire purchase instalments and trying to find temporary jobs during erratic adjournments in the trial.

They were an unanswerable argument for universal suffrage. The Afrikaner in Glencoe station had implicitly expressed a view commonly held, even by liberals, that voters must achieve a certain standard of education. During the trial the judge, referring to the ANC's objective of 'one man, one vote', questioned the value of 'people who know nothing' participating in the government. Mandela, usually restrained in court, reacted angrily: people were perfectly capable of deciding who would advance their interests, he declared, citing his own father, who had not been formally educated but who would have had the ability and the sense to vote responsibly.

Beginning with a defective indictment, the trial promised to be a prolonged and boring test of endurance, a cruel farce. Indeed, the State's handling of the trial resembled Lewis Carroll's *Barrister's Dream*:

> And the judge kept explaining the state of the law
> In a soft under-current of sound.
> The indictment had never been clearly expressed,
> And it seemed that the Snark had begun
> And had spoken three hours, before anyone guessed
> What the Pig was supposed to have done . . .*

Focusing on the policy of the ANC and its allies between 1952 and 1956, the prosecution monotonously read into the record thousands of documents seized at innumerable meetings and police raids. In the often incoherent evidence of police witnesses, every wart on the face of the ANC was studied as

* *The Hunting of the Snark*, Zodiac, 1948.

through a strong microscope. The key document was the Congress Alliance's Freedom Charter. The defence, repudiating the charge that this was treasonable or a step towards a communistic state, set about proving that it was not 156 individuals who were on trial 'but the ideas that they and thousands of others in our land have openly espoused and expressed'.

The State's expert witness on Communism was Professor Andrew Murray, a political scientist from Cape Town University. In analysing documents, he was given to using selected phrases as examples of Communist doctrine. Counsel for the Defence was Vernon Berrangé, auburn-haired, sharp-featured, with piercing blue eyes, renowned for relentlessly incisive cross-examination. Reading a series of extracts from speeches and books, after each he asked Murray whether it showed Communist tendencies. 'Yes,' came the reply. Could Murray identify the authors? 'No,' was the reply. Berrangé then disclosed their identities: Woodrow Wilson, Franklin D. Roosevelt, Dr Malan and Professor Murray himself.

After several months the prosecutor announced: 'I am now going to call evidence of actual violence during the Defiance Campaign of 1952. I will show that bloodshed and incendiarism were engineered by the ANC . . .' Alerted by a member of the defence team, I hurried to the court. In the witness box was a confident, bespectacled, middle-aged man. A woman seated beside me in the spectators' section whispered that his name was Solomon Mgubase: a lawyer, according to the prosecutor. Dramatically he alleged that 'Mr Sisulu and Mr Bopape' had arranged for 'ammunition and a certain gas powder to set off Mau Mau' and to murder Europeans in the Transkei. The rigmarole continued, to the open derision of the accused, who for this outrageous nonsense were separated from families and on trial for their lives.

The defence proceeded to elicit Mgubase's past record: he was no lawyer; he had served four terms of imprisonment for forgery and fraud and had once been a police interpreter.

Had the highest law officers of the government believed that they could get away with Mgubase's lies? But of course, for generations successive governments had effectively touted the *swart gevaar* – the black peril – fear based on ignorance which was deliberately used as a political weapon. Much of the 'evidence' produced in court showed contempt not only for the law but for public opinion. Meanwhile, the ANC, despite ever more violent repression of its protests, consistently maintained non-violence.

Through the trial the government succeeded in hamstringing many leaders and organizers of the liberation movement for an indefinite period. Mandela spoke to me one day about what it meant to be confined to Johannesburg and its townships. He was giving me a lift to a meeting at the Bishop's house and suddenly his voice, which usually expressed a powerful energy, grew wistful as he told me how he missed the spacious country-side of his youth, how he used to dream of having a small house there. But for years, like so many others, he had been restricted to Johannesburg, first by bans and now by the trial.

But the circumstances of the trial also meant, as Lutuli remarked, that 'What bannings, distance, other occupations and lack of funds had made difficult – frequent meetings – the government had now insisted on. We could at last confer *sine die*, at any level we liked.' Innumerable visitors turned up at the Drill Hall. Some were messengers or domestic servants wanting to show support for their leaders, others were distinguished foreigners – lawyers, academics, politicians, journalists. And significant figures in continuing protests urgently consulted leaders during lunch-breaks: they included organizers of Alex-andra township's successful bus boycott and of a stay-at-home strike on 26 June initiated by Lutuli in support of a demand for £1 a day basic wage.

Meanwhile, outside the City Hall and, later, in 'Freedom Square' in Fordsburg – a mainly Indian section of Johannesburg – Bishop Reeves, Alan Paton and women of the Black Sash movement, as well as speakers from the Congress Alliance, addressed crowds of all races protesting against the Group Areas Act and the Pass Laws.

Early in December a multi-racial conference, inspired by Reeves and hailed as the most diverse in South Africa's history, was held at Witwatersrand University. Leading churchmen, academics, activists, lawyers, trade unionists and liberals took part and among the more impressive speakers was Govan Mbeki from the Eastern Cape. Lutuli, prevented by bans from taking part, met individuals in the cafeteria. The 650 delegates, after condemning apartheid, optimistically agreed on the objective of a common society with universal adult suffrage. In a moving conclusion we all rose to sing the ANC anthem, '*Nkosi Sikelel' iAfrika*'.

A last chore for the Treason Trial Fund took me to Johannesburg station to buy scores of train tickets for excited defendants about to return home for Christmas. Then I had to resign and Freda Levson, with whom I had been staying, became secretary of the Fund. Now it was my turn to be a patient in 'our' hospital in Pretoria, where doctors gave an ultimatum: only a form of cortisone – a drug which might have harmful side-effects – could reverse the dangerous deterioration in my condition. Soon I was convalescing, and within weeks I had set out to visit friends in the Cape and in Natal.

Among them was Ismail Meer, a lawyer and one of the Indian Congress leaders on trial for treason. As a student in Johannesburg, he had been an organizer of the passive resistance in 1946 and had known Michael Scott well – indeed, had collected £30 to help Scott on his way to the United Nations in 1947. Meer and Ahmed Kathrada, another key figure in the Indian struggle, had shared a flat which became a centre of lively and radical activity. Mandela, a fellow-student, had stayed there, as had Scott. Now I spent a few days with Ismail and his wife, Fatima, a sociologist at the university in Durban. It was to be the first of many experiences of Indian hospitality – an eager sharing that was a revelation – but it was also a brief experience of what life was like under the Group Areas Act. The Meers and their three children lived in a small house in an area near the seafront which had been designated 'white'; the law, in an attempt to force them to move to the distant area designated 'Asian', prevented repairs being made and the house had become quite ramshackle.

Before returning to London to work on the biography of Tshekedi Khama, I paid a last visit to the Drill Hall. On 30 January 1958 the State withdrew charges against sixty-five of the accused, among them Lutuli, Matthews and Tambo. Ninety-one men and women were committed for trial on a charge of High Treason. On the previous day, the Treason Trial's Defence Fund had been permitted to hold a street collection in the city; the public had given generously to the defence and the welfare of the 'traitors'.

Nearly two years later, on the way to Bechuanaland, I attended the trial proper, transferred to a disused synagogue which had been converted into a 'Supreme Court' in Pretoria. A further sixty men and women had been discharged. Among the remaining defendants were Sisulu and Mandela, Kathrada and Helen Joseph, a British-born social worker who felt honoured to sit alongside such leaders in the dock and who would soon have the added distinction of being the first individual of any race to be placed under house arrest.

In between sessions I lunched with defendants in a vicarage garden opposite the court and dined with members of the defence team, which now included two Queen's Counsel; Isie Maisels, brilliant and imposing, who had not previously appeared in a political trial, and the distinguished Afrikaner and Communist, Bram Fischer, as well as a young advocate, Sydney Kentridge.

The State, undeterred by humiliation in the Preparatory Examination, again called Professor Murray as its 'expert' on Communism. Again he spent days analysing speeches and documents written by defendants, concluding that they were Communist-inspired. Now Maisels cross-examined him on 'certain objective facts in South African life', to see whether there might not be a simpler explanation, such as 'the right of a human being to be treated as one'.

Murray was reminded of the last census figures: 'Europeans', 3 million; 'Natives', 9 million; 'Asiatics', 431,000; and 'Coloureds', 1,300,000. Grudgingly he conceded that 79.2 per cent of the population had no vote and that a mere 13 per cent of the country was available for 67 per cent of the population. Maisels questioned him on every aspect of apartheid, exposing the cruelty and injustice of the system. The accused men and women were inspired not by Communism, Maisels reiterated, but by 'the actual miserable conditions under which they live . . . When one considers the position in South Africa one hasn't got to look for any foreign influences . . . [Do] you agree with me,' he asked, 'that Government policy is designed deliberately to keep them in a position of inferiority, if not subjection?'

'Yes,' replied Murray.

In what would become the forty-first page in the record of

this cross-examination, Maisels took Murray through a litany of deprivations:

'It is clear, is it not, Professor, to summarize this position, that the laws of the white man – and I use that not meaning of this government but of successive South African governments – all these laws in which the black man has, and has had, no say, are such that for a Native and, to a somewhat lesser extent, the Indian and the Coloured – they prescribe, and just listen to this catalogue, where he may live. Correct?'

'Yes.'

'Where he may work?'

'Yes.'

'What work he may do?'

'Yes.'

'What he is to get paid?'

'Yes.'

'What schools he may go to?'

'Yes.'

'Where he may travel to in South Africa, in his own country?'

'Yes.'

'In these circumstances,' Maisels asked, 'do you not think that the Native may well regard himself as oppressed and exploited by the white man?'

'I think in certain spheres of life, yes,' replied Murray.

'And by the capitalists?'

'I don't like the term capitalists in this connection, but by certain groups, yes.'

'And this is so, whether he is a Communist or non-Communist?'

'Yes.'

Having established that the ANC's protest campaigns and the Freedom Charter were a natural and understandable reaction to the injustices, Maisels concluded: 'We know, of course, as a fact that no single act of violence was committed over the whole period of this indictment by any [of the accused], notwithstanding all the grievances and exploitation of grievances – you know that, don't you. Professor?'

And Murray replied, 'Yes.'

The trial had dragged on for three years. And it would drag

on for another eighteen months before all the accused were found not guilty.

In those days, before banning orders were extended to social as well as political gatherings, the banned could go to parties, and whites – however awkwardly – as well as blacks danced the 'Kwela'. Meanwhile, from cars parked obtrusively in the street outside, the Special Branch noted each arrival, and waited. But when they burst in, hoping to trap Africans 'illegally' being served alcohol, they found black hands innocently holding cans of Coca-Cola – hosts and guests were adept at this game.

Parties might be 'multi-racial' but in cinemas apartheid prevailed: however radical or well-intentioned whites might be, everyday life was fraught with compromise. At the local suburban theatre Bishop Reeves, his family and I joined other whites celebrating New Year's Eve at *Some Like It Hot*. As we drove home, still laughing helplessly at Jack Lemmon's tipsy, maraca-rattling dance, midnight struck and with it came an almighty din as countless sticks were banged against telegraph poles – the servants' traditional act of welcoming the New Year, a clamorous assertion of their black presence in those white suburbs.

Towards the end of January 1960 I flew from Johannesburg to South-West Africa. A letter had come from Chief Hosea Kutako. 'I hope that you shall be able to meet me before I return to my last resting place,' he wrote, reminding me that he was now eighty-nine years old. And he referred to the death of sixteen men and women: 'As an old man the brutality of the shootings in that night of December caused great despair in me.' They were among people who had gathered in Windhoek location to protest against forced removals. Police had fired into the crowd. Apart from those killed, a further thirty had been wounded.

Arriving in Windhoek, as before I took the hotel car to the Continental, wondering how to contact the Chief. It was difficult now to visit the location; a journalist from the *New York Times* had recently been arrested for going there without a permit. Berthold was no longer able to help. His story left a bitter taste: Michael Scott had raised funds for him to study at an Oxford college of education and he had applied for a passport. The government refused to grant it. Soon after, Berthold had developed a tumour on the brain. A specialist in Cape Town could do nothing. In his early thirties, Berthold remained partially paralysed. 'Oh Mary,' he had dictated a letter to me. 'As Milton "On his Blindness" said "Stand and wait", I am impatiently waiting for better days with lots of courage too.' He had not long to live.

As I registered in the hotel I noticed a young Herero hovering near the entrance. I strolled toward him and, when he whispered my name, followed him outside, where he began polishing a shop window while giving me a message from the Chief. Next morning at seven a car would pick me up at the corner opposite the Methodist Church.

It was a Sunday morning, the streets deserted; distant church bells were ringing but there was no sign of life at the Methodist Church. My shadow was immensely long, the sun still low and mild. Each passing minute seemed like ten – was it simply 'African time'? At 7.20 a black sedan with two Hereros in front drew up. Greeting me cheerfully, they ushered me into the back, where the blinds had been pulled down, and told me to remain on the floor until we were out of town.

Soon we'd left the smooth roads and were bumping along. 'You can come up now!' one said. Winding through anonymous bush they joked about how difficult the Security Police made hospitality. We stopped under a large thorn tree. Before long a truck rumbled towards us. Beside the driver sat Hosea Kutako. I hurried to him as he climbed stiffly down and stood, upright and alert. There was no need for words. It was wonderful to see him again. I felt as if he were the grandfather I'd never known.

Tall young men jumped from the back, bringing chairs. He introduced his new councillors and we sat in a circle, the Chief beside me holding my hand. We all made light of meeting surreptitiously but, he explained through his interpreter, police activity had been intense. Trouble had been brewing for more than a year, ever since whites had begun building houses near the location and the 17,000 black inhabitants had been ordered to move some miles away to a fenced-in ghetto of concrete block houses. New rents would be £2 out of an average wage of £10 a month, whereas in the location they paid 3/6. And there would be ethnic grouping, a system which had already proved destructive of community relations in South African townships. The Chief had petitioned the UN in April 1959, warning that the people were not prepared to accept any scheme based on apartheid, 'as they have suffered terribly under this inhuman policy'.

By November people were almost unanimous in refusing to move from the location. 'This is our home, rebuild here!' they demanded. For the first time nationalist movements had been formed, the SWA National Union and Ovambo People's Organization, and their leaders, who included Sam Nujoma, like the traditional chiefs, insisted on non-violence. Nujoma had joined Hosea Kutako and Frederick Witbooi of the Namas in warning that the situation was critical. Herero women marched to the administration offices and people boycotted buses, the municipal beer hall and cinema. Then, on the evening of Human Rights Day in December, an angry crowd gathered in the location.

'*Hy wat nie wil hoor nie, moet voel!*' (He who won't listen, must feel!), the Mayor of Windhoek threatened, before sending armed police to order the crowd to disperse within five minutes. No loudspeaker was used. Only those in front heard and when they tried to retreat, others from behind, curious, pushed forward. Five minutes up, the police fired. Not tear gas, but bullets, the Chief explained.

An official inquiry found that the main cause of the violence was 'African provocation'. No action was taken against the police.

'For fourteen years now, we have been appealing to the United Nations,' the Chief pointed out despondently, 'and our position is worse than before. Should we go on trusting that justice will be done? Is there any point in petitioning them again?'

Before replying, I thought about those annual resolutions at the UN, how misleading they were, promising action that came to nothing. When the UN had at last sent a Good Offices Committee to Windhoek, it did not bother to meet Chief Hosea and the other leaders. What if they appealed to the Principal Allied Powers, who had originally consigned them to South Africa's rule, I asked, in the form of an Open Letter? The British Prime Minister, Harold Macmillan, had just delivered his speech to the South African Parliament, declaring, 'A wind of change is sweeping through Africa!' And, under Britain, Tanganyika, a Mandate like South-West Africa, was moving towards independence. De Gaulle was getting tough with white extremists in Algeria and the Belgians were planning to grant self-government to the Congo.

The Chief was enthusiastic: the letter should, of course, describe the shootings. A councillor urged that it must also expose the lie that their protests had been inspired by outside agitators: 'As if we need to be told of our sufferings! We must speak of the pass laws, of starvation wages and loss of our lands!' All agreed that Macmillan's tolling bell should be included.

The roar of an engine startled us. A small plane, flying low, approached over the treetops. We hid our faces and remained silent as it hovered. When it moved off, we resumed the discussion. But soon it returned, circled and withdrew. The Chief sighed. 'You should get back to your hotel. We do not want to cause you any trouble.' In Herero he blessed me and we said goodbye. He climbed into the truck, I into the car. We were driven off in opposite directions.

Surely in the nine years since I had visited Windhoek one or two 'liberals' must have emerged among the 66,000 whites. Frank, the architect, was away. In the repressive dry heat a sense of *déjà vu* assailed me as I went the rounds, meeting an affluent young businessman in an air-conditioned office on Kaiserstrasse, a bearded layman in the Methodist Church and a German businessman just back from skiing in the Tyrol. Awash with tea and whiskey I returned to the hotel, their words resounding in my mind: 'No white, however sympathetic to Natives, dares to express it openly.' 'Why must the Natives cause all this trouble?' 'We must consider our families, our businesses.'

In breathtaking contrast to that secretive drive into the bush was the sudden arrival in the hotel of four very tall, young, dark-suited Hereros, the Chief's councillors, who strode through the lobby and up the main staircase to knock on my door. They crowded into my room to discuss Chief Hosea's Open Letter. It referred to Macmillan's speech and the policies of the three governments, then continued:

After forty-one years of rule as a Mandate we have no secondary school for the vast majority – the 473,000 Africans and other Non-Europeans; when Europeans covet lands we have to move on, we have no security, no hope for the future. Is this what the Principal Allied Powers intended by their conception of a 'Sacred Trust', where the indigenous people would be helped to stand on their own feet?

We implore your respective governments, now, to be true to the ideals that have moved you in the reforms brought into other countries in Africa. We, too, are your responsibility, and as long as we remain oppressed, so long will you not be able to point with pride to your other achievements. The bell may toll for us, it tolls for each and all of you as well.

They deputed me to convey their disillusion and anger to the British and American ambassadors. Flying off to Cape Town I looked down on Windhoek's showplace, the cemetery. Nearby were the small houses and shanties of the location. 'Why don't they move?' a Christian minister had asked, not attempting to hide irritation. 'The new township is really no further away.' But there it was, shoved way out on barren land: Katutura, the regimented mass of block houses was called; Katutura, which means 'we have no permanent dwelling place'.

The British Ambassador spared me ten minutes, the American, forty-five. They listened with apparent sympathy. The former gave me a copy of the Wind of Change speech. Macmillan had referred to the rest of Africa, to Asia, the Commonwealth, the United States and Europe. He did not mention South-West Africa. He spoke of Durban and Johannesburg, Pretoria and Bloemfontein. He did not mention Windhoek. He quoted John Donne's 'Any man's death diminishes me'. What of the dead in Windhoek location?

When the Open Letters reached London and Paris and Brussels, would they be read? Filed? Or tossed into waste-paper baskets? Would no government ever act on such appeals, however often and passionately reiterated? Must it always be violence that brought about change?

Wretchedly I wondered whether my well-intentioned involvement only led to further frustration? Surely I should rather have insisted that only by their own actions, in their own territory, could they ever hope to win their freedom. The Preamble to the Declaration of Human Rights states: 'It is essential if man is not to be compelled to have recourse, as a last resort, to rebellion against tyranny and oppression, that human rights should be protected by the Rule of Law.' But where could they get arms and how could they repel South Africa's massive military force?

Sam Nujoma and SWAPO, which had grown out of the Ovambo People's Organization, restrained themselves to non-violence for fourteen years before resorting to armed resistance against that violent and illegal regime. But with Britain and America adamantly refusing to use any pressure except words of condemnation, the South African government was long able to flout the entire world's demand that Namibia – as the territory is now named – should have free elections, leading to independence. Meanwhile, British and South African mining companies have been plundering the mineral wealth of the country.

When I met Hosea Kutako under the thorn trees, I handed him a modest gift from a friend in London: £200 for some of the victims of the shooting. His councillors brought me the chief's meticulous receipt, listing the twenty-eight most needy cases among whom the money had been shared. They included:

Rheinhardt Kuiiri: Dead. Mother and children aged 4 and 5 £15

Martha Nurises: Broken lower leg, both bones, has two children aged 5 and 3 £15

Albanus Karange: Shot through the chest left arm paralysed – £5

Bartholomews Kahliko: Dead. Survived by widow and three children aged 8, 3, 1 years respectively £20

Dominicus Kashipuku: Shot through the stomach and the back £2.10.0

Annah Mungunda: Dead. Survived by old uncle £2.10.0

I was never to see the Chief again. He died in 1970. After his death, disputes over the chieftainship drastically weakened the Hereros. Hosea Kutako, the leader who first brought the plight of all the people of South-West Africa to the attention of the world, like his spokesman and friend Michael Scott is barely mentioned in modern histories of the struggle.

*

Returning to Johannesburg, I was taken one morning by women from the Black Sash to the Bantu Commissioner's Court in Fordsburg: the Pass Laws Court.

In the main entrance of the cluster of low-lying buildings an African woman waited. 'Why are you here?' asked a Black Sash woman. '*Ek soek my man*' (I am looking for my husband), she replied. A few nights ago he had not come home. She knew the inevitable routine and had gone the round from local police station to pass laws courts, dread that he had been imprisoned only less than hope that he had not met with an accident. She was only one of tens of thousands who suffered this dread, who went through this routine. She held a crumpled pound note in case she should trace him and be able to pay a fine. The Black Sasher remained to assist her.

The rest of us, who now included Peregrine Worsthorne, a staunchly Conservative journalist from London, went into Criminal Court C, a drab room, to a wooden bench reserved for white members of the public. Not that any but the Black Sash or an occasional employer ever occupied it. Worsthorne, in dark suit, sat amongst a group of middle-class women wearing obligatory hats or headscarves. Through a window we could see a crowd of Africans huddled in a wired-in enclosure, some sullen, some dejected – there was none of the laughter which enlivened the Treason Trial.

The Bantu Commissioner, neat, white-haired, entered. The black interpreter called for the first defendant. Earnest, tall, unshaven, he had been arrested over the weekend and now was accused of altering the date in his 'reference book'. 'Guilty or not guilty?' he was asked. He explained that when he'd been discharged from his previous job, his employer had written the wrong date in the book. He had therefore altered it. 'This is a serious matter,' said the Commissioner. 'In future, take the book back to your employer and get him to alter it. One pound or seven days.' Thump of a rubber stamp as the man was replaced in the dock by another, carrying a bright pink hat. He had lost his book. 'Eight pounds or eight weeks.' Thump of the stamp.

A boy came next, very young and very frightened. 'I was working in the school holidays when I was arrested,' he said and bowed humbly. He was not yet sixteen, the age covered by the law. He went free, but he had spent the weekend in police cells.

Several more men followed – they all seemed dazed – then came one who was aggressively defiant. He had left his book at his workplace and the police had refused to let him fetch it. 'Five pounds or five weeks.' Thump of stamp.

I could no longer control the tears flooding my eyes. Worsthorne handed me his large handkerchief. Never had I felt so white, so privileged, so guilty: we were a part of it, witnessing, patronizing with our pity, emasculating.

Five more men were sentenced to five pounds or five weeks. Three were remanded for police evidence. Only one was well-dressed and probably able to pay the fine, the rest were shabby, ragged even, surely destined for jail. Number 35 was quite young. 'Guilty or not guilty?' He took his reference book from a pocket; the police had not asked him to produce it. 'Case withdrawn.'

At teabreak the Commissioner withdrew. He had tried thirty-five cases in forty-five minutes.

As for us, we went from there to have tea and scones at the Country Club.

A few days later, at the end of February, I returned to London, where I was able to tell organizations and press what the pass laws meant for the hundreds of thousands imprisoned each year, and for their families. Anger had reached boiling-point. Both the ANC and the rival Pan Africanist Congress were planning protest campaigns, and under Bishop Reeves liberal and left-wing organizations, with an unprecedented display of unity, were calling for the abolition of the pass laws.

On Monday, 21 March, the PAC's day for demonstrations, the news came that police had shot dead sixty-nine men and women and children and wounded 180, at a township called Sharpeville.

Next morning came the news that police had killed yet more protesters in the Cape, a thousand miles from Sharpeville, at a location called Langa.

Just as, three months earlier, they had shot down demonstrators in the location at Windhoek.

7

The African National Congress

As the plane flew south above the Transvaal's cultivated pattern of farmlands and occasional dorps, I wondered what hazards lay ahead.

'A history of the ANC must be written,' Anthony Sampson had said, 'and you're the one to do it!' Time was running out, he'd explained; the organization had been established in 1912, most of its founders had already died and the survivors, now very old, must be interviewed soon. My protests that I had no academic qualifications and anyway thought an African writer would be more appropriate were overridden. Why not you yourself? I'd asked. Anthony had been a brilliant editor of *Drum* magazine, but, backed by Philip Mason, Director of the Institute of Race Relations in London, he argued that my work with the Treason Trial Fund had given me invaluable connections.

Eventually I agreed and, with a princely advance of £200 from my publisher, set off, excited but also apprehensive. A year earlier, after Sharpeville, the ANC had been outlawed and under the Suppression of Communism Act merely talking about it could be legally construed as 'furthering the aims of a banned organization'. Quite apart from myself, I was anxious not to endanger the people I interviewed, and I began devising a code for my notes: Nelson Mandela would be Traf – for Trafalgar; Z. K. Matthews would be Man at UN; an Eastern Cape leader, bearded and melancholy in appearance, would be El Greco; while anything to do with Communism would be Golders or Green, where I mistakenly believed Karl Marx to be buried.

It promised to be an eventful, precarious time. Within weeks, on 31 May 1961, South Africa was to become a Republic – a white Boer Republic in the eyes of blacks. Mandela had gone underground in order to organize a countrywide stay-at-home protest strike. Would there be a repetition of Sharpeville?

At Jan Smuts Airport I went smoothly through Immigration. No sign of the Special Branch. Relieved, I joined Poppy and her family, who welcomed me at the barrier.

'So Miss Benson flew in this morning!' a member of the Special Branch remarked to Ruth First, when he happened to encounter her in the city that day. So much for my powers of observation.

Ruth, as always chic and vital, quickly put me in the picture: police searching the country for Mandela had arrested thousands – most of them black – and several leaders had been charged with 'furthering the aims' of the ANC. Her husband, Joe Slovo, was to defend them.

Headlines in the Press reflected the growing tension: POLICE CONFIDENT ALL IS UNDER CONTROL; CAPE WHITES FORM VIGILANTE GROUPS; RAND RUSH FOR ARMS; NEWSHOUNDS ARRIVE IN LATEST TROUBLE MISSION. As Mandela continued to elude the police and regularly issued statements calling on workers to 'Stay at Home!' on Monday the 29th, the press dubbed him the Black Pimpernel. At night helicopters flew low over townships, flashing searchlights down on to houses to frighten the occupants. Police announced they would force people to go to work and employers threatened to sack those who responded to Mandela's call.

Yet on the first day of the strike, when I met Patrick O'Donovan, an old friend from the *Observer*, for lunch in the city, the usually bustling streets were almost denuded of Africans. Clearly many thousands had resisted the massive intimidation. Leonard Ingalls of the *New York Times* told us that in Johannesburg the strike was estimated as 50 to 75 per cent successful. But over the State radio came an announcement from the head of the Special Branch: the labour position was 'normal'. Next day he was to announce that it had 'returned to normal'. (In a subsequent trial police admitted that 60 per cent of the workers had struck.) In Port Elizabeth, always the most militant area, 75 per cent stayed at home, while in Durban many Indians responded to Mandela's call. Even in Cape Town there had been unusual support from the Coloured community.

Nevertheless, next morning came news that Mandela had called off the strike. Feeling excitingly conspiratorial, Patrick and I, with Robert Oakeshott of the *Financial Times*, were driven

My Mother

My Father

Off for a walk with Nanny; Pretoria Prison in the
background

Mom, Poppy and me

(*Left*) Dad, Poppy and me

(*Below*) The New Hospital and our house, seen from the koppie

(*Right*) Pretoria Girls' High Tennis Team

James Stewart at a première – I am the fan on the right

Judge Brinton

John Murray in Cairo

Captain Pixie Benson

Alan Paton

Tshekedi Khama and Michael Scott

Michael Scott

(*Above*) Chief Hosea Kutako

(*Left*) Nelson Mandela at lunch in London, 1962

(*Above*) Chief Albert Lutuli
(*Above right*) Walter Sisulu
(*Right*) Bram Fischer

Athol Fugard and Serpent Players

With Pa at Jan Smuts Airport, 1966

by Ruth First to a block of flats in Yeoville – one of the less prosperous white suburbs. In a sparsely furnished room dimmed by drawn yellow curtains, with a single electric bulb hanging from the ceiling, we were welcomed by Nelson Mandela. He was far from conspiratorial, relaxed in striped sports shirt and grey trousers, slanting eyes closed to slits as laughter reverberated through his huge frame.

I was content to listen as the 'pros' questioned him. The disappointing response to the strike and his decision to call it off, did he concede it had been a failure? asked Robert.

'In the light of the steps taken by government to suppress the Stay-at-Home, it was a tremendous success,' he retorted. The mobilizing of army as well as police was 'striking testimony of African strength and a measure of the government's weakness'.

What about the ANC's policy of non-violence? asked Patrick.

'This was not just a question of belief, but a selfish consideration. In face of a highly industrialized state, a sensitive economy and a government armed to the teeth, the ANC has to be realistic.'

Patrick referred to the moderation of the Africans and was forcefully corrected: 'Moderation is not the appropriate word! Our feeling against imperialism is intense. I detest it! But,' Mandela went on, 'credit must be given to the ANC as the only political organization that has gone out to preach the question of discussing problems in an atmosphere of goodwill.'

His supporters, weren't they worried about cooperating with whites?

'Once the average African is convinced that this cooperation is genuine, and that whites support his claims and aspirations, he gives full support to this policy.' Mandela gave as examples Michael Scott, living among Africans in Tobruk shantytown, and Father Huddleston's opposition to the Sophiatown removals. Unfortunately, he added, other countries in Africa misunderstood this cooperation, but he thought this would soon be cleared up.

It was time to go. At the door he turned to face us and, his face suddenly sombre, he declared: 'If the government reaction is to crush by naked force our non-violent demonstrations, we will have to seriously reconsider our tactics. In my mind we are closing a chapter on this question of a non-violent policy.'

Three weeks later a friend dropped me at a bungalow in a white suburb, again the drawn curtains but this time, as well as a bearhug of welcome from Nelson, a friendly Alsatian loped in, nuzzling for attention. A tray of tea stood ready. All the police in the country were on the alert and here was their quarry, sociably recollecting the past.

He told of his upbringing as the son of a chief in the royal kraal of the Tembu people, of how at night by the fire he'd listened fascinated to tales told by the tribal elders about the days when the land was theirs, when they'd governed themselves, before the wars against invading Europeans. I mentioned my great-grandfather, who had led a commando against the Xhosa – it made us smile to think how once our ancestors had been at war but now he and I were on the same side. We were also almost the same age; I had thought he was the younger, but in fact he was a year older than I.

At twenty-two, he had run away from the Transkei to escape an arranged marriage. In Johannesburg the only job he could get, this young aristocrat and university student, was as a mine policeman. 'I sat at the compound gate, watching people come and go. I wore a uniform and carried a knobkerrie and whistle!' He laughed heartily at what must have been a humiliating experience.

Walter Sisulu had rescued him, 'pushed' him towards studying law and provided a 'decent' suit for graduation. In 1944, along with Oliver Tambo, a friend from university, he had been encouraged by Walter to join the ANC. With other young Nationalists they had formed a militant Youth League. The Defiance Campaign, repeated bannings, imprisonment, the Treason Trial, followed.

I did not realize how important every detail of Mandela's personal as well as his political life would become and concentrated on the theme of his association with the ANC; nor did I use a tape recorder. During the twenty-six years of his imprisonment, the outside world has heard his voice in only one brief interview, secretly made by a British television journalist during that May of 1961. Pictured in a bleak room and wearing a winter jacket, with a side-parting clipped in his hair (a momentary fashion), he speaks – as he had to us – of the crushing violence of the state which, finally and inevitably, had put an end to the liberation movement's policy of non-violence.

Mandela had eluded the police for more than nine months. One night in mid-November, I waited expectantly in the living-room of that same modest bungalow. As he came in, looking very fit, thinner and bearded, he cast off the chauffeur's white coat and peaked cap he'd been wearing. He was in ebullient mood, just back from touring Natal and the Cape. 'A wonderful experience, visiting the rural areas!' he said. 'You can't comprehend unless you stay right there *with* the people.'

It was eight years since he had been confined by bans to Johannesburg. I recalled our first encounter at that time. In the Indian Congress office I'd come upon him in the thick of a loud and furious quarrel with Yusuf Cachalia. Quite unembarrassed they broke off to respond to my questions about the Defiance Campaign. Neither he, nor Yusuf later, remembered the incident and he had long ago learned to control his hot temper.

Now he could spare only an hour, he said apologetically. Pressure was mounting. But he seemed amazingly relaxed as he described the narrow escape he'd had a few days earlier: 'I was waiting on a corner in town, wearing that chauffeur's outfit, when the car due to pick me up failed to arrive. It's vital,' he broke off to explain, 'to be absolutely punctual when you're functioning underground. And I saw, coming towards me, one of the Special Branch – an African member I knew by sight. He looked straight at me. I thought, it's all up! But he went on by. And as he did so, he winked and gave the ANC salute!'

The incident made Nelson roar with laughter, but he also regarded it as an example of the hidden support the ANC had, even among the police.

When the hour was up he offered me a lift and, after putting on the coat and peaked cap, led me out to a car that was very much the worse for wear. We drove off, with me, as madam, in the back and he, as chauffeur, in front. But the engine kept spluttering to a stop. Each time it seemed an eternity before he managed to rev it back to life. At any moment a police car could have driven by and stopped to see what was wrong. He joked about it, but this was the only transport available to him. At last the car coughed its way to within walking distance of my sister's flat and we said goodbye.

A few weeks later, on 16 December, sabotage broke out in Johannesburg, Port Elizabeth and Durban, launching *Umkhonto we Sizwe*, Spear of the Nation. I realized then how precious even that hour must have been to him, an hour spared from planning the action which had been implied by his remark '. . . we are closing a chapter' on the policy of non-violence.

Six days earlier in Oslo, as if – unwittingly – stamping a seal on that chapter, the King of Norway awarded the Nobel Prize for Peace to Chief Albert Lutuli in recognition, so Lutuli insisted, of the ANC's long record of non-violence and its stand for a non-racial democracy.

The award had been announced on 23 October and Walter Sisulu and Duma Nokwe had asked me to assist 'Chief', who was virtually besieged by journalists and swamped with communications from all over the world. After flying to Durban, I was driven northward through lush green sugar plantations and teeming, brightly coloured Indian villages with silvered temples, white planters' mansions and golf-courses in the distance, until we reached Stanger, a small town sited near a sugar mill. There, E. V. Mahomed, an accountant and friend of Chief's, escorted me to the Bantu Affairs Commissioner to apply for the permit required to visit Lutuli, who was confined by bans to the neighbourhood of Stanger. Duly granted, this read:

PERMIT
(In terms of Section 24(1) of Act No. 18 of 1936)
Permission is hereby granted to Miss Dorothy Mary Benson . . . to enter the Umvoti Mission Reserve on the 25th October 1961 for the purpose of visiting Ex-Chief A. J. Lutuli.
1. This permit expires on the 1st November 1961 but may be withdrawn at any time without reason assigned.
2. The permit holder must make his own arrangements for board and lodging. Lodging with bantu is not permitted.
3. Under no circumstances must the holder hereof interfere with or in the domestic affairs of the bantu.
4. In his dealings with the bantu, the holder hereof must behave in a dignified manner and refrain from criticism of the Administration of the Government or of any of its officials.

As E. V. drove me along a rough road, past neat homesteads and beyond hedges of bougainvillaea and amatungulu, he expressed his veneration for Lutuli, a man with 'fire in his belly'. Because of that veneration, for years he had put himself at Chief's disposal.

When we arrived at the humble red-roofed house marked by two tall cypresses, we were welcomed by Mrs Lutuli, Noku-khanya, a spare, motherly woman. Chief was in the dining-room, seated at a table covered by telegrams and letters. Our first task, he said, was to reply to *the* cable. I promptly did so, sending the historic message from the EUROPEANS ONLY section of Stanger's post office:

GUNNAR JAHN, NOBEL COMMITTEE OSLO. FILLED WITH SENSE OF GRATITUDE AND APPRECIATION. SHALL BE APPLYING FOR TRAVEL PERMIT. LUTULI.

In one of numerous subsequent trips to the post office, Chief accompanied me, walking with calm dignity through the separate doorway to the NON-EUROPEAN section. Each morning, at E. V.'s office, he met correspondents from London, America, Europe, Johannesburg and Cape Town, coming freshly to each encounter, giving to each question his full attention, sometimes closing his eyes as though he turned inward to peruse the past, insisting that the credit was not his at all. 'My regime of the African National Congress,' he repeatedly explained, 'inherited policies that go back fifty years which I have been happy to carry out.'

I was staying with E. V. and his quietly submissive wife. Although he was a staunch member of the Liberal Party, according to Indian custom, and to my embarrassment, she cooked and served meals but could not join us at table. I slept in one of their two garages, empty but for a narrow bed. Cries emanating from the next-door garage, in which their Zulu maid lived, announced the birth of a baby. That was the least of the night-time disturbances. No sooner had I switched off the light and darted into bed, than squads of Natal's notoriously gigantic cockroaches advanced from all four walls towards the centre of the garage where I lay, petrified. Only drenching rain kept them at bay, enabling me to sleep through one night, rain which became a deluge on the Saturday of the meeting we had organized to celebrate the Nobel award.

Lutuli was refused permission to attend the celebration. The authorities also blocked the use of buses to transport people from Durban. But nothing could daunt the crowds; convoys of cars packed with Africans and Indians drove into Stanger, disgorging their occupants, who formed umbrellaed queues outside the hall we'd hired. Lutuli, with his wife – ignoring the bans under which it was illegal for him to be with more than one person at a time – joined Alan and Dorrie Paton for an informal lunch given by Indian friends. To Chief's delight, Alan recited a 'praise song' he was to give at the meeting:

> You there, Lutuli, they thought your world was small
> They thought you lived in Groutville
> Now they discover
> It is the world you live in . . .

Then, to the freedom song 'Somlandela Lutuli' – we will follow Lutuli – we all formed a line behind his imposing figure to perform a dance, at once thoughtful and jubilant.

Still elated, Chief settled in a corner of a friend's garage, adjacent to the hall. From there he could just hear sounds coming from the packed meeting and imagine what was happening: the sibilant, long-drawn-out 'Shame!' of disgust which greeted the reading of the magistrate's telegram refusing him permission to attend the meeting; the women's ululations as his wife was presented with a scroll of honour on his behalf; the applause greeting Fatima Meer when she spoke of his vision of a free South Africa, the vision which taught people to demand freedom with love and tranquillity, which had led to the martyrdom of many, the vision the world was heralding. Loud and clear he heard the wild excitement following each verse as his close friend M. B. Yengwa declaimed a Zulu praise song:

> . . . The great bull that enemies tried to fence in a kraal
> Has broken the strong fence and wandered far,
> As far as Oslo!
> *Nkosi yase* Groutville! *Nkosi yase Afrika*! *Nkosi yase* world!

Meanwhile, in the front row, grim-faced members of the Special Branch laboriously made notes.

On my last day I took a stack of correspondence to the Lutulis' house for his signature. He was very tired. Leaving him to tackle the work at leisure, I played with his grandson in the garden. A photographer from an Afrikaner newspaper drove up – the picture he took of Msomi seated on my lap featured in a caustic article about a white woman assisting the prizewinner.

I was having tea with Chief and Nokukhanya when the telephone rang. A Johannesburg journalist wanted to know how many cables Lutuli had received from important people. His wife joined in his chuckles as he replied, 'But each person is important in his own way.'

My final task was to prepare his application for permission to go to Oslo. Within twenty-four hours a passport was granted.

Alan Paton said Lutuli was 'the shadow of a great rock in a weary land'. In his day he was unique in uniting people of all races. The government, therefore, having failed to crush his rapidly growing influence by a one-year, then a two-year ban, or even a charge of high treason, finally confined him to his home district for five years, a restriction that was reimposed until, in 1967, he was run down by a train and killed.

In my research into the ANC's history, I came to know my country as never before. I travelled by rail, road and air to cities and towns, to remote villages such as Inanda in Natal and Thaba'Nchu in the Orange Free State, as well as townships and Bloemfontein location, where I visited the hall in which the ANC had held its inaugural conference in 1912 – a bioscope now, standing among red and yellow brick houses under dusty trees. And I came to know our history, so rich and complex compared with the arid distortions learned in school. This history flowed partly from recollection of individual lives, from people's opinions of each other and, of course, from what it meant to be black. And as these men and women of all races and from various organizations and backgrounds, spoke of their experiences through decades of protest and struggle, the past grew in my imagination. Despite the risk, they spoke with extraordinary frankness. I checked and counter-checked in an effort to be as accurate as possible, but found that the truth often lay deep in a bottomless well.

Eventually, I sent what I had written to the individuals

concerned. The response I treasure most came from Port Elizabeth: 'The manuscript has been read and corrected by Mr Caleb Mayekiso and Mr Vuyisile Mini . . .' Vuyisile, the finest singer in the Treason Trial choir, was found guilty of ordering the death of a State witness and was hanged in Pretoria prison in 1964. Caleb died while held in solitary confinement in 1969.

One of the few survivors of the ANC's inauguration in 1912 was Mweli Skota, who had an office not far from the Law Courts in Johannesburg. He was a courteous old man, formerly an editor, who vividly recalled attending that first conference which Pixley ka Izaka Seme, newly returned from studying law at Columbia and Oxford universities, had called. Chiefs, intellectuals and others came together and Seme emphasized that tribalism must be buried; on its ashes they would build a united African nation. Skota spoke of the remarkable abilities, humour and good looks of Charlotte Maxeke, who had led African women in their 'quite revolutionary' protests against the pass laws at the time of the First World War. 'People felt wonderfully optimistic during those early years,' he said. 'To them, freedom was only round the corner.' Disillusion came, he added sadly, when not one of the deputations they sent to London to appeal for support from the British Government achieved their objective. 'People became very despondent.'

Across the corridor from his room was Walter Sisulu's office. I was pleased to find that it was more prosperous than the one I'd visited nearly ten years earlier. Since Walter's movements were dogged by Sergeant Dirker of the Special Branch, a thoroughly lugubrious man, it was difficult to relax and get on with our interview. Late one afternoon, therefore, a friend gave me a lift to Orlando, where mile upon mile of bald little houses covered sloping ground, hardly a tree to be seen, all regimented brick and concrete against brown earth, the only softening element the pall of smoke from a multitude of stoves cooking the evening meal. It made a grim contrast to Sophiatown's anarchic vitality. One day this conglomeration would be officially named South-Western Townships, with the acronym Soweto.

The night was bitterly cold. There were no street lights. Along dirt roads bumpy with potholes people cycled or trudged home. The Sisulus lived near a railway line. Albertina, a nursing sister, generous of spirit as of build, was expecting me. The small front room was lit by lamps and candles. Walter arrived, in overcoat and woollen scarf, and over tea we continued our interview, with Albertina joining in, since she had been the solitary young woman member at the inception of the Youth League in 1944. Their wedding picture hung on the wall, he slender and rather wistful, she modestly smiling – now she was the mother of five and the youngest girl was called Nonkululekhe, Freedom. What struck me when I came to write about Sisulu was that he, more than any other African leader, knew just what it meant to be a 'native'. He had been a kitchen 'boy', studying English grammar in his spare time, a miner and then, working in a bakery for £2 a week, he'd led a strike for better conditions and been sacked. That, the first of countless experiences of jail, had resulted from protesting against a white man's ill-treatment of a black child. Aged forty-one, he had visited Russia and China in 1953, passing through Israel and London, and for the first time had been treated – as he put it – 'like a dignified human being'. From interviews with a variety of men and women, I had learned that he was quite as important as Mandela and wondered, but did not ask, how much he knew of the continuing, sporadic acts of sabotage.

Afterwards, he led me down the road past a barren area, a danger-ground, he explained, where *tsotsis* preyed on returning wage-earners, on to the Mandelas' house, facing a hill. Inside, it was colourful and full of Nelson's books. I had met Winnie several times at dinner with Nelson in the past. She was putting their baby daughters, Zeni and Zindzi, to bed. A social worker with Child Welfare, her married life had been continually disrupted, first by the Treason Trial and the months of Nelson's imprisonment during the 1960 State of Emergency, then by his disappearance underground. In her youthful prettiness could be descried the strikingly beautiful woman whom the State failed to crush by repeated bannings, by solitary confinement and by banishment. The resulting isolation would tragically lead to scandal as she became a law unto herself.

Driving the eight miles back to the city along a winding road dangerously crammed with weaving bicycles, past mine dumps and labour compounds, I thought about the Mandelas, the Sisulus and the Lutulis, about their homes. In any other country such political leaders would live in mansions, if not in Presidents' palaces. Had Mandela been white, as a successful lawyer his house in Johannesburg's northern suburbs would have been substantial, even luxurious. In half an hour's time I would again be enjoying that suburban social life of dinner parties and weekends by the pool, and soon I would be in the Cape. Most of the people I had been interviewing were prevented by bans or by the pass laws from travelling freely. How ironic it was that Mandela could only move about the country of his birth because he was a fugitive.

Looking back twenty-seven years, perhaps the most significant encounter was with the Rev. James Calata in the small town of Cradock. I had met him when he was on trial for treason; he was among those released in the early stages. Now I set off by train from Port Elizabeth on a bitterly cold night, arriving before dawn at an ill-lit, old-fashioned station. Finding a taxi, I took a chance and asked for the Grand Hotel – there was sure to be one – but when the driver knocked on its door there was no answer. '*Verdomde kaffers!*' he cursed and drove me on a few blocks to a verandahed single-storey hotel where the African porter led me to a room. My fitful sleep was interrupted by a clanging bell. Quickly and as discreetly as possible I telephoned Calata, who gave me instructions on how to get to his house. Emerging from the hotel after breakfast into Cradock's Church Square, I almost bumped into a heavy white man in a hat. Backing away, as I hurried down a side street I checked to see if he was following, but the chilly street was empty. Ahead was a stretch of rough ground. On the far side, as described by Calata, tall trees sheltered a red-roofed church and a whitewashed house. Beyond, a sprawl of brown clay houses marked the location. In the distance, flat-topped hills gave an austere beauty to the arid landscape. I was distracted from the scenery by the appearance, across the road from the church, of a Volkswagen: in it sat the heavy man and, beside him, an African. They watched as I approached the house and knocked at the front door.

Calata welcomed me in and, when I gestured apologetically to the Security Police, he shrugged. After introducing me to his wife, a fragile, shy woman, he led me through to his study. In his sixties, thin, very dark-skinned, he had a slight cast in one eye. Before we settled down he pointed through the window to one of the hills, 'That is where Olive Schreiner is buried.' He had no need to indicate the decaying houses and gulleys running with waste in the foreground. Under the Group Areas Act, he explained, the location was to be moved two miles away and meanwhile it was illegal for people to repair their houses.

Shelves were stacked with books and on the walls, but for a space which bore the mark of pictures recently removed, hung religious paintings and photographs of bishops, of clergy and African boy scouts. A few weeks ago, he said with a hoarse laugh, he had been arrested for a picture taken in 1942 of an ANC delegation to the Deputy Prime Minister and a 1939 photograph of himself as President of the Cape ANC. Imprisoned for twelve days before coming to trial, he had been found guilty of 'displaying' pictures of an unlawful organization and was sentenced to six months. His appeal would soon come before the Supreme Court. Now, as he committed the further offence of describing his membership of the ANC and his long years as its Secretary-General, his manner was matter-of-fact. He had a rich voice; it was a pleasure to listen to him. I knew that he was a fine musician, both in his church and when composing those freedom songs which had inspired volunteers to the Defiance Campaign; and that he, more than any other individual, had rescued Congress during its serious decline in the thirties, although he'd been ill with TB and almost penniless.

Proudly he showed me his church, airy and simple, lit by candles and colourful with flowers. 'Those police, they have no respect for religion. When they raid my church they throw their cigarette ends on the floor.' For the first time anger was revealed. 'They are raw in the true sense of the word. We have one consolation,' he added. 'We can laugh at the whites. It helps to know that when you look at them, you are not looking up but down, and that you are suffering for the right thing.'

When I left him at lunchtime, there was no sign of the Volkswagen. That evening rain sheeted down. Making sure I was not followed, I found a taxi in the square and asked to be taken to St Matthew's Church. Would the driver report a white woman going to the location at night? But Calata scoffed at my anxiety and ushered me into the church hall, where I sat beside his wife among several rows of Africans. He settled at the piano, erect in a black suit as he waited for quiet. His choir of young men and women filed on to the platform, he touched a note to give the key and they sang.

They sang in celebration of the women's vast protest gathering in Pretoria in 1956 which told the government, 'Hey, when you strike a woman, you strike a rock!' They sang about the Treason Trial and about the Bishop of Johannesburg assisting the wounded at Sharpeville. Finally, they sang a song he had composed in 1952: 'Join Congress ye youths, The time has come, Write down your names . . .' Calata conducted vigorously, the young people sang with a powerful beauty – all of them risking arrest, he especially with that prison sentence hanging over him – while the rain beat down and outside lay the threatened location.

Next morning he drove me to the station in his rackety car and we waved until we lost sight of each other.

It was during the journey back to Port Elizabeth that I suddenly realized I felt wholly South African, involved in the fate of my country, belonging. As if I had had a crash course in what it meant to be – as Michael Scott once put it – born there, of my parents, at a particular time and, as a result, with a certain responsibility.

A month later, in September 1961, Calata's appeal was heard. The judge confirmed the sentence of six months' imprisonment, suspending it for three years.

'The picture case,' Calata wrote to me, in his small, neat handwriting, 'was not too great a disappointment except the criminal stain in the face of the public. I did not expect the judge to stoop down to politics. I feel no breach of my conscience over those pictures. It is one of those persecution measures which I have become used to and am leaving it to God, who can turn it to some good.'

Arriving in Cape Town, I found the policy which Cousin Tiny implemented now plumbed new depths of inhumanity. Prime Minister Verwoerd had decreed that under Section 10 of the Urban Areas Act, the Western Cape must be rid of 180,000 Africans. Most would remain anonymous. One family made headlines because of the birth of triplets. Mrs Wenie Ntlonti was the mother and, shortly afterwards, she was 'endorsed out' –

ordered to leave her husband and go with their children to the Transkei, several hundred miles away.

The Black Sash had taken up her case and with their assistance I found Mrs Ntlonti in a 'Site and Service' *pondok* on Great Dutch Crescent – part rutted-earth road, part sewer – in Nyanga East township. Coming from rows of tightly packed, rusty shacks among hot sand dunes incessantly blasted by the wind, the moment I entered her little home I felt an affecting sense of a safe refuge. A bright-faced young woman, she was accompanied by her two older children, Derick, aged four, and Winston, aged one. The twins – for one triplet had died – were still in hospital. Mrs Ntlonti explained that part of the £30 which she had received from readers of the newspaper report had gone towards funeral expenses for the baby. She hoped that part of the remainder would help to send Derick to school. But most of it would have to go on train fares to the Transkei. All their savings from the £12 a month her husband earned in a glass factory had gone into making their home more comfortable. In the course of five years he had divided it into two rooms and a tiny kitchen, put in wood floors – a great luxury – as well as firm doors and covered the cardboard inner walls with yellow paper. On the table was a clean cloth, a Bible and some tumblers and, on the wall, a baptism certificate. She had no idea where in the Transkei she would go, nor how they could exist there. Her young husband, whose framed picture stood on the dresser, would be sent to live with other husbands similarly bereft, in 'bachelor' dormitories.

On the drive back to Cape Town I passed those dormitories in Langa: shabby cream-coloured buildings with tiny windows which, at the time of the police shootings in March 1960, had housed 18,000 men.

All one could do was to write articles about the Ntlontis, point out that they were among hundreds of thousands of Africans whose family lives were ruthlessly destroyed under apartheid and send on to her via the Black Sash the small gifts donated by sympathetic readers.

I could no longer feel unalloyed affection for relatives or for friends from the past who, through prejudice or through apathy, condoned apartheid. To my delight, Poppy had become warmly supportive, but I seemed unable to convey to our cousins how life had been excitingly transformed by coming to know these fellow-South Africans of all races. 'You mean you were alone with Natives!' one exclaimed, after seeing me drive up with an Eastern Cape leader.

Even self-styled liberals said: 'Don't be so impatient, things are moving. Just give it time.' Couldn't they see how every moment mattered when black youths were being driven to become *tsotsis*, their mothers frantic? In this, their only life, in this world of ours? *Time*. What did that matter to the Ciskei babies dying of starvation, babies whose vast eyes had gazed coldly at me from their Belsen-faces? Men claiming to be Christian had committed the subtlest cruelty: depriving fathers and mothers of the humblest and greatest need, to dream dreams for their children.

I wondered how I dared to be stimulated in spite of the persecution and suffering I had witnessed, but there was no doubt that tension sparked adrenalin. Everyone in the 'movement' seemed almost casual about the intrusions of the Security Police, as the Special Branch were renamed. Professor Z. K. Matthews met me in Alice, the small town where he had been an eminent figure at Fort Hare University until he'd resigned in protest against Bantu Education. As he led me from my hotel to his car, he indicated a Volkswagen waiting nearby: 'The Security Police in these dorps have nothing better to do than harass us,' he remarked. 'Well, we'll give them a little thrill!' And he proceeded to drive round and round the square, peering into the rearview mirror and chuckling at the sight of the police stolidly following our gyrations. He might chuckle but I, not so accustomed, flushed my notes down the toilet on returning to the hotel.

The Security Police turned out in force, senior officers included, for a celebratory meeting on Afrika Day, 15 April 1962. In a field at Kliptown, where the Congress of the People had been held seven years before, they loitered around the fringes of the crowd. Posters of Lutuli and Lumumba were held high. Albertina Sisulu and Winnie Mandela wore Xhosa dress, while men in Zulu warrior garb vociferously approved speeches made from an improvised platform on a lorry. Interspersed with the rhetoric were sober references to the huge sums spent on arms, money desperately needed for better housing and food for the malnourished. 'It's true, it's true!' a young man beside me wearing a silver miner's helmet passionately affirmed.

Next day I had lunch with a visitor from Britain, Robert Birley, the headmaster of Eton. It was not all that startling a social leap because this huge, immensely erudite man would soon be teaching in the most deprived areas of South Africa. Over lunch with Robert Loder, one of his former pupils, now with the Anglo-American Corporation, Birley spoke of his intention to resign from Eton in order to become Visiting Professor of Education at Wits University. He thought his work in Germany after the Second World War should be relevant – he had been in charge of de-Nazifying education. He evinced a lively interest in my ANC researches and expressed a determination to meet people of all races, of all political persuasions and all ages. Each time I had returned to South Africa I had been struck by how cliquish the various dissidents were, out of touch with each other, even mutually suspicious in what, after all, was a lonely situation. Birley's unusual lack of any such caution was very endearing.

One afternoon in May I went to Orlando with Nat Nakasa and Peter Magubane, *Drum*'s star reporter and photographer. We had tea with Zeph Mothopeng, who earlier that day had been released from prison. A tall, jovial, middle-aged man in a loose-fitting suit, he was one of the Pan Africanist Congress leaders jailed for organizing anti-pass demonstrations just before the Sharpeville shootings occurred. During the two years in a cell it was, he said, 'the isolation and cramping-in feeling' that he'd felt most sharply. 'I never liked to see a bird in a cage,' he explained, 'but it never struck me it was something of an inconvenience for the bird – now I know what it is like. For an open-air man . . .' He broke off to accept a joyful welcome home from old friends. He was to return to jail again and again for his militant role in Africanist resistance.

Exhilarated by his spirit, I returned to my sister's flat to learn that in my absence the Security Police had called. They left a message ordering me to take my South African passport to the local passport office. There it was confiscated. Shock was dulled by the urgent necessity of getting a British passport since I had assignments for the *Observer* in Nyasaland and Tanganyika. Fortunately, the British Embassy quickly granted a passport, on the grounds that Dublin, at the time of my father's birth, had been part of the Empire.

A different kind of assignment took me briefly to Khartoum. To further Chief Lutuli's call for international sanctions, I met an official of the Foreign Ministry who listened sympathetically to the request that the Sudanese Government should lead the way in preventing South African Airways flights over their territory. Then I flew on to Egypt for a weekend with the Brintons, who now lived in Cairo. The Judge, while admiring the adventurous nature of my work, would have preferred it to be less political, more creative; but he never failed to give encouragement. We walked in the grounds of the Gezira Sporting Club – only Egyptians were there now and, for me, the ghosts of Gavin, of John.

In London I lived in the flat in St John's Wood which once I had borrowed for the dinner with Alan Paton. A terse note in my diary for Thursday, 14 June 1962, states: 'Cooked. 7 P.M Tambo.' Oliver Tambo, Chief Lutuli's deputy, had for two years been organizing the ANC-in-exile. A knock at the door and, when I opened it, standing beside him was Nelson Mandela. 'And N. Gorgeous!' the note continues, compensating for the brevity. 'Talked till 1.30.'

Nelson, immaculately suited and looking superb, gave a thrilling account of slipping across the border to tour Africa. Pacing the small room until the floor squeaked, he described the reception he'd been given in country after country, the experience for the first time in his life of being 'free'. Now, marvellously, he could spend a few days in London. On the Saturday, through David Astor, he met Hugh Gaitskell and Jo Grimond, leaders of the Labour and Liberal parties. On the Sunday, Freda Levson and her husband, Leon, and I, took him sightseeing, to Parliament and Westminster Abbey, then along the Thames to lunch at their house in Chelsea.

Early in August came the news that he had been captured, a few days after his secret return to South Africa. Betrayed by an informer? Horrified and dreadfully sad, I tried to keep busy and helped draft a profile of him which Cyril Dunn wrote for the *Observer*.

He was sentenced to five years for 'inciting' the Stay-at-Home in 1961 and for leaving the country without a permit. He was imprisoned in Pretoria jail.

8

To Mississippi and Back

I have always felt at home in America, perhaps because in childhood I was an avid reader of Milly-Molly-Mandy stories in the *Christian Science Monitor*, as well as such classics as *Huckleberry Finn*, *Little Women*, *Girl of the Limberlost* and the *Anne of Green Gables* series, which I inherited from Poppy. Then, of course, there was my long love-affair with the movies. I was naturally delighted when the publication in New York of *The African Patriots*, my history of the ANC, led to invitations to speak and give seminars at a number of universities across the continent.

James Coleman, a pioneer in African Studies programs, was my host at UCLA in March 1963. Returning to Los Angeles twenty-four years after that first trip to Hollywood, I had a small apartment at Malibu Beach – not the glamorous end, but with a fine view of the Pacific. From there I went to Berkeley and Stanford, across to Chicago, then to Howard, the Negro College in Washington DC, before paying brief visits to colleges in New England and finally to Boston University and Columbia. Well aware of my nervousness as a speaker and of a flat voice, I was relieved to find my subject-matter aroused a warm response, while my 'English' accent was widely admired.

In Washington, a friend in the State Department suggested that it would be useful to inform members of Congress about the ANC. He initiated me into the complexities of lobbying on Capitol Hill. Much depended on the impression one made on Administrative Assistants, usually very bright and personable young men. The close friend I gained on the staff of a liberal Democratic Senator proved a positive asset for years to come.

One of my objectives was to describe the events and intensifying repression which had provoked the ANC's decision to turn to sabotage. I found that men proud of forebears who had achieved independence from British rule through armed revolution became squeamish at the thought of blacks resorting to force. Another objective was to convey the quality of the ANC leadership. And there were questions about the role of the Communist Party. I explained that since the 1920s a handful of Communists had been the only whites to provide education in trade unionism to blacks, the only whites to call for a universal franchise. Quoting Lutuli and Professor Matthews on the long years of support and self-sacrifice from white as well as black Communists, I gave an example of American neglect: whereas Sisulu had been hospitably received in Russia during the early fifties, no such invitation had been extended to Mandela to visit the United States. However intriguing the glimpses I had of Washington's political scene, the arguing was exhausting; but even more of a strain was the walk from office to office along great stretches of marble floors – painful despite the cloth 'Jiffies' which were the only shoes soft enough for my arthritic feet.

Early in May a member of the UN Secretariat asked if I would testify before the newly formed Committee on Apartheid. In the over-heated, gloomy Great Northern Hotel on 57th Street I tussled with the question. However much I had written and spoken out, this was the ultimate in verbal attack on the government. But in South Africa, under the Ninety Day Law, detainees were being tortured, and the country was toppling into ever greater violence. It would be inadequate simply to recount facts; if I spoke, I must also recommend action. I felt contempt for those living in safety overseas who glibly called for 'armed struggle'. The 'ordinary' people were always the ones to suffer. Chief Lutuli had called for economic sanctions as the international community's only effective alternative to outright violence. Why should trade always be regarded as sacrosanct?

I would be the first South African to testify. Surely this would make it difficult, perhaps impossible, to return home? I valued gathering material there for books which could then be written in the freedom of England; as writer and lobbyist I could only function confidently on the basis of first-hand experience. Above all, I had developed a profound love for my country.

There was one final question: would my testimony be useful? So many fervently worded statements had already sunk without trace in the morass of international bureaucracy. Besides, I felt cynical about the human rights record of some of the governments to whom I would be appealing.

I telephoned David Astor in London, who consulted Michael Scott, Bishop Reeves and Colin Legum, a South African journalist on the *Observer*, before calling back to say they all urged me to go ahead.

Tense at the thought of the responsibility, I worked hard on writing the statement. After four days it was done and a subcommittee of the UN approved my credentials.

The next morning – a Friday – in a committee room of the UN, I was shown to the lonely seat, with its microphone and a glass of water, facing the Committee, which consisted of four Africans, three Asians, a Haitian, a Costa Rican and a Hungarian. To one side sat the Secretariat staff; beyond, in glassed-off boxes, interpreters mouthed like fishes in bowls. Friends sat in the public gallery, where there was constant movement as spectators came and went.

'I am honoured to be the first South African given a hearing by your Committee,' I began, and went on to explain that to speak out seemed the least I could do, so desperate were the times in my country. Since the facts of apartheid were already known, my testimony would concentrate on the effects on living human beings, within my experience.

Successive governments, I then pointed out, had used the weapon of fear, yet if we considered history, it was the blacks who, ever since the time of the slave trade, had suffered far more at the hands of whites; it was the blacks, therefore, who had more to fear. I spoke of the special culpability of English-speaking whites and of Afrikaners, who had cut themselves off from the world in 'deliberate, deluded self-isolation', whose government understood only one language, that of force. 'And the only non-violent way of applying force is the one the United Nations has already chosen, that of economic pressures.' My great fear was that the UN would fail, 'due to the refusals of the British and American Governments to support its efforts; in other words, to their virtual abandonment of South Africa to a violent solution'.

'But,' I concluded, 'how marvellous if you succeed! If in this age of nuclear dangers you can find the way to use non-violent economic pressures *firmly* towards achieving justice for that tragic country, a country that is the crux of the greatest issue in the world today, whether we, and you' – and I paused to glance at the Africans and Asians facing me – 'can live together in mutual confidence and understanding.'

The statement had taken forty-five minutes. Drained, I went on to give radio and television interviews. But what mattered most to me was that my testimony should be reported in the *Observer*, so on Sunday I hurried to Times Square to buy the airmail edition. It was not mentioned.

'Back to life' a diary note proclaimed on Monday. And in the *Christian Science Monitor*, which often reflected the conservative views of its South African readers, Earl Foell wrote an unexpectedly appreciative article of the testimony.

The following evening Josh, a black journalist I had met recently, took me uptown to Harlem. It was drizzling as he guided me down steps to the rosily lit Red Rooster bar, crowded with men and a few stunning girls, drinking and talking against the juke-box jazz. I liked being there as his friend and not a sightseer, although I could not help being conscious that I was the only white in the bar. While he chatted to an acquaintance, I studied the slanting planes of his face, the thick, curling lashes, the up-turning mouth which could be mocking or amiable.

In the street the drizzle had cleared. He tucked my hand under his arm. 'What about some real jazz?' and he indicated a club on the corner. A glance at my face and, impulsively, he hailed a cab. In silence we rode downtown to the hotel where he was staying.

We were not in love. But, as he put it, we wanted each other and we were both adult. It had taken me a long time to recover from the emotional defeat I'd suffered over Michael and from the illness which had permanently deformed my hands; I found reassurance, even bliss, in the relationship with Josh. Everything about me amused him, amazed him: when he discovered I was assisting lawyers working on the South-West African case, he asked how much they were paying me. 'Nothing? You mean you do it all for free!' He laughed until the tears came.

During the days that followed, whereas in Harlem we walked arm in arm, downtown – in 'white' surroundings – we were circumspect, relaxing only when we reached the privacy of his room. Our times together were intense. Soon I would have to return to London.

But first I wanted to visit the South, which seethed with Civil Rights protests, to witness for myself the drama and to compare it with my experience of South Africa. Since Josh was not directly involved a friend of Michael Scott's, Bayard Rustin, gave me introductions to leaders in three centres.

In the less illiberal state of North Carolina I visited the prosperous town of Greensboro, which had been the scene of the first student sit-ins in 1960. From the airport we drove through a familiar contrast of lushly gardened white suburbs and the crowded and often dilapidated black area. There, two student leaders, Bill Thomas and Jesse Jackson, welcomed me. With others from local colleges, with Negro ministers and young whites from the Congress of Racial Equality, they had been holding protest marches to demand an end to segregation. Hundreds had been arrested and briefly imprisoned. In the Baptist church the crowd sang freedom songs, and so jazzy grew the rhythmic clapping and swaying that Bill rebuked us. A lanky twenty-year-old with a casual surface to considerable inner strength, he played a key role in their discussion of future action. When a Negro minister told students, 'I want to see you young men piloting airplanes and you young women as air hostesses', I remembered that African minister in the Transvaal who spoke of his dream of a black ship's captain.

Staying with a hospitable black undertaker and his family, I shared in their excitement over the action of 1,300 whites who had advertised in the local Sunday newspaper to call for 'the equal treatment of all persons, without regard to race, color or religion' and to pledge support for businesses which abolished the colour bar. It seemed that whenever we turned on the radio a fresh development in the overall struggle was reported: a new victory in the Supreme Court, another town desegregated, the latest mass gathering in California or Chicago to be addressed by Martin Luther King, or a meeting between Bobby Kennedy and black leaders. But beyond the ferment, beyond the victories, there was real cause for fear, as I found when I flew on to Jackson, Mississippi, the 'snakepit of the South'. The main street was packed with police, and crowds of whites were milling around Woolworth's, where Negro students and two whites, one of them a girl, had staged a sit-in at the soda counter. In Windhoek I had felt uneasy when driven by a hostile white taxi driver to the location; in Jackson I was alarmed and incredulous when the cab-driver remarked that whites who took part in sit-ins 'oughta be nailed to a cross and burned', and this as he was taking me to Lynch Street in the Negro quarter, where my destination was the office of the National Association for the Advancement of Colored People.

Medgar Evers, Field Secretary of the NAACP, was greeting the young demonstrators who had just returned from Woolworth's, where white bystanders had assaulted one of them and smothered the others in catsup, mustard and sugar. Pearlena Lewis, a delicate twenty-two-year-old, told in a calm but strained voice how the man who had daubed the word NIGGER on the back of her dress had apologized for not writing it more legibly.

That evening on the way to a mass meeting I had a sense of the mythical South, scent of magnolia drifting through Mississippi's sultry heat and, out of the heavy silence, the sudden cry of mocking birds, the chirrup of crickets.

In the Pearl Street church the crowd was black but for a handful of whites from Tougaloo College and from the media. Medgar Evers was introduced as 'the man who for nine years had fought longer, harder and more knowingly than anybody here'. Cheers broke out when he declared: 'Yesterday the mayor talked about his wife and his children and *his* rights. Today when we saw him he talked about *our* rights! We are beginning to be free in Jackson.'

Whereas in South Africa the apartheid laws were being challenged, here their delegation to the mayor had argued for the hiring of Negro policemen and school crossing guards and the upgrading of job opportunities. 'You must all register as voters, everyone over twenty-one, go down and register!' The injunction set off a freedom chant which grew to a roar of certainty. Whenever a section of the crowd realized the TV cameras were focusing on them, they gestured fiercely, then burst into laughter.

'My heart is filled with joy,' Pearlena told the crowd when she and other sit-ins were called to the platform. 'To think that you, the Negro community, has been unified so as to say we are going to be free *now*! As I sat on a stool this morning and asked for a cup of coffee, it was unbelievable that anyone could refuse. It made me realize that we have to struggle yet harder.'

The older men who had negotiated with the mayor were optimistic, but a black student warned: 'If a man can preach to me how much he hates me and lets police stand by while he beats me and yells "nigger, nigger", he can lie over other things too. Be prepared. Tomorrow we have workshops on non-violence and direct action. No swinging back. No knives. If they throw mustard and catsup, *feel* good! And don't do nothing.'

The crowd rose to sing rousingly 'We shall not be moved' and a collection was taken to the singing of 'This little light of mine, I'm gonna let it shine'. People danced along to the collecting bowls. Then came the blessing: 'Beloved, let us love. There is no fear in love, perfect love casteth out fear. He who loveth God shall love his brother also.'

'Three hours of racial violence,' the local *Clarion Ledger* reported, while the mayor described the meeting as 'a deliberate attempt to heighten racial unrest'.

Late that night came a message that a petrol bomb had been thrown into Evers's carport. 'We are not going to run,' he said next morning. 'We will fight all the harder.'

Willie Ludden and a strikingly elegant couple, Dave and Mattie Dennis, were among student organizers preparing for a surprise picket of Capitol Street. After breakfast with them I called on the head of the White Citizens' Council. Proudly he told me that his organization exchanged propaganda with the South African government. He, like a local newspaper, regarded those composed young blacks as 'arrogant, aggressive and hate-inspiring'.

On Capitol Street, under a brazen sun, brisk blue-shirted police were on the alert and patrol cars crawled by. Then, as if the cops were their pointers, a pack of teenagers in gaudy checks and jeans moved deliberately in, hungry for action. Paunchy, crewcut, grinning men were around too; their necks really were red. 'Move along! Keep moving!' an officer dispersed the congestion. Four of the black students strolled unobtrusively towards the chosen targets. Willie Ludden approached, casual as any shopper, gave the merest flicker of an eyelid as he passed me. Suddenly all four simultaneously unfurled their placards: DON'T BUY ON CAPITOL STREET. JACKSON NEEDS A BI-RACIAL COMMITTEE. The press swiftly gathered as police raced to arrest the picketers and white men cursed and spat: 'Knock hell out of the bastards!' 'See the apes perform!' Violence seemed imminent. It was hard to believe all this was simply because some dark-skinned beings were claiming their right to have a hot-dog and coke at a lunch counter, to enter the library, to use restrooms in shops only too willing to sell products to them.

Mattie Dennis appeared with her placard. Three men followed and the pack of youths tried to tear it from her. I had remarked to Jack Langguth, the representative of the *New York Times*, about the beauty of several of the black girls. 'That is one of the troubles,' he had replied. As I photographed the scene a bony, middle-aged man lunged at my camera, but I swung away towards Langguth's comforting grey-flannel-suited presence. Meanwhile, the police were arresting the demonstrators, among them an elderly woman who laughed gleefully. They all promptly sat down on the kerb. Soon a paddy wagon drew up and out sprang four young blacks. Under orders from the Deputy Sheriff they lugged demonstrators to the van. They were trusties, prisoners with a special rank for 'fidelity'.

That night at the meeting in a church on Pasacula Street two schoolboys reported that they had dared to go into the library and had not been insulted. 'We had a wonderful time,' said one. 'We did learn something,' the other added. 'We learned that we are not afraid.'

Evers prepared the crowd to face arrest next day. 'What if the police use dogs as in Birmingham?' someone asked anxiously. 'Just grab the leash,' quipped a man, 'throw the dog up in the air and he's strangled!' Laughter roared out.

Two weeks later, on 12 June 1963, Medgar Evers was shot dead on his doorstep by a sniper. Incriminating fingerprints were found and a member of the White Citizens' Council was identified. A local jury found him not guilty.

In Birmingham Alabama – ole Burninghell, blacks called it – I met King's two young assistants, Andrew Young and James Bevell, both ministers, at the Gaston Motel. A few weeks earlier the motel had been petrol bombed, triggering riots which had police attacking with dogs and fire hoses, but on this day all seemed calm.

Young explained that lunch counter sit-ins had been the first step to encourage people to unite. In South Africa, I said, such action had only been briefly attempted in cafés in Cape Town. Bevell, shaven-headed, handsome as the young Brando, declared that in America as in South Africa struggle was necessary for people to become creative and to be purified. 'What matters,' added Young, 'is the vote, becoming part of the power structure.' Of course, that was a far less remote possibility in the States, where the Constitution spelled out the principle of equal rights.

King was out of town, but the regular mass meeting carried on, this time in a shabby church, its windowpanes painted with streaks of blue and green to imitate stained glass. Most of the men, including my escort, Mr Nelson, wore overalls. The only whites apart from myself were two dark-suited men, conspicuously from the FBI. A speaker teased them: 'Talk about integration, we have been integrated about four, five years. Such fine men too, and they know how to take their seats and be quiet. They've heard more preaching here than they ever heard in their lives!'

The speeches sparkled with imagery and humour, arousing the traditional responses of 'Yeah Lord!' 'That's the truth!' When Mr Nelson suddenly announced that a South African was in the audience, I was asked to speak. I told them how much their struggle reminded me of that back home, where Albert Lutuli resembled their leader, Martin Luther King.

The choir sang passionately, soaring gravelly voices, shouted song, to an organ and rickety honky-tonk piano until the building shook with 'Go tell it on the mountain'. Then, as the organ thumped out the familiar notes, we all rose and everyone's hands joined to form a chain as we swayed and confidently sang: 'We'll walk hand in hand, Black and White together, We shall overcome some day!'

To crown profoundly moving days, however frightened I had felt that hot morning in Jackson, as we were leaving the church from the gallery cheering black children tossed an American flag to me.

Four months later a dynamite bomb which was hurled from

a passing car destroyed the 16th Street Baptist Church. Four children were killed and nineteen were injured. Not until fourteen years later was a white man finally charged with the murder of the girls; he was a member of the Ku Klux Klan.

A young black mother in Greensboro had said to me: 'I don't think we'll get anywhere until we open up the apple that is the American way of life. But I'm afraid that what we'll find at the core will be so rotten that we'll shut it up quickly again.'

Soon after my return to London, in July 1963 news came of the arrest of Walter Sisulu, Govan Mbeki, Ahmed Kathrada and several others, in Rivonia, a suburb of Johannesburg. When they were brought to trial in Pretoria's Palace of Justice, Nelson Mandela was named Number One Accused. Charged with membership of the National High Command of the *Umkhonto we Sizwe* sabotage movement, they faced a possible death sentence. A worldwide campaign was mounted to put pressure on the South African Government and prevent the men being hanged. At the UN the anger of the international community was expressed in a vote of 106–1 condemning the South African Government for its policies and calling for the release of the Rivonia defendants. Protesting crowds demonstrated outside the UN and at the White House, among them black actors such as Ossie Davis and Ruby Dee, and the novelist John Oliver Killens.

Oliver Tambo, Vice-President of the ANC, testified before the UN Committee on Apartheid, followed by Miriam Makeba, the singer, and representatives of American anti-apartheid organizations. I was asked to speak specifically about the men on trial, since I knew or was acquainted with several of them, and in March 1964 I flew from London to New York. 'The press here,' wrote Govan Mbeki from Pretoria prison, 'have carried the news of your intended visit across the Atlantic.' Having spoken of the Rivonia defendants, I went on to describe the lives of African families under apartheid and the role of foreign investment in sustaining the South African Government, and then, in desperation, concluded: 'To tell the truth, my heart is so sick at the endless churning out of the horrible facts, which we all know too well, and have known for years, when all the time the iniquities we tell each other about, ceaselessly and so unnecessarily are hurting human beings – and this is their only life. Therefore, I beg that we stop cataloguing facts, and plan action and then *act*. Economic sanctions are surely the obvious civilized form of action when diplomatic and moral pressures long ago failed to make any impact on the South African government.'

Meanwhile a group of experts appointed by the Security Council tussled with the commendable but hopelessly optimistic task of finding a way of bringing about peaceful change in South Africa. Mrs Alva Myrdal, aided by Sir Hugh Foot, the British Ambassador, headed the group and I was hired to do research for their wide-ranging historical and political survey. In essence, the group recommended the establishment of a National Convention, representing the whole population of South Africa, to set a new course for the future. If, the report continued, that government was not prepared for such 'free discussion', the Security Council would be left 'with no effective peaceful means of assisting to resolve the situation, except to apply economic sanctions'. Not unexpectedly, the South African government treated the recommendations with contempt.

During three months in Manhattan, interrupted by trips to Washington and to Greensboro, I shared an apartment with Josh. After living alone for so long, I relished the unusual domesticity, even the chore of rising before daylight to make breakfast on the occasions when he must set off for an out-of-town destination – he was covering an industrial dispute.

'What if I come to London?' he teased.

'It would shake up my life,' I said.

'Your life needs shaking up,' he retorted.

Our times together gave new meaning to that life. The drive towards political action, my lecturing and lobbying, seemed to represent the masculine element in my nature, pleasing Dad, delivering the goods. I felt happier when reflective, strolling in Central Park, pausing to watch some insect or to gaze at leaves against sunlight and, now, this contentment flowing from the heart of my being.

Thrilling black plays appeared Off-Broadway, an outcrop of the Civil Rights struggle and of intensifying concern about South Africa. *In White America*, Langston Hughes's *Jerico-Jim Crow*, Genet's *The Blacks*, and *Dutchman* by a new playwright,

LeRoi Jones, were all running simultaneously, along with Athol Fugard's *The Blood Knot* and a musical based on Alan Paton's story about a reformatory boy, *Sponono*. Listening to the harsh hot-gospel singing in *Jerico-Jim Crow*, I thought we could have been in Alabama, even the breathy twiddles and scrolls of the Hammond organ sounded authentic, but we were safely in New York City. The throbbing splendour of young Gilbert Price's singing of 'Is Massa Gwine Sell us Tomorrow?' stirred memories of Mrs Ntlonti and countless black families in South Africa. *In White America*, a dramatization of documents of what whites had done to blacks during 200 years, laid bare a truth so terrible that many in the audience could not contain sorrow. And there was James Baldwin's *Blues for Mr Charlie*, not entirely successful theatrically, but a shattering experience of black and white in confrontation.

On a rainy night in April, by appointment I met Baldwin in Junior's Bar, just off Broadway. We sat in a corner, enveloped in the murkiness typical of American bars. With the physique of a cricket and great popping expressive eyes, he was the most immediately loving person I had ever encountered; and he was melancholy at the approach of his fortieth birthday.

We were both possessed by a sense of the past, of his country and of mine. 'The truth about the past,' he said, 'is really all we have to guide us in the present.' I thought of Nelson and Walter and so many others back home, of messages telling of fresh arrests and torture, of appeals to 'do something immediately!'

'Sometimes,' I said, 'the present truth is unendurable. How, then, can you bear to go on living?'

'I will tell you what I think,' he replied. 'It is very tentative. Someone said to me a long long time ago, about twenty years, somebody said: no matter how terrifying civilization may seem to be now, imagine what it would have been had there been no Socrates, no Jesus Christ, no Dostoyevsky. It is like a train going through a place of high mountains at night, everything is dark but there are lights here and there. They are the lights. I don't know what those lights do. People fall to their death in spite of them.' He paused. 'Despair is the only sin.' That, I said, I understood to be a Jesuit saying. 'We black people,' said Baldwin, 'have to be very Jesuitical.'

When I spoke of my longing to go home but of my apprehension, he confided that he had felt compelled to return to America from France, not because he was not afraid to do so, but because he *was* afraid. 'You will find,' he declared, 'that you will have to return to South Africa.' Perhaps . . .

It was time to leave New York and Josh, and return to London.

Meanwhile, on 23 April in the Palace of Justice in Pretoria, Bram Fischer, QC, leading the defence, had announced that Mandela would make a statement from the dock, the statement which has become historic with its concluding, noble affirmation:

During my lifetime I have dedicated myself to this struggle of the African people. I have fought against white domination, and I have fought against black domination. I have cherished the ideal of a democratic and free society in which all persons live together in harmony and with equal opportunities. It is an ideal which I hope to live for and to achieve. But if needs be, it is an ideal for which I am prepared to die.

On 11 June Nelson Mandela, Walter Sisulu, Govan Mbeki and all but one of the others in the Rivonia trial were found guilty on all counts. What would the sentence be? In St Paul's Cathedral we kept vigil through the night. Next day came the news: they had all been sentenced to life imprisonment with hard labour. Nelson and the other black defendants were flown to Robben Island, a small rocky outcrop in the south Atlantic, some seven miles from Cape Town. Dennis Goldberg, the only white, remained in Pretoria prison.

I received a message that their spirits were tremendously high. They felt they would not become forgotten men. 'To most of the world,' said the *New York Times*, 'those men are heroes and freedom fighters, the George Washingtons and Ben Franklins of South Africa.'

A Negro Leadership Conference on Africa was to be held in Washington in October. Giving only a day's notice, a representative of the ANC asked me to fly there to speak on the organization's behalf – at that time they had hardly any members lobbying in exile. Civil Rights leaders were backing the event and the Secretary of State, Dean Rusk, was guest of honour, Martin Luther King the chairman. Chief Adebo, Nigeria's impressive ambassador to the UN, was the main speaker, and I followed.

After comparing the leadership and methods of the American freedom movement with that in South Africa, I spoke of recent events: leaders such as Nelson Mandela and Robert Sobukwe imprisoned on Robben Island, further arrests, interrogation under torture, innumerable political trials. What lay ahead, I asked, if non-violent resistance was met by massive crushing by the State, by killings, as at Sharpeville, and the outlawing of African political organizations? If underground action and sabotage led to death sentences and prolonged terms in prison? If Britain and America continued, in deed if not in word, to support the status quo of racial tyranny because of trade and investment?

In South Africa, as in the United States, I pointed out, the great majority of black leaders had steadfastly refused to be driven by white racialism into black racialism, and in both countries courageous whites had played a significant role in the struggle. I paid tribute to Martin Luther King, James Farmer, Roy Wilkins and other leaders in the United States for exerting moral authority – the American nation had cause to be profoundly grateful to them. They had already supported UN calls for economic sanctions against South Africa and I was confident that their determination would be strengthened by recent events in South Africa. Surely now they would exert renewed pressure on their government, and also on American investors who helped to bolster apartheid. Emphasizing the increasing significance of the Negro vote, I urged that they set about transforming government policy.

The Conference called on the American Government to impose an oil embargo against South Africa but, as in the UN, the words fell on deaf ears. Nor, I realized, after speaking to several black leaders, was any follow-up likely. However sympathetic they might be, however many powerful resolutions they passed, when it came to action, they were naturally preoccupied with their own immediate struggle.

A few months later Martin Luther King arrived in London on his way to receive the Nobel Prize for Peace, three years after

Chief Lutuli had done so. He was a disconcertingly impassive man, very relaxed. It was extraordinary to think of him calmly leading huge crowds in those perilous Southern cities.

He addressed a packed meeting in a hall near St Paul's Cathedral. The poetry and rhythm of his speech was intoxicating. Bayard Rustin had asked me to write some notes about South Africa which King could include. I was startled when he abruptly broke the beat of his oratory and, bringing my typed pages from his pocket, began to read dryly: 'In our struggle for freedom and justice in the United States, which has also been long and arduous, we feel a powerful sense of identification with those in the far more deadly struggle for freedom in South Africa.' He went on to pay tribute to Mandela and Sobukwe, among the hundreds 'wasting away in Robben Island prison' and, reading on, asked, 'In a world living under the appalling shadow of nuclear weapons, why do we not recognize the need to perfect the use of economic pressures? . . . Why does our government, and your government in Britain, refuse to intervene effectively now? It is as if only when there is a bloodbath in South Africa – a Korea or a Vietnam – that they will recognize the crisis.' Eventually, putting the paper back in his pocket, he reverted to his inspiring oratory.

Then, hand in hand with Andy Young and Ralph Abernathy, we South Africans and the British surrounding King on the platform sang, 'We shall overcome some day . . .'

When, I wondered, would Victor Hugo's axiom become appropriate? 'Greater than the tread of mighty armies is an idea whose time has come.'

During the summer of 1964 Ruth First had settled in London with her three daughters. It was wonderful to see her again. She had endured 117 days in solitary confinement and long periods of gruelling interrogation. Some found her intimidating, since she did not suffer fools gladly, but close friends knew her to be an intensely private person whose dedication was lit by warmth and a sense of humour which deflated pretension and sentimentality. For the time being she would devote her brilliant intellectual powers to political and academic activity in Britain. (After returning to Africa, to academic work in Mozambique, in August 1982, Ruth was assassinated by a letter bomb – an intolerable loss to family, to friends and to her country.)

Bram Fischer also turned up in the autumn. Unexpectedly he had been granted a passport – unexpected because he had just been arrested in Johannesburg and, with twelve others, had been charged with membership of the illegal Communist Party. In London he was leading an appeal before the Privy Council on behalf of a commercial company. He had given an assurance to the South African authorities that he would return to stand trial.

I had first met him during the Treason Trial. What struck me was his courtesy: it never faltered, even when some remark by the prosecutor, some action by the police, angered him, hardening the expression of his blue eyes. Not physically impressive – short, ruddy-faced, with silver hair – he was an immensely captivating man.

His visit was both arduous and celebratory, seeing old friends and new, fitting in theatres between serious discussions. He seldom spoke of himself, was concerned rather to convey precisely what was happening under the Ninety Day detention law. To Hugh Foot (now Lord Caradon), who was on leave from the UN, Bram described the effects of police torture. Suliman Saloojee, a young Indian held in solitary, had somehow managed to smuggle a message to his wife. 'Pray for me,' he'd appealed. Bram could hardly contain wrath and grief as he explained that Saloojee was not a religious man and that, a day or two later, while being interrogated in Security Police headquarters, he had fallen seven storeys to his death.

In London influential politicians were profoundly impressed by Bram's dignified courage. They tried to persuade him to remain in Britain rather than go back to almost certain imprisonment. 'But I gave my word,' he told them. And from the bar of the Privy Council, Abram Fischer, QC, prepared to return to the dock in a Johannesburg Magistrate's Court.

I discussed with him my longing to go home. Apart from nostalgia for friends and family, as well as country, I felt it would be a small token of commitment when so many liberal or left-wing whites were leaving South Africa. And there was the continuing dislike of 'agitating' abroad without returning to experience developments in the country. London seemed increasingly a neutral zone, an area of withdrawal from Johannesburg or from Jackson. But a lawyer in Cape Town advised me that, since I had advocated sanctions against the South African Government, I could be charged under a law which carried a minimum sentence of five years. Other friends in Johannesburg and in Port Elizabeth thought I would probably be followed by the Security Police and could harm the very people I wanted to assist. Bram, however, was convinced that all would be well and hoped I would decide to go. And I recalled James Baldwin's grave insistence that I would find I would 'have to' return to South Africa. Finally, a perceptive English friend cut through my habitual inner arguments and uncertainties: 'It's obvious you want to go, so go!'

Before leaving London I asked my doctor for something to calm me should I encounter the Security Police. He prescribed a seasickness pill. As the plane flew over the Transvaal on Christmas Eve, I swallowed one and by the time we landed at Jan Smuts Airport I was feeling euphoric. The friend who had sat beside me throughout the flight, a South African academic living in America, made himself scarce. Entering the terminal I glanced around: there, the big man in flannels and blazer, eyes narrowed, hair cropped, surely he was one? A voice over the loudspeaker called: 'Will Miss Benson go to the BOAC counter?' Oh God, I thought, this is it! But at the counter a young woman wanted simply to confirm my return booking. In line for Immigration Control I wondered if they were checking names against a list. It seemed not. When my turn came the official studied my passport: 'Hm, so you're a writer!' He smiled. 'Well, have a good time in South Africa.'

Home again. Even the weeds looked beautiful. And the night sky, when you gazed up at the Milky Way and the constellations – Sirius, Canopus and the Southern Cross – surely nowhere in the world were the stars so opulent and yet so intimate. While crickets shrilled, unceasing.

9

Bram Fischer

'It's like the coming of a whole battalion,' Bram welcomed me extravagantly, that New Year's Eve of 1964. A few days later I attended his trial, in the 'whites only' gallery, sitting nervously among families and friends of the thirteen who had been accused of membership of the outlawed Communist Party. Bram entered the court by a side-door and stood for a moment, looking directly at me. No greeting, only the acknowledgement of my presence. I was glad I had come.

The chief State witnesses were Gerald Ludi, a police spy who had been a member of a Party cell, and Piet Beyleveld, who had been a friend of Bram's – an Afrikaner, long a leading member of the Party. Both witnesses agreed that the activities of the Party centred largely on propaganda about injustices. The very issues about which the English-language press and the Liberal and Progressive parties legally protested, became illegal when taken up by Communists. But Ludi also declared that the Communists aimed to overthrow the government by violent revolution. Beyleveld contradicted this: revolution, he contended, did not mean violence but change; the Party had condemned acts of terrorism and insisted there must be no bloodshed.

'For years, Piet and I were comrades,' Bram had told me. 'I do not believe that when he comes into court, when he looks me in the eyes, he will be able to give evidence against us.' But Beyleveld came into court, he stood in the witness box and he evaded Bram's gaze. When asked by the defence why he was giving evidence, he said he had agreed after persistent questioning by the Security Police; there had been no ill-treatment. Questioned further, he gave a startlingly accurate account of Bram's nature and influence: Fischer, he said, was well known as a champion of the oppressed, with political views that had never been concealed; a man widely respected in all parts of the community. He himself, he added, still revered Fischer.

I could imagine the distress this admission must cause Bram, who seemed to feel no bitterness towards his old friend, only anger at the system which manipulated such an easy betrayal. The defence counsel must have been astounded. 'I was interested to hear you say that,' he remarked to Beyleveld, and then asked, 'I don't like to put this in my client's presence, but he is a man who carries something of an aura of a saint-like quality, does he not?'

'I agree,' Beyleveld replied.

On a Friday afternoon I met Bram in a coffee-bar. His gaze was unusually intense, but I put this down to our activity over the previous days. I had encouraged him to write an article expressing his views about the crisis in the country which would be suitable for the London *Observer*. Coming from him it was a seditious, illegal document and he was worried lest I be incriminated as a fellow-conspirator. Security Police made no attempt to hide the fact that they were following him, but he was sure that on this occasion he had given them the slip. He handed me the final copy of the article. Then, gripping my hands, he asked me to be sure and come to court on Monday. Of course, I said. With a light kiss and a '*Totsiens*' – till I see you – he left.

All weekend I brooded miserably on what lay ahead. Perhaps Bram intended to make a deliberate challenge to the State from the dock, an action that would precipitate his imprisonment? How little I knew him.

On Monday, 25 January a friend who was staying with the Fischers stopped me as I approached the court, drew me into an empty waiting-room and handed me a letter. 'Bram has gone underground,' she confided.

'I feel incredibly dishonest and have ever since our talk on Friday,' Bram wrote. 'This is not because I am about to "jump" my bail. The other side has never played according to the rules and has changed the rules whenever it has suited them. That is the least of my "moral" worries. But throughout our talk I had to act to you and pretend I would see you on Monday and that was a singularly unpleasant experience.

'In some ways I suppose this would seem to be a crazy decision. Yet I feel it is up to someone among the whites to demonstrate a spirit of protest. It must be demonstrated that people can fight apartheid from within the country even though it may be dangerous. That is why I returned here from London. I have left the trial because I also want to demonstrate that no one should meekly submit to our barbaric laws. I'm sure we shall meet again.'

In the court everything seemed normal. Police and officials, defence and prosecution teams were present, and the other twelve defendants filed into the dock. Except that there was no sign of Bram. As soon as the magistrate had taken his seat, leading counsel for the defence rose to announce that he had a letter from Number One Accused, Abram Fischer, who had decided to absent himself from the trial. There was commotion in the court. The twelve defendants appeared flabbergasted and their families strained to hear as counsel read the letter. Bram stated that he had not been prompted by fear of punishment; indeed, he realized that his eventual punishment might be increased. He believed that white complacency in the face of the monstrous policy of apartheid made bloodshed inevitable. 'To try to avoid this becomes a supreme duty, particularly for an Afrikaner,' he declared. 'If by my fight I can encourage even some people to think about, to understand and to abandon the policies they now so blindly follow, I shall not regret any punishment I may incur. I can no longer serve justice in the way I have attempted to do during the past thirty years.'

'The desperate act of a desperate man,' the prosecutor called it. 'The action of a coward'.

Conflicting opinions were vehemently expressed, in private and in public. Some thought it a futile gesture. A lawyer felt 'let down' because Bram was 'the one man who could have united everyone'. Others were elated at a magnificent act of protest. Among them was my father, who had met Bram on New Year's Eve, and I was moved by his understanding. Fischer, commented the editor of the Johannesburg *Sunday Times*, was 'a paragon, the model of gentleness and respectability', who, when young, 'had been regarded as a future Prime Minister or Chief Justice'. The tragedy was that now he had become a 'hunted fugitive ostracised by society'.

Under the byline 'From a Special Correspondent in Johannesburg', Bram's article, which I had mailed to the *Observer*, was headlined WORD FROM MISSING QC:

The State thinks it has crushed the liberation movement, but it has not . . . If the struggle for freedom is smothered in one place or for the time being, it flares up again before long . . .

World opinion has positive and constructive tasks to perform. It must prevent torture from being used again . . . and should work for the release of our thousands of political prisoners; the wives and dependants of these prisoners must be cared for . . . But most important is the extension of human rights to all citizens. This is not Spain. It is 1965, not 1935 . . . The United Nations can bring home to white South Africans the recognition that the maintenance of white supremacy is doomed.

Bram's message to the outside world, written with passionate urgency more than twenty years ago, has gained the weight of prophecy:

A peaceful transition can be brought about if the government agrees to negotiation with all sections of the people and, in particular, with the leaders at present jailed on Robben Island or in exile.

He concluded with a vision of a free South Africa: at last the country would fulfil its great potential internally and in African and world affairs.

When copies of the newspaper appeared for sale in Johannesburg, the article had been excised.

Within days of Bram's disappearance, the Johannesburg Bar Council – of which he had once been Chairman – applied to have his name struck from the roll of advocates. FIRST WORD COMES FROM BRAAM [sic] FISCHER, the evening paper announced on 5 March. In protest against the Council's action, he had written to lawyers, requesting legal opposition to the proposed expulsion.

Weeks passed. The English-language press enjoyed taunting the police. BRAM FISCHER STILL FREE. The authorities said he might be disguised as a black-haired priest with dark glasses, or as an elderly invalid woman swathed in shawls. FISCHER COULD BE ANYWHERE FROM MALMESBURY TO MOSCOW.

Curtains drawn against the night, two women sat beside me

on a sofa. They had asked to see me urgently. One signalled a warning that the room might be bugged. Gaps in their soft, quickly uttered sentences were filled by words they wrote on paper. They had seen Bram. He was known as Max. I watched the hand as it wrote, 'Max is depressed and isolated, will you visit him?'

'Of course,' I said, and wrote, 'When?'

'Tomorrow.'

The word took me aback, set off inner turmoil. It gave me no time to prepare. Besides, I did not drive; I would have to take a taxi. Might not the police follow me? But how wonderful to see him again, how proud I felt to be asked. What were the implications of meeting a fugitive? But I cared greatly for him. 'Yes,' I said.

One of the women drew a map, showing the street, the house, a shopping centre some blocks away where I could be dropped, and a discreet route to ensure no police would follow. 'Try to look as unlike yourself as you can,' was the final warning.

Writing now of those events, in the detail made possible by my coded notes, I can feel again the apprehension – and exhilaration – of being caught up in such a drama.

On a bright autumn day, wearing heavy suntan make-up and a headscarf to obscure my face, I took a taxi to the shopping centre. From there I walked until I arrived at an ugly yellow-brick house with ornamental iron railings. Head held high but with shaky knees, I went up a long drive past an unkempt garden and tennis court. No one was visible in the neighbouring house. Pressing the doorbell, I heard its chime but no movement. I rang again and this time the door was opened by an African woman. There had been no mention of a maid. 'Is the master in?'

She motioned me through a bare hall to a large room furnished only with cane garden chairs and a table. I noticed an ashtray with pipe and matches. But Bram did not smoke. A sound made me swing round. A man was standing there, staring at me. Auburn-bearded, balding with receding auburn hair, his eyes blank behind rimless spectacles. Jesus, I'd come to the wrong house! How could I explain and get out?

'Good God!' he said. It was the familiar voice, warm, slightly accented. 'What are you doing here? How wonderful!'

It felt weird to embrace this strange-looking man, but the voice, the smile, were Bram's. He was delighted and reassured by my failure to recognize him. 'You look like Lenin,' I teased. He had not lost a mannerism of clearing his throat, nor a certain gesture of the hand.

He picked up the pipe. 'I've taken to smoking. It helps disguise my voice. And see how thin I've got. My walk,' he demonstrated, 'not so bandy-legged!' I had heard his health was troublesome, but he said the high blood pressure was now under control. Seeing a doctor had been one of the tests of his disguise, a disguise achieved by dieting, by shaving the crown of his head, then dying hair, eyebrows and beard to a colour natural to his reddish complexion.

The maid, Josephine, brought tea. As we talked, I began to realize just how cut-off he was, he who had led an immensely active professional and social life. Clearly he desperately missed family and friends. Too soon the time was up. I would come again in a week on Josephine's day off.

In the days that followed I marvelled that he was living in the heart of Johannesburg, within a mile or so of his old home, while the police were scouring the country. A substantial reward had been offered for his capture. I thought of him, alone but for the maid, in that dreary house. It was sickening that a man of his integrity should be forced to resort to subterfuge and lies.

'Get yourself a hat,' he had said. In the OK Bazaars I bought one, emerald green, to match a borrowed green-and-white suit. The object was to look normal when leaving my sister's flat, where I was staying, and to arrive at Bram's house looking, I hoped, like a district nurse. Barney Simon, a close friend, drove me. He was ignorant of my ultimate destination, knowing only that I had to be dropped at the shopping centre – in a time of such tension and complexity friends were careful not to ask dangerous questions. When I nonchalantly put on the green hat, the sight reduced him to uncontrollable laughter, setting me off until we rocked with mirth. Sobering up, absurdly hatted, I strode into a fruit shop while he drove off. By the time I had reached Bram's front door, the hat was in my hands.

I was glad that he chose to have tea in the front garden rather than in the house, which was sparsely furnished, he explained, because he did not want to use his limited funds on unnecessary comforts. He was enjoying the informality of his new life, wearing sports shirts and flannels, and each week he grew more confident. A leading member of the Security Police had passed him in the street, a judge he knew well had stood beside him in a lift. Someone he had met for the first time had thought he was in his thirties. But he wondered if he should go on with his hermit's existence or join the local bowling club, become a new personality. He rehearsed me in preparation for a possible encounter with the police. I was to say I had met 'Max' only recently, through friends. I found it hard to think of him as Max, although he was not quite Bram either.

I had just handed him a cup of tea when footsteps crunched up the drive. I glimpsed a white man before I turned away, saying to myself, 'Good heavens, no, his name is Max!' But Bram rose to intercept the stranger and lead him to the house. He had come about the electricity. I thought of how Bram could be caught over something quite trivial. Josephine was having problems with her pass-book. What if just coping with that led to his capture?

When we had relaxed again, he fed crumbs to sparrows in the dry grass. How different it had been three months earlier at his old home, when he had given a Sunday lunch party for family and a few close friends. He led me towards a cool corner by the front door. 'Look, Molly's special garden.' Small rare plants his wife had set in evergreen grass. 'It's a real monument to her,' he said.

In 1961, when Bram was in Rhodesia on an important arbitration case, he had telephoned Molly every evening. I was staying with her and their son Paul while I completed research for the ANC book. After more than twenty years of marriage, she was like a girl preparing to meet her lover as she chose a new outfit for Bram's return. Then, in 1964, the night after he had concluded the defence in the Rivonia Trial, he and Molly set off for Cape Town to celebrate their daughter Ilse's twenty-first birthday. Crossing a bridge, in the darkness Bram swerved to avoid a cow and crashed into a stream. Molly, trapped in the car, drowned.

Bram without Molly. The triumph of saving the Rivonia men

from hanging had just been muted by the anguish of their life sentences, and then came this cruel, intolerable tragedy. There was no way I could even try to console him.

In his letter telling me he was going underground Bram had concluded: 'It is very early in the morning and a glow is touching the garden that Molly and I tended for more than twenty-five years. I have wondered and wondered what she would advise in the present circumstances. I think she would have approved.'

BRAM SEEN CROSSING BECHUANALAND BORDER.

FISCHER SEEN IN DAR ES SALAAM.

He had said he would not leave South Africa. 'Our place is *here*.' How often I heard him say that. And I had witnessed the extremes of his feelings: his fury when he heard that a comrade had fled the country, fury aroused not by the man but by the Security Police, who tortured and broke people and drove them to flight; his exuberance when I'd returned.

I did not want to know what he was doing or who he was seeing. The Ninety Day detention law had been suspended but could be brought back at any moment; the less I knew, the better. Clearly, he was having to start from scratch.

Usually we met once a week. He loved to hear about friends. Alan Paton was in town and Bram wished he could see him. 'I'd give anything . . .' During the Rivonia trial he had visited Alan in Natal to ask if he would speak in mitigation of sentence. He had hardly made the request when Alan agreed. 'But you've not heard all the facts,' Bram protested. To which Alan replied, 'You told me that it's a matter of life and death.'

On judgement day in the trial of Bram's comrades, I waited in the main street of Benoni, a mining town where my brother-in-law had his office. Bram's Volkswagen approached, on time, and we headed for the southern border of the Transvaal. I was happy to be with him and relieved to avoid the tension of the court.

We talked of his children, who were never far from his thoughts. Ruth and her husband were in London and, before going underground, Bram had sent his teenage son Paul to join them. Ilse was in Johannesburg. He worried about her having to cope with letting their old home.

Packing before the move, Ilse had shown me family papers

and mementos removed from Bram's chambers. Among yellowed pages of letters was one from Ouma Steyn, widow of the President of the Orange Free State, to Bram on his twenty-first birthday: '*As kind en as student was jy 'n voorbeeld vir almal, en ek weet dat jy nog 'n eervollig rol gaan speel in die geskiedenis van Suid Afrika.*' (As a child and as a student you were an example to everyone, and I know you will play an honourable role in the history of South Africa.) As Bram and I drove through the dried-out veld, I said how moved I had been on reading Mrs Steyn's letter. 'What would Ouma say if she could see me now?' he asked wryly.

We began to discuss the Afrikaans language. Wanting to lighten his mood I recited the poem which still lodged in my memory, about midnight and the Zulu warriors creeping like snakes around the laager, '. . . *middernag, Nader kruip die Zulumag* . . . It's so ugly and guttural,' I protested.

'But it's a poetic language!' came his impassioned retort. 'Listen: *motrëen*, moth rain, that soft rain. And *douvoordag*, dew before daybreak.' I had to concede that when he spoke those words, they sounded beautiful.

The Transkei homeland had recently chosen English as the first language in schools and this, I said, was good. 'Why *good*?' Bram asked. 'On the contrary, it's sad that my people, through their actions, are turning Africans against Afrikaans. Now it's the Transkei; ultimately all will be lost. In my ideal state we would try to preserve the language.'

When he spoke of his people, perplexity, anger and love clashed. Their historic Great Trek from the Cape had been precipitated by the desire for freedom from British control, but they also wanted the freedom to own slaves, so were they freedom-fighters or oppressors? He thought Piet Retief had some fine ideas. 'His manifesto in 1837 spoke of upholding the "just principle of liberty". His followers would not molest others nor deprive them of property. They wanted peace and friendly intercourse with the African tribes.'

Bram reverted to his family, what made them rebels was the Boer War. His grandfather, a Member of Parliament from the age of twenty-five, had tried to mollify President Kruger, while keeping at bay 'the wily old Imperialist, Milner'. When such efforts failed and war broke out in 1899, grandfather Fischer rallied people to the Boer cause, addressing endless meetings in dusty little dorps, coaching Hertzog, who was among the more extreme of their generals, in politics, while keeping in touch with the moderates, Smuts and Botha.

Listening to Bram talk of the war, I was struck by how real it seemed for him although he was born six years after it ended. His family had town and country houses in the Free State and, like many Afrikaners, they were left with little but a few ornaments. British soldiers tore pages from the family's set of Dickens to stuff pillows.

When the British ceded power to white South Africans under the Act of Union, Bram's grandfather, by then Minister of Lands, pushed through the 1913 Natives' Land Act, dispossessing Africans of their land, restricting 4 million of them to less than 8 per cent of the country. The million whites obtained access to more than 90 per cent. 'Even up to 1926,' Bram said, 'Afrikaner Nationalism was a progressive force for whites – against big monopoly capital and *for* the working class, *for* the Jews.' I thought he was over-romantic about the past. 'In the early forties,' he added, 'I had lunch with Verwoerd. He was trying to make up his mind whether to be a Nationalist or a Socialist!'

Bram laughed at that recollection, but the laugh turned to a sigh. 'Today in all South Africa Afrikaners are only about 8 per cent of the population, and who in the outside world backs them?' Perhaps, he mused, oppressed people are always progressive until they get power. So, once Afrikaners attained power, their Nationalism escalated into domination over the blacks, a domination to which it seemed there was no limit.

It struck me that Bram's sacrifice of family, career and freedom had essentially been inspired by his Afrikaner heritage. He had implied as much in his letter to the magistrate: as an Afrikaner, he sought to make some reparation for the misdeeds of his people.

Considering this as we drove on that day, for me there was also an intensely personal revelation. Just as reading *Cry, the Beloved Country* had shattered my prejudice against the blacks, so now Bram had blown away the cobwebs of my childhood perception of Afrikaners as alien. My father used to joke that he'd left Ireland to escape a bunch of rebels, only to find another lot in South Africa, but, of course, he was not speaking of our few Afrikaner friends. I mentioned the Griffiths family to Bram. The Welsh name was misleading; the father was proud of having been President Kruger's secretary, but then, they were Christian Scientists rather than Nationalists. And now we were driving through a farming area of the southern Transvaal where my family had often spent weekends with the Mosterts, in a luxurious house designed by the Imperial architect Herbert Baker. Its Italianate gardens, I recalled, were somewhat incongruous among the mealie-fields and eucalyptus plantations. Oubaas Mostert, a wealthy patriarchal farmer, actually *was* a Nationalist, with a bust of Kruger prominently displayed under the chandeliers in the great panelled dining-room. His wife, however, a cultured German, was a Christian Scientist, and that to us made all the difference.

Bram announced that we'd reached our destination, Volksrust. Drawing up at the post office, he mailed letters to Helen Suzman and to his fellow-Afrikaner Beyers Naude. He wanted to express appreciation for their courage and tenacity in opposing apartheid, but it was also a way of demonstrating that he was still in the country. Such gestures soon staled. His letters to newspaper editors, sent from each of the four provinces, had already been publicized. Besides, as a 'listed' Communist, his actual words could not be quoted. He wanted to support black political action, but that had been crushed through massive arrests and political trials. His success in evading capture seemed to me in itself a potent form of protest.

'Molly and I often brought the children here.' He turned off the main road to drive down a track to a *kloof*. 'We were both so busy and picnics were the times we could all be together.' In his pleasure at returning to familiar spots, I sensed how profoundly he missed Molly. Yet he was a perfect host – the fire deftly made, the chops well grilled, the drinks iced. Each picnic became a festive occasion. He identified birds and trees and shared a letter from Paul, proud of the boy's literary style and amusing comments on life in London.

The sun, lighting the shaved area of his head, exposed white roots where the auburn hair began. 'Your hair,' I said. 'It's beginning to show.' Later, when we arrived in the suburbs, he stopped at a chemist, where I bought the dye that he used.

12 REDS ARE FOUND GUILTY, the evening paper proclaimed. Bram's old friends Eli Weinberg and Ivan Schermbrucker had been sentenced to five years, the others to two. Five years. That was the sentence he would have been given.

That winter I spent six weeks in the Eastern Cape, reporting on political trials, and exchanged postcards with 'Max'. Speculation about him continued in the press: 'Throughout South-West Africa police are manning roadblocks on all the main highways after tourists reported seeing Abram Fischer at the Etosha Pan.' And: 'A Johannesburg professional man was detained at Warmbaths police station; he was mistaken for Abram Fischer, QC.'

Bram had been underground for more than six months.

Back in Johannesburg, I found that he had moved. To my relief he was much more security-conscious and when one evening he drove up in his Volkswagen to where I awaited him on a corner, he asked me to close my eyes until we had driven in the gate to the new house. It was semi-detached but he hardly saw his neighbours, a young couple. He no longer employed a maid. Inside was the same garden furniture. Two garish paintings remained unhung in the nondescript sitting-room.

Warmed by an electric fire, we drank sherry to celebrate our reunion. He was eager to hear about my experiences and I told of the trials held in obscure village courts from which the families of defendants were barred, of the trumped-up charges, of Security Police beatings and bribing and schooling of witnesses. He was not surprised to hear that magistrates accepted blatantly parroted evidence.

And I shared the moment when Govan Mbeki, whom Bram had defended in the Rivonia trial, arrived at the courthouse in the village of Humansdorp. Handcuffed and flanked by police and armed soldiers, he had been flown from Robben Island to give evidence for the defence in a trial. After a year of labouring with other 'lifers' in a lime quarry, he had aged considerably and it seemed to me that weariness had settled on him like fine dust. But, as I told Bram, his spirit was strong: when the magistrate called on the press to withdraw, since it was 'not in the interests of the State' that we should report the evidence of this 'important political prisoner', Govan stood in the witness box radiating irony.

Bram recalled an incident two or three years earlier when Mbeki, Mandela and Sisulu had been functioning from underground. A leaflet circulating in the townships incited people to kill informers. The three leaders strongly opposed such actions and, when a policeman was murdered in the Eastern Cape, Mbeki was sent there to order such acts of revenge to stop.

Later that evening, when Bram drove me to a taxi-rank, I encouraged him with one further anecdote. A lawyer who regularly visited prisoners awaiting trial told me that the first thing they asked was: 'Is Bram still free?' When assured that he was, they were jubilant.

I had grown quite accustomed to the strange double-life. Dining with friends, spending Sundays in and out of their pools, it was odd to hear their speculations about Bram. But when such speculations embraced me, I grew anxious. A diplomat remarked on how curious it was that the police hadn't taken any action against me and surmised this might be because, knowing I was a friend of Bram's, they hoped I would lead them to him. However, my only encounter with the Security Police in Johannesburg was when I attended a political trial and Sergeant Dirker, the policeman who had made life a misery for Walter Sisulu, asked for my press card. I watched as he showed it to Ludi, the former spy, who was assisting the prosecution and who gave him some instruction, whereupon he left the court. Meanwhile, I had swallowed the seasickness pill prescribed by my doctor and slipped away to visit academic friends, who were amused when I suddenly dropped off to sleep.

On a day bathed in winter sunshine, Bram and I drove along a road straight across the vast, breathtaking spaces of the Transvaal, the bare veld which previously I had seen as monotonous. The glorious day suited our mood. During the past weeks the *Rand Daily Mail* had published a series of articles by Benjamin Pogrund on prison conditions and the *Sunday Times* had followed with revelations from a white prison warder. Police raided the newspaper offices several times, interrogating the writers of the articles. Laurence Gandar, editor of the *Mail*, had written increasingly provocative editorials. The Minister of Justice, Vorster, remained uncharacteristically silent.

'Do you think it's the flaring up of a new flame, or old ashes dying?' Bram asked, his broad smile revealing what he thought, and before I could reply, he exclaimed, 'I believe it is a new flame! If, now, people could be brought together, a whole new opposition working together . . .' I knew how divided were the remnants of opposition, but who was I to judge between a last spark and a phoenix? Cautiously, I said that the most likely outcome was a penal reform committee of academics and lawyers.

The establishment of a non-racial government in South Africa stirred his imagination. He could envisage the country becoming the industrial supplier for the entire continent. The conflict between white and black would then no longer endanger investments. But we both suspected that the short sight of Western investors and multinational companies would prevent their supporting economic pressures, taking a temporary loss now rather than losing everything in the future.

We picnicked under a cluster of thorn trees. Suddenly, African women materialized from the bush – there was no sign of a village – and sat beside us, displaying their handiwork. Bram bought grass mats and seed necklaces. After the women had withdrawn we had a last cup of coffee. There was always a slight melancholy when the time came for packing up.

Bumping over the veld in search of the main road, we returned to our discussion, to Verwoerd's assertion that by 1978 the 'tide would be turned', blacks would be drained from the cities and confined to Bantustans. Bram derided the idea. 'And by 1978,' he added, 'Verwoerd will no longer be Prime Minister. Others will reap the terrible whirlwind. We've done all we can to avoid that holocaust – has anyone done more? The last thing Communists want is violence. But the Nationalists don't mind shedding blood. After Sharpeville, Karel de Wet, a member of the government, expressed regret that so few had been shot!'

He turned to me for a moment. 'Listen, Mary. The struggle here is not a Communist one. The Africans' concern is for the liberation of their people and for a just way of life. They say, we don't want violence, we hope it won't be inevitable.' He paused. 'No, it *is* the phoenix. I'll never believe we are dying ashes! We are glowing embers that will soon be part of a new flame.'

One evening I brought him a gift, German poetry with translations, to mark his seven months of 'freedom'. It was a kind of milestone for me too. I had found that when you do something risky without being caught, each day is an extension of life that you truly value. Bram and I had separately seen a local production of *The Caucasian Chalk Circle*. Now I wanted to share with him Brecht's poem '*An die Nachgeborenen*' – to those who come after – which I felt expressed the question Camus put, the most important of our age: How cease to be victims without becoming executioners?

> . . . We went
> Through the wars of the classes, despairing
> When we saw only injustice and no rebellion.
>
> And yet we know:
> Hatred even of cruelty
> Distorts the features.
> Anger even at injustice
> Makes the voice hoarse. Alas, we
> Who wished to prepare the ground for kindness
> Could not ourselves be kind.
>
> But you, when the time at last does come
> And man can care for humanity
> Do not judge us
> Too harshly.

Was repression inherent in Marxism or was it rather that successful revolutions deteriorated into repression? I had read somewhere the Levellers' appeal to the future Charles II: 'We have lost our way, we looked for Liberty, behold Slavery.' But before I could express such thoughts, Bram had responded by reading from Brecht's *Galileo*:

On our old continent a rumour started: there are new continents! And since our ships have been sailing to them the word has gone round all the laughing continents that the vast dreaded ocean is just a little pond. And a great desire has arisen to fathom the depth of all things: why a stone falls when you drop it, and how it rises when you throw it in the air. Every day something new is discovered . . . And because of that a great wind has arisen, lifting even the gold-embroid-ered coat-tails of princes and prelates, so that the fat legs and thin legs underneath are seen; legs like our legs. The heavens, it has turned out, are empty. And there is a gale of laughter over that.*

'That's how it is,' Bram exclaimed. 'The great wind of Socialism, do you see?' He put down the book and stood confronting me: 'Come over to us, Mary! Become a part of something great, be with the people!'

His appeal rang in me. Although I loved and admired him, I could not join him.

During the thirties, while I was a politically ignorant and racially prejudiced teenager, he had been a Rhodes Scholar at Oxford, alive to the intellectual climate and to events in Europe. On student tours of the Continent he had witnessed Nazism and Fascism at first hand. The Italian invasion of Ethiopia, hunger marches in England – these too had been part of the realities of his world. Returning to South Africa he found Oswald Pirow, Minister of Justice, leading the Greyshirts. Only the Communist Party militantly opposed the spread of Fascism abroad and at home, regardless of the risks. Only Communists were prepared to work alongside blacks and demand 'one man, one vote'. Bram joined the party, as did Molly, and they became active in politics, Stalin was our great ally. During 1946, while I was in Germany working among Displaced Persons, many of whom had suffered under both Hitler and Stalin, Bram and other Communists were assisting African miners in their momentous strike. He had seen the violent suppression of the African Mineworkers' Union by the Chamber of Mines, aided by Smuts's army and police.

Our discussion that night, typically, was amicable and ani-mated, interrupted by the occasional burst of exasperation. When Bram talked of the exploitation of one class by another, I remonstrated, 'But in Vienna I saw the way Russian officers treated their men!' And when he patiently explained dialectical materialism, my mind went blank. I had been influenced by the

* *The Life of Galileo* by Bertolt Brecht, translated by Desmond Vesey, Methuen & Co., 1960.

ideas of Camus, Lewis Mumford and Simone Weil, but my arguments were imprecise, inspired as I was by the human spirit, by its capacity for transformation and transcendence.

Bram mentioned that he was studying the methods of the Portuguese Communist Party's underground. It was necessary to be ruthless even with your own family. But I knew that he was taking the considerable risk of regularly meeting Ilse. To my surprise he added that he had been reading the Bible – how much love there was in it, he said, and goodness, qualities inherent in Communist ideals. (It later transpired that he used it as a code in letters sent overseas.) In South Africa, he pointed out, Communists had always tried to work with Christians, with Michael Scott, for instance, and with Bishop Reeves. The future lay with Socialism, he insisted with unquenchable optimism.

On a Sunday morning towards the end of August we drove to the north-west, through veld barren and strange under a sickly yellow sky. Again the weather matched the news. Vorster had at last reacted. Splashed across the morning's front pages were reports of Security Police raids on the *Rand Daily Mail*. They had seized the passports of Laurence Gandar and of Benjamin Pogrund, and had arrested those who had given information about prison conditions.

On our return journey we drove past the Atomic Research Centre at Pelindaba. The network of highways, empty of traffic, confirmed the belief that the country's sophisticated road system had been conceived for speedy movement of military transport, just as African townships, isolated and virtually treeless, were easily sealed-off targets.

Spring was heralded by snow in the mountains and cold rain in the city. Ominous portents. On the Witwatersrand, one of the perpetually overcrowded trains of black workers crashed. Ninety-one passengers were killed. Survivors battered to death a white man coming to their aid.

FISCHER SEEN ON KAUNDA'S FARM.

FISCHER NOT HERE – KAUNDA.

On the wind that swept away the clouds came a host of yellow and white butterflies. Green shoots sprang in the veld. In a *kloof* below a high rocky *krans* Bram and I spread our rugs and cushions under blossoming trees. Kingfishers plunged towards the nearby stream. We gathered wood for our *braaivleis* fire.

Lunch over, I read to Bram from the final chapter of the history of the ANC, which I had been bringing up to date for a paperback: 'Laski once wrote, "The political criminals under a tyrant are the heroes of all free men."' I broke off to ask, 'That's a good quote, hey?' He smiled agreement. As I read on, shouts broke out from the woods on the opposite bank and from downstream.

'Your scarf!' he urged. The shouts sounded nearer and nearer. I quickly tied the headscarf under my chin and, as helmeted heads appeared among bushes across the stream, Bram calmly offered me a banana. Voices now came from behind us. We turned to see soldiers in full battledress running towards us. This is it, I thought.

'*Gooie dag!*' called one brightly.

'*Dag!*' said Bram.

'*Dag!*' I said as they trotted on by. We watched their booted feet climb the almost vertical cliff. More shouts sounded and more men ran past. We were in the middle of army training manoeuvres.

With studied casualness we packed the picnic basket and rugs and drove up the track to the main road. There a jeep was parked. Three senior officers stared out at us and smilingly saluted. We waved back and speeded away.

A few days later came the inevitable but horrifying announcement that Vorster had brought back and doubled the Ninety Day detention law. One hundred and eighty days of solitary confinement. You had no access to lawyers or courts while the Security Police interrogated you.

A man named Isaac Heymann was the first to be so detained. In prison he attempted suicide. I did not know him but was sure he was one of Bram's contacts. Bram's face was grim when next we met. Yes, he confirmed, Heymann was a close friend. 'Do you know anyone who would put up a fugitive?' he then asked. I thought about it. I was renting a room in a friend's house; Athol Fugard and his family were also staying there while he rehearsed a new play. 'No,' I said apologetically, ashamed that I did not want to expose myself or test my friends.

The net was closing in. He confided that he was having sleepless nights. He had assumed a new name, Peter West.

On 2 November came an event he had been dreading: the Judge President of the Transvaal, responding to the application from the Johannesburg Bar Council, ruled that Abram Fischer, QC, should be struck from the roll of advocates. Bram was bitterly angry. 'Dishonest! The Judge President called me dishonest and dishonourable!' he burst out as soon as I joined him in his car. He had just read the evening paper. He expressed disillusion and anguish in a torrent of words. For thirty years he had worked hard to uphold the law, had done all a man could to struggle for justice. Surely colleagues who had known him well should have the sense, the feeling and courage to understand his reasons for the drastic step he had taken in going underground. 'Why couldn't they let the government do its own dirty work?' he cried out.

We drove to a suburban hotel. 'Let's have a gin and tonic to cheer ourselves up!' he said. We sat on the verandah under a rapidly darkening sky. There was only one other customer, a man at a nearby table. Was he observing us, the tall woman and the short, bearded man? Sensing my unease, Bram said, 'If anyone you know comes up, don't forget to introduce me as Peter West, from out of town.'

'Open your eyes!' We had arrived back at his house. A jacaranda tree was in bloom, glowing phosphorescently in the light from the street. For the rest of the evening, we hardly talked, just listened to music.

A few days later the woman who had been my contact with Bram was taken into detention: 180 days. When I had last seen her she said that on some days she felt well and was confident she could cope, but on days when she was feeling ill, she was not so sure. Women detainees were usually made to stand while interrogators questioned and threatened them, made to stand all through the day . . .

Would Bram want to put off our appointment for the coming evening? I telephoned his house from a shop. There was no reply. Knowing the number worried me, but it was necessary in case of a change of plan.

Teams of interrogators worked in relays, night and day,

banging on the table: 'Wake up!' Yelling: 'We will crack you!' Mocking: 'You are going to land in Weskoppies asylum!' . . .

Bram and I met, as arranged. In his house he took me through to a small room where a bed was ready. So this had been for the 'fugitive'. 'It was too late,' he said. And shut the door on the room. He was distracted from his grave anxiety for what his friend might be going through only by the desperate need to get away from this house. He had found a suitable place, but the owner could not see him to conclude negotiations until the following Sunday.

He wanted to post an important airmail letter. We drove to the main post office in the city. I watched him cross the road in front of a line of cars drawn up at the traffic lights.

Standing, standing, night and day . . .

Next morning, the morning of Thursday, 11 November, I telephoned Bram. He had asked me to arrange an appointment with a visitor from London and, although I had tried to dissuade him from so risky a venture, he had insisted. 'Your appointment on Saturday,' I told him, 'it's all right.' He was delighted.

That evening was the first performance of Fugard's *Hello and Goodbye*. On the way to the theatre came news of Rhodesia's Unilateral Declaration of Independence. Surely, I thought, Britain would not stand for Ian Smith's rebellion. This crazy act must help our struggle. I felt suddenly exhilarated, but also sad that the Rhodesian whites could be so deliberately self-destructive. Bram must have seen the evening paper; we would discuss it when we met in a few days' time.

Early next morning an acquaintance called by to collect some photographs. She said: 'Bram Fischer's been caught!'

I did not believe it. There had been many false alarms; how he and I had laughed at them. I began to feel nauseated. She handed me a newspaper:

JO'BURG DRAMA: FISCHER IS ARRESTED

Security Police arrested a heavily-disguised Abram Fischer in a northern suburb of Johannesburg last night. Brigadier van den Bergh said Fischer was in a car when police, who had been shadowing him, cut off his car and stopped him. The arrest took place very near his old home, and he handed himself over without any trouble. For 290 days the police have searched far and wide for him in probably the biggest manhunt they have ever undertaken.

Die Transvaler had a picture of him beside the gross and malevolent Swanepoel, the most notorious of all the Security Police; his fist clutched Bram's arm, while Bram's other hand adjusted his rimless spectacles as he stared into the photographer's flash.

A day of mourning. Athol sat with me on the balcony looking out on the wild garden where we lived. We did not talk. A day interminable, somehow to be survived. 'You've saved my sanity, bless you,' Bram had said when we parted on that last evening.

The semi-detached house was pictured in the press. It was called *Mon Repos*. A lorry stood outside, stacked with furniture – the garden chairs and table we had joked about. In the foreground was the mulberry tree from which we had picked leaves for Athol's small daughter's silkworms.

SURGERY CHANGED FISCHER'S FACE. A plastic surgeon, after studying pictures of Bram, opined that it looked like the work of an expert, probably outside South Africa.

Die Transvaler assured readers that the police had been watching Fischer's house for a considerable time. Associates and friends who had visited the disguised fugitive would be 'snuffed out'.

The corridors of the Magistrates Courts clattered with uniformed police. Photographers' flash bulbs flickered – press or police? Ilse was absent but Ruth and Paul, back from London, were taken to see their father in the cells below the court. They returned, grinning at the list of chores he had given them to do.

The courtroom bristled with Security Police. A handful of spectators, white on our side, black on theirs, sat in the public galleries. While we waited I counted the police milling around the dock. I had reached forty-nine when up the steps from the cells and into the dock came Bram.

He turned once, deliberately, calmly, to look at us, and once to look at the black gallery. He had shaved the beard and reverted to his old, half-rimmed spectacles. He was no longer Max, but not quite Bram – I felt doubly bereaved.

It took only a few moments for the magistrate to announce a

remand. A glance from Bram at Ruth and Paul and he was gone, a prisoner, to be held behind bars and locked doors in a cell in Pretoria prison. I was never to see him again.

At his trial early in 1966, largely on the evidence of a black turncoat, Bram Fischer was found guilty of conspiring to commit sabotage with Nelson Mandela and the other men he had defended two years earlier in the Rivonia trial. Guilty also of contravening the Suppression of Communism Act and of forging documents with assumed names. He made a statement from the dock in the course of which he spoke of 'a strong and ever-growing movement for freedom' amongst blacks, a movement supported by virtually the whole membership of the UN, both West and East, a movement which could never be stopped. 'In the end it must triumph. Above all,' he declared, 'those of us who are Afrikaners and who have experienced our own successful struggle for full equality should know this.'

The sole questions for the future were whether change could be brought about peacefully and without bloodshed, and what the position of the white man would be immediately following the establishment of democracy, 'after the years of cruel discrimination and oppression and humiliation which he has imposed on the non-white peoples of the country'.

The extreme intensification of the policy of apartheid had led to the Afrikaner being blamed for its evils and humiliations. 'All this bodes ill for our future. It has bred a deep-rooted hatred for Afrikaners, for our language, our political and racial outlook amongst all non-whites – yes, even amongst those who seek positions of authority by pretending to support apartheid. It is rapidly destroying amongst "non-whites" all belief in future cooperation with Afrikaners.

'To remove this barrier will demand all the wisdom, leadership and influence of those Congress [ANC] leaders now sentenced and imprisoned for their political beliefs. It demands also that Afrikaners themselves should protest openly and clearly against discrimination. Surely, in such circumstances, there was an additional duty cast on me, that at least one Afrikaner should make this protest actively and positively even though as a result I faced fifteen charges instead of four.

'It was to keep faith with all those dispossessed by apartheid that I broke my undertaking to the court, separated myself from my family, pretended I was someone else, and accepted the life of a fugitive. I owed it to the political prisoners, to the banished, to the silenced and those under house arrest, not to remain a spectator but to act . . .

'All the conduct with which I have been charged has been directed towards maintaining contact and understanding between the races of this country. If one day it may help to establish a bridge across which white leaders and the real leaders of the "non-whites" can meet, to settle the destinies of all of us by negotiation and not by force of arms, I shall be able to bear with fortitude any sentence which this court may impose on me.'

He was sentenced to imprisonment for life.

The two women who had been his contacts were each sentenced to two years' imprisonment.

He concluded by quoting the Boer leader Paul Kruger. 'Prophetic words,' Bram said, 'when spoken in 1881.' Words which remained prophetic: 'With faith we lay our whole case bare to the world. Whether we win, whether we die, freedom shall rise over Africa as the sun out of the morning clouds.'

Bram wrote to me: 'I tried very hard to reach my fellow-Afrikaners, but that does not seem to have worked.'

I remember once saying to Bram that he was a source of strength. He was silent for a moment, then rounded on me as 'a silly ass!' He was really cross. 'It was Molly who gave strength,' he exclaimed, 'Molly, not I!'

During his fifth year in prison his son, aged twenty-three, died suddenly. One of Bram's brothers came to Pretoria prison to break the news. They stood, divided by a partition, two warders behind each of them. Bram was told that Paul had died that morning. Afterwards he was taken directly to his cell and locked in for the night. Not until the next morning did his fellow-prisoners hear of his bereavement. He was not permitted to attend the funeral.

In 1968, when I was allowed back briefly to South Africa, I applied to visit Bram. The Commissioner of Prisons was a man of few words: 'Your request to visit A. Fischer cannot be acceded to.'

We were able to exchange occasional letters, 500 words the limit, and no mention of politics or world affairs. For the most part he referred to his studies: he had passed Economics I and was reading 'Native Administration'. And he described the plants he was growing in the courtyard of their special section: gazanias and roses, Iceland poppies and freesias. He was experimenting with grafting guava and grenadilla and if it bore fruit he would name it guavadilla. He fed crumbs to sparrows, doves and rock-pigeons. 'Then we have a thrush coming after worms occasionally and can sometimes hear a Cape robin before dawn.'

And he wrote of a thunderstorm, the lightning glimpsed through the barred window of the cell, and in an instant I was back in the little house next door to the jail, with the pain of exile and missing him added to the violence of that never-to-be-forgotten storm.

'Of course I remember the Trafalgar starlings,' Bram replied to an inquiry in September 1974. 'When you see our host again, please give him my regards.' He was referring to the evening we'd spent with Hugh Caradon in his apartment overlooking the birds' shrill nightly invasion of Trafalgar Square. 'Also remember picnics,' he added – his turn now to test my memory. 'The famous one where we watched youngsters practising crossing rivers, climbing crags.

'Seven lines left,' he concluded, 'to serve for Xmas greetings, for I shall have to keep some months for family obligations. Celebrate happily.'

That Christmas he was in hospital – the hospital I remembered so well – guarded by two warders. After a fall in prison, cancer had been diagnosed. Throughout his dreadful, slow dying he was said to be calm and cheerful, but exhausted. Despite the increasingly urgent appeals of family, friends and innumerable people from many countries, the Minister of Prisons and Justice refused to release him to the care of his family until he was incapable of appreciating their companionship.

Bram Fischer died on 8 May 1975. After the funeral, the authorities demanded that his ashes be returned to Pretoria prison.

10

Athol Fugard and the Eastern Cape

On a Monday night in September 1961, Athol Fugard's play *The Blood Knot* opened before a multi-racial audience expectantly cramming the small, suffocatingly hot rehearsal room of Dorkay House. This rundown factory in Johannesburg's carshowroom district had been adapted as the African Music and Drama Association. For blacks, theatre was a relative novelty, although a handful had seen the musical *King Kong* and skits, while English-speaking whites were accustomed to classics or drawing-room comedies from Britain. What would this unknown young writer/director come up with? All we knew was that the play was a two-hander, with Fugard himself in one role and, extraordinary for South Africa, a black actor, Zakes Mokae, in the other.

'A play that never ended,' is Fugard's recollection of that night – it went on for four hours – 'on a terrible little stage, only about six inches high at one end.' Egg-boxes had been glued to the walls to shut out traffic noise by Barney Simon, an aspiring young director, but through blacked-out windows on one side came the beat of drums from a nearby mine compound. In my diary I recorded: 'Fugard play, brilliant, an experience, but was very tired'. It was about Morrie and Zach, half-brothers, one white and one black, living in a squalid *pondok* in Korsten, a slum I had recently visited in Port Elizabeth, but, South Africa being a land of paradox and Fugard true to his creation, their wretchedness was lit by dreams, by absurdity and ferocious comedy. In telling their story, the play told about all whites and all blacks: if we were not prepared to live together in brotherhood, we were doomed.

Describing that humble debut, I wrote in the London *Times*: 'South Africa has produced a playwright whose *Blood Knot* gives the indigenous theatre international status.' Certain local critics, however, considered it too regional, too specific to find an audience overseas. Twenty-seven years later the play, along with Fugard's subsequent works, continues to be performed at home and abroad, and he is recognized as one of the great dramatists of our time.

Dorkay House throbbed with activity when I returned a few days later to interview him. A trombone clashed with scales from a piano, a woman's voice belted out 'Never on Sunday', raucous laughter came from men improvising an urban farce, and through it all typewriters rattled. Talking at the top of his voice against the cacophony, Athol described the Karoo dorp in which he'd been born in 1932, and how his family had moved to Port Elizabeth, where he'd been brought up in the back streets – 'A damn good experience!' His father, of Irish and, possibly, Polish descent, had played the piano in a jazz band; his mother was an Afrikaner, a Potgieter. Athol, after dropping out of Cape Town University, hitch-hiked up Africa, then joined a British tramp-steamer, as 'captain's tiger', sailing round the world, the only white member of the crew. Back in South Africa, he spent a traumatic, revelatory stint as clerk in the Pass Laws court in Johannesburg and it was the friendship of black writers and musicians in Sophiatown – Bloke Modisane, Can Themba, Lewis Nkosi and Zakes Mokae – that sparked off his first two plays. 'All worthwhile art in South Africa,' he told me, 'is stimulated by work between the races; creative impetus and vitality must come through cooperative efforts.'

In *The Blood Knot* I'd thought his language, a fusion of English and Afrikaans, beautiful. 'There are certain things about South Africa,' he explained, 'which achieve their truest statement from the Afrikaner background. The tragedy is that their love of country has become a passionate but shrivelling emotion. Afrikaans has become the language of violence. The Afrikaner has done this to himself.'

Coming away from the interview and walking down Eloff Street Extension under the evening sky, I could still hear the trombone, now competing with a trumpet. A line of men trotted by wearing a mixture of tribal and Western garments, clutching bulging suitcases and bundles, sewing machines and guitars, heading for the railway station – they were miners

187

returning to tribal areas. Trendily dressed city Africans took no notice of them. The two groups seemed to me part of the amalgam from which black musicians, actors and writers were eagerly creating a thrusting township culture, dreaming of the day when they might follow Miriam Makeba or Hugh Masekela to stardom. Among the organizers of Dorkay House were Dan Poho, Ian Bernhardt and Robert Loder, a young Englishman recently down from Cambridge who had been drawn to South Africa by Father Huddleston. Athol thought the venture encapsulated 'the whole of the South African experience – every reason for despair, every reason for courage, real work and also bad work'. By the 1980s the fruits of that work were visible in productions successfully touring Europe, America and Australia.

After seeing *The Blood Knot* again – it had transferred to the YMCA theatre – I visited the Fugards and their baby daughter, Lisa, in the poorly lit flat they rented in a down-at-heel block, romantically named Braes o'Berea. Zakes, when he stayed there, had to use the servants' entrance at the back. Sheila, a composed, quiet woman, seemed to provide Athol with a certain stability.

I was increasingly drawn to the burning energy of this sinewy, hungry, intense young man who made outrageously honest remarks, provoked as much by social hypocrisy as, in those days, by brandy. Around the time that I was starring as Red Riding Hood at Arcadia Primary School – I must have been seven or eight – Dad had taken the family to a matinee of *Queen High*, a musical comedy from London. All I remember of the occasion was coming home, flinging myself face down on the box ottoman and, in a paroxysm of tears, crying out, 'I want a brother like that man in the chorus!' Some thirty-five years later I finally acquired a brother, adopted by mutual consent and, like so much else in life, a far cry from my original desire or expectation. Indeed, Athol was everything I'd been brought up to be snobbish about – heavy Eastern Cape accent, darkly bearded and unkempt, with a tendency to be loud in his enthusiasms – and while my relatives were in the management of the South African Railways and Harbours, Athol and one of his uncles had actually worked as part-time stewards on trains. The only common experiences we could find in the past were a good grounding in Scripture from our respective fathers and ballroom dancing. As a teenager in white tie and tails, with his sister he had entered competitions in Port Elizabeth, while I was unwillingly roped in by Poppy, who taught ballroom dancing, to partner the females, who greatly outnumbered the males among her pupils.

Athol was struck by my responsiveness to his work and to the other tremendous excitements of that time, epitomized by a production of Tagore's *King of the Dark Chamber* in Durban, which was enthusiastically backed by the Meers and other Indian leaders, and by the country's first Jazz Festival. In Johannesburg City Hall an audience of 1,200 Africans with a few whites was enthralled by the pianist Dollar Brand, immensely tall and stylish with an unforgettable stillness, by the incomparable Kippie Moeketsi on saxophone and by Chris McGregor, pale face hardly visible under a tweed cap. After midnight we were still cheering for more, despite the problem for Africans of returning to their remote townships at that late hour.

Meanwhile, Mandela continued to elude the police and Lutuli was awarded the Nobel Peace Prize.

In Cape Town I again saw *The Blood Knot*, first in a crude village hall, then in the city's multi-racial Labia Theatre. Athol had begun the process of pruning the play. Wherever possible, he and Zakes performed to mixed audiences, but most theatres were segregated, as were the trains in which they had to travel. Since Zakes, as 'non-European', was restricted to third class, Athol tipped the Coloured bedding attendant to take food and (illegal) alcohol to his friend.

On a sun-filled day I accompanied the actors to the beach, to a beautiful stretch of empty sand and empty surf where black and white *were* permitted to mix, a freedom due entirely to the dangerous currents washing back under the waves. Zakes, lean and bearded, laughing maniacally, headed for the water with great leaps, while Athol followed at a steady trot, and as they dived through crashing breakers I watched in alarm, imagining the entire cast of *The Blood Knot* swept out to sea.

The following evening Athol braced himself to address a gathering of liberal and left-wing intellectuals. Albie Sachs, a young lawyer, was chairman. Very nervous, Athol had resorted to an extra-large brandy. As he rose to speak, he became aware that no one was looking him in the eye; indeed, everyone stared fixedly in one direction, while Albie was urgently whispering, 'Your fly's undone!' Zipping it up, Athol, quite unabashed, proceeded with his talk on theatre – a talk which inspired me to write an appreciative letter. His prompt reply began: 'Sincerely, many thanks for your note. I was quite honest on Sunday night when I said I was "high". In fact, all I can clearly remember of that evening is zipping up my fly with considerable aplomb.'

Our friendship flourished through occasional encounters, each one unforgettable, and a lively correspondence: 'What I cherish most about our relationship,' he wrote, 'is the extent to which we've "made" it, literally with our hands. There was something there to begin with of course, a raw material, but like good Brechtian workmen we've used it well.' Before long, we had come to regard each other as Sissy and Boetie.

In 1962, a time of intensified arrests, he described a journey to Johannesburg to discuss his new play, *People Are Living There*: 'I can't begin to tell you how important that trip was for me – just the trip, the twenty-four hours in the compartment going up, and again coming back. I think I came nearer to understanding my purpose than ever before. It is to love the ugly – the unloved because that is all that ugliness is, the thing that isn't loved. The focus of all these thoughts was very specific in that 2nd Class compartment. It was South Africa itself. Has this poor, blighted country ever been uglier? Is it possible for the stain of injustice on this earth to be deeper? I don't think so. At some point in the new play Milly says: "When the worst becomes worse". We have reached that point – a madness in which degrees of comparison lose their meaning. The worst has come, and can only get worse.

'Yes, South Africa is ugly – so ugly that even those who really loved her are now beginning to hate – and this is tragic! Never before has the need for love been greater . . .

'There is a heart-breaking lot of talk in Johannesburg about leaving – getting out while the going is good . . . I literally cried out to them How much fucking poorer do you want to make this country!

'Believe this, Mary: I would do more good with my life if from now on until the day I died I did nothing more than walked, every day, the length of some back street, in some town or dorp, and loved what I saw . . .

'Forgive the emotional tremble in the higher registers – but I feel strongly about all this and know I am talking to someone who feels just as strongly.'

'The sea is at our doorstep,' he wrote in December 1964, after moving with his family to a seaside cottage in the village of Skoenmakerskop, seven miles down the coast from Port Elizabeth. 'There is enough land and need for the highly moral activity of tree-planting and the beginnings of a vegetable patch that has kept us in lettuce, carrots and spinach for the past month. I've never realized fully how much of an Afrikaner I really am, until this moment when I kicked off my shoes and stood barefoot on the earth. I keep looking at my toes to see if roots haven't appeared. All this plus the sea – an even greater passion than the earth.

'I want to, need to talk to you again.'

I understood. My toes retained a memory of digging into stony ground when I went barefoot up the koppie.

Over the years Athol's letters were rich in quotations from Camus, Malraux, Beckett, Olson, quotations which often provoked him into sharing his deepest thoughts, and he opened my mind to areas of beauty in what before had seemed arid or crude – stones, desert, pain, dregs – small things and large. While I tussled with city life in London or New York, he gave me a vivid sense of the Eastern Cape: 'This afternoon a walk with Azdak in the bush'. Azdak, his *brak* of a dog, part Dobermann, was named after the rogue in *The Caucasian Chalk Circle*. 'Ended up on a high sandy ridge, almost a dune, the harsh grey scrub cropped close to the earth by our savage south-westers. One was blowing, long cool and clean; in the distance the sea, brilliantly blue and settling down after two days of rough weather . . .'

When I returned to South Africa in 1965, during a brief visit to him and Sheila and five-year-old Lisa in the cottage at S'kop, Athol handed me a draft of his new play, *Hello and Goodbye*, and left me alone to read it. Afterwards, I found him sitting on a rock overlooking the sea. 'Good, very good,' I told him. It was the first response he'd had to the play. There was no need to say more. We sat contentedly while the wind blew freshly from the

Indian Ocean, stirring the aromatic heather which surrounded us.

In years to come, discussing his plays with him face to face or by letter and seeing them performed in Johannesburg and London, New York and Paris, my feeling of familiarity for the region was continually enlarged: the back streets of Port Elizabeth where Johnnie Smit roamed, those small railway stations through which Hester's train travelled, the marshes and mudflats in which Boesman and Lena scratched to survive, the heart of New Brighton where Sizwe Bansi's friend Buntu stole a *dompas* from a dead man, and the tearoom in St George's Park where Sam shared in the young Master Harold's education. 'I know that I have mastered the code of one time, one place,' he said. 'My life's work is possibly to witness as truthfully as I can the nameless and destitute of this one little corner of the world.' And because the plays were rooted deep as the aloes of the landscape, their truth about those characters in that region became universal.

His work as a writer was repeatedly interrupted by crises in the work of Serpent Players, the black theatre group he had helped to form in Port Elizabeth. Soon after *The Blood Knot*'s successful tour of South Africa, he had been approached by men and women from New Brighton township who, as he put it, had a hunger for experience in the realm of ideas. They were school teachers, a bus inspector, a lawyer's clerk and a cleaner who was also a leading blues singer. They began to rehearse in the evenings, two or three times a week, sometimes in a trades union hall, sometimes at the Fugards' cottage.

In 1963 Athol wrote to tell me of their first production, an adaptation to a New Brighton situation of Machiavelli's *Mandrake*. 'Hilarious and deliciously vulgar. I am staging it very strictly in the Commedia del Arte style – bare stage, a few props but lots and lots of fun.' The group's 'sudden and newfound excitement and hope and making of meanings is so fragile,' he added. And, 'As if the physical disadvantages we work against weren't enough, the Special Branch are also making life difficult for us. They've already broken up a rehearsal, taken names and addresses, etc. The night they burst in on our rehearsal I got the impression they thought they had found another Rivonia. Then one of them sat down and read the Machiavelli through from beginning to end – and laughed, "A good play, man!"'

The production, first in a township hall with inadequate stage and poor lighting, then before a mixed audience at Rhodes University in Grahamstown, was warmly appreciated. 'A small masterpiece in improvisation,' a local critic called it, 'something new and significant for South African theatre.' Next came Büchner's great play and Athol wrote: 'I see *Woyzeck* as Man brutalized, got at, pushed around, ridiculed – and in all this also *a* man with his little portion of loving and fearing and jealousy – but intensely felt! This would have been an ambitious project even with an experienced Johannesburg cast at my disposal – I intend mounting it almost as a Brechtian musical with original songs and music provided by a good jazz "combo". If I can realize the images forming in my mind this production will be unlike anything yet seen in this country . . . Hold thumbs for us . . .'

Again a success, 'another step forward'. To my offer to raise funds for the group, he replied, 'I really don't know if we can accept any money yet. No false humility believe me – but I' mean, are we worth it? A group of inexperienced, green would-be actors and one crack-pot has-been playwright!' It was some time before he requested assistance, and then it was for the modest sum of £25.

The following year Serpent Players staged Brecht's *The Caucasian Chalk Circle*. 'A beautiful production,' wrote Athol. 'We were all patting ourselves on the back, preparing for the township performances, when out of the blue my leading actor was taken in for ninety days – twelve hours before a performance. What the papers don't report is that this warm and wonderful man was savagely assaulted by the police in his home (1 a.m.) in front of his family and dragged away to jail crying for mercy. I felt suicidal. The whole substance of my life seemed – No! *was* – rotten with self-indulgence. My simplest pleasures turned sour. If I hadn't had to go on in the part I don't know what I would have done.'

Two months later and, during my visit early in 1965, Serpent Players considered what next. In the Fugards' small sitting-room I listened to their high-spirited reading of *La Ronde*, but

agreed with their decision that it was not appropriate. Afterwards, as we all relaxed with the customary gallon of Tassen-
berg wine, Athol began to sing. I can never hear Bob Dylan's
'Don't think twice, it's all right . . .' without seeing him, sitting
cross-legged on the floor, swaying to the rhythm, until the
actors one by one joined in the chorus, while Azdak lay
slumbering.

Back in Johannesburg, I was having the first of my secret
meetings with Bram Fischer and Athol wrote to say he was
applying himself with renewed vigour to *Hello and Goodbye*. But
he was also preoccupied by a fresh crisis facing Serpent Players.
The government had placed a nationwide ban on performances
before multi-racial audiences. 'The banning has provoked a
situation which, although depressing in one respect, is also
fertile with new (and needed) purpose. Let's hope we are mature
enough to rise to it. I can't tell you how meaningful our last
meeting was. We shelved the discussion of our next production
to ask and try and find answers for the really basic why's? and
what's? of our existence.'

Out of that self-examination came their choice: *Antigone*.
They saw the relevance to their lives of this play, written in 400
BC, about the corruption of authority and the moral and
religious justification for rebellion against such authority. But
their leading actor, Norman Ntshinga, had been arrested. Held
in solitary confinement while awaiting trial, he wrote to Athol:
'The day you started rehearsing *Antigone* I did not worry much
as I knew that for a few meetings you would be doing nothing
but reading and I hoped I would be released in time to catch up.
But when I learnt that you were moving ahead with the play I
paced about for hours in hysterics. I reproached myself bitterly
for losing my nerve, I tried to sleep but sleep would not come.
I got up again and paced about. Towards the early hours of the
morning I lay down but not to sleep and when the dull day light
came all support vanished and I seemed to be sinking into a
bottomless abyss. God help me if I ever endure greater anguish
than I did then. As time went on I grew worse week after week
and my melancholy took a fixed form . . . I do not think any
person except those who have gone through such a crisis can
comprehend what it is. I never knew what solitary confinement
can do to a person. But I understood enough to be convinced

that any person who has gone through it can assure himself that there is nothing on earth that he need dread. But all that is over now. I'm trying to explain that of all the things I'm missing there is nothing I miss like my family and Drama. Acting is my second love.'

When I returned to S'kop in June 1965 to report on political trials, Serpent Players were surreptitiously rehearsing *Antigone* in a Coloured kindergarten on the outskirts of Port Elizabeth, the only place they could find since Athol was now barred from New Brighton, the township where they all lived. Nomhle Nkonyeni, a factory worker, was Antigone, and George Mnci, a schoolmaster, Creon. As Creon balanced precariously on two small tables representing his palace steps, Athol directed: 'In an MGM production there would be trumpets to announce you. We have no trumpets. *You* have to sound them: the glory has to be there in your performance.' Mabel Magada as Eurydice had the line, 'I'm not unacquainted with grief, and I can bear it.' She was the wife of Norman Ntshinga.

The schoolmaster playing Haemon particularly impressed me, but before opening night he too was arrested and would be sent to Robben Island. Nevertheless, although Athol was refused a permit to attend the dress rehearsal in New Brighton and the company was refused a permit to perform in Port Elizabeth, the production went ahead as if actors and directors were inspired by Antigone's words: 'I honoured those things to which honour truly belongs.' And the day came when Norman Ntshinga, in Robben Island prison, improvised a production which in turn generated *The Island*, a play created by Athol with John Kani and Winston Ntshona, two new recruits to Serpent Players. From a workshop production in Cape Town, they went on to perform at the Royal Court Theatre in London and then in the United States.

Since Athol had to discuss the forthcoming production of *Hello and Goodbye* in Johannesburg, and the family accompanied him, I stayed on in their cottage with Azdak. For the past three years I had been hearing reports of police brutality in New Brighton and Kwazakhele townships and of the subsequent arrest of hundreds of men and women. Only local Port Elizabeth newspapers and, before it was banned, the left-wing *New Age*, had mentioned these events and it was with trepidation that I set off early one morning to attend a political trial in Addo.

I managed to get a lift with a young lawyer who had come from Johannesburg – such was the atmosphere in Port Elizabeth that it was almost impossible to find local lawyers to take on the defence, which was paid for by a Defence and Aid Fund, successor to the Treason Trial's Defence Fund. From the city the road ran past New Brighton, through mudflats and on through winter-arid brushland where trees were sparse and stunted and only the red candelabra of aloes brightened the landscape.

Beyond a steep rise a fertile valley appeared, the valley of the Sundays River, where orange groves stretched in all directions and a polo ground symbolized the lifestyle of these prosperous farmers. A railway siding, trading store and police station with hairdressing salon above constituted the entire settlement of Addo. The fresh-faced lawyer was, to judge from our conversation, politically naïve, but I had elicited from him the disquieting fact that families of the defendants were barred from the trials. Now, leading me into a large room attached to the police station, he informed the solitary policeman that I had come to report on the trial. The policeman fetched a chair and I was seated to one side while the young lawyer settled at a table adjacent to one for the prosecutor, a lean, swarthy man with drooping moustache named Klackers. Nearby a blonde woman adjusted a tape-recorder, which crackled noisily. Two members of the Security Police, one white, one black, sat at the prosecutor's elbow. The defendants entered and huddled on a backless bench. Around their necks hung squares of cardboard with the numbers 1 to 8. Number 2 marked a young man in leather jacket. Two of the women were also quite young, wearing cotton dresses with coats. The third was older, in threadbare coat, green bedroom slippers and traditional *doek* on her head. It transpired that she was the wife of a clergyman, mother of several children; she sat in stony misery.

'Rise in court!' The magistrate entered, bulky against the winter sunlight streaming in from two big windows, and sat on a low platform. The policeman whispered to him and he glanced in my direction with an expression of distaste. Klackers rose and

Number 6 walked jerkily into the witness box. Cross-examination was continued from the previous day, the prosecutor putting questions and a black interpreter translating from English into Xhosa and back. Number 6, continually tugging at his thick beard, head cocked as though to hear better, denied belonging to the banned ANC, denied attending tea parties to raise funds for it, denied distributing leaflets. The cardboard square flapped in a draught of air and he put up a hand to still it.

Number 7 went stolidly into the box. He also denied the charges but said that many years ago he could remember having seen the black, green and gold flags of the ANC, at street-corner meetings. The magistrate made an occasional note.

During tea-break I remained seated. The young defence lawyer, who had been remarkably silent so far, suddenly began to sing, 'Che sera, sera', and before he'd reached the second line, Klackers, with a grin, joined in. I watched with amazed horror as they executed a sort of soft-shoe shuffle, then, still singing, left the court and crossed the yard to the nearby store. The accused men and women, whether disgusted or apathetic, took no notice, only sat without speaking under the policeman's guard. Nor did they react when later the prosecutor pleaded for the maximum sentence. Defending counsel protested to no effect. The interpreter called on us to rise. The magistrate withdrew. In the silence, occasional trains shunted back and forth at the railway siding.

'Rise in court!' The magistrate climbed back on to his platform. The eight accused stood. The magistrate pronounced: Numbers 3, 4 and 5 – guilty on two counts. The others – guilty on three counts. All, sentenced to four and a half years.

The accused just stood. Then Number 6 began to weep. They were herded into a prison van and driven away. Magistrate, prosecutor and Security Police drove off together. Through the long journey back to Port Elizabeth with the young lawyer, I clamped down on thought and feeling. Arriving in the Fugards' cottage, I tramped restlessly from room to room, with 'Che sera, sera' ringing in my brain. Compulsively I rearranged crockery on kitchen shelves. I could see Klackers with the Security Police beside him and hear the magistrate's, 'Four and a half years'. Seizing a broom I strode to the outside lavatory and swept it out, stroke after stroke, opening the door wide for a last, hard go at the grit. Fetching disinfectant and brush, I scrubbed the round wooden seat with its handled lid. Back in the house I pulled on my swimsuit and hurried as fast as I could along the clifftop road, but in memory the cardboard numbers flapped and the older woman's blank face accused me. I moved down steep steps to the small beach and ran into the sea, into shock, an extremity of cold, plunging deep in the salt water until my tears and the tears of the bearded man were washed away and straining lungs forced me to the surface, where I floated, gazing at the empty sky.

As I went from trial to trial in courts hundreds of miles apart, I realized that the roots of this widespread repression lay in history. After the British had invaded the area, the Xhosa people there had been the first blacks to be educated by Victorian missionaries back in the 1830s. They were the only Africans to have the vote, until disenfranchized in 1936. Many of their national leaders came from the region and were active in founding the ANC and the PAC. In the Defiance Campaign of 1952, volunteers from Eastern Cape townships had proved the most militant, crowding the jails, disciplined and good-humoured. Now the Security Police were taking revenge and although sabotage had been crushed, the machine ground on, bulldozing every crumb of political dissent. The people in the dock were ordinary men and women, many of whom had tried to continue protesting and raising funds even though the ANC and the PAC had been outlawed after Sharpeville. If they'd had anything to do with sabotage or even spontaneous violence, they would have been brought to trial in the Supreme Court in Grahamstown. The police, after arresting suspects by the hundreds, detained them in solitary confinement while interrogating them. Those who held out were 'guilty', those who cracked were schooled as State witnesses. If torture was necessary, if evidence needed embroidering or concocting, why not? The accused were guilty. At all costs the State must be defended from the 'Communist' threat.

Evidence about the past was blatantly manufactured and, as neither magistrates nor many of the defence lawyers knew the history of the ANC and the PAC, such evidence repeatedly went unchallenged. From all I had learned since 1961 I could assist defence lawyers with certain facts, although, however able,

198

tenacious and brave these men were, they had little chance of success in face of the rigging. Over it all reigned two members of the Security Police: Detective-Sergeant du Preez, a big pink-faced blue-eyed man destined for rapid promotion, and his black assistant, Sergeant Gazo, thick-set with greased-down hair and highly polished shoes. As a result of their activities, the townships were riddled with informers.

Zebia Mpendu, a nursing-sister I had met in New Brighton in 1961, was the next defendant to be brought to trial in Addo. She had already been held in prison for sixteen months. 'There are others who were more important, who have waited longer,' said du Preez.

No one was allowed to talk to the accused, but in any event I pretended not to know her lest this add to her troubles. A bespectacled woman in black cloth coat, white furry hat, grey darned stockings and black gloves, she hunched over a note-book, making notes throughout the 'evidence' given by State witnesses. She looked very tired, alone on the backless bench, but her gaze, when it encountered Gazo's bold stare, was steadfast. Now and then, she and I exchanged smiles.

Allister Sparks, from the *Rand Daily Mail*, now sat beside me, a very welcome arrival. The trial, said Klackers, centred on the disposal of a motor-van. Zebia was accused of selling it to raise funds for the ANC. Because that organization had been out-lawed under the Suppression of Communism Act, local news-paper headlines labelled such a trial 'Red', and when Klackers abruptly announced there was a plot to murder a State witness, the headline read: MURDER OF WITNESS 'PLOT' – TRIAL OF NURSE. Nothing more was heard of the 'plot'. Zebia was sentenced to four years' imprisonment. Allowing for the eighteen months she had by this time been held, it meant another two and a half years to go. (Upon release, she was expelled by the Nursing Council for her 'communistic' activities.)

Allister and I were joined by Joe Lelyveld, newly arrived representative of the *New York Times*. The Fugards had returned and over dinner together, with black humour, we swopped examples of the appalling farce which ran through procedures in these tinpot courts.

On my own again but for an elaborately hatted local journalist with the improbable name of Mrs Marx, I was covering a trial to which Govan Mbeki and Terrance Makwabe, a fellow-prisoner, were brought from Robben Island to give evidence for the defence. Under heavy guard, Mbeki was led into court, handcuffed. A policeman produced a key but was unable to unlock the handcuffs. Another policeman tried another key, the same result. In the confusion, Govan grinned his enjoyment at their predicament. Mrs Marx, meanwhile, had rummaged in her handbag and, offering the police a huge bunch of keys, said in bright explanation, 'The servants you get nowadays!' One of her keys did the trick. With hands freed, Govan was led into the witness box.

The prosecutor promptly sprang up to request that the press withdraw. 'It is not in the interests of the State that this man's evidence be reported. He is an important political prisoner.' Predictably, the magistrate agreed. Mrs Marx and I had to file out. Brigadier Aucamp, head of Prisons Security, who had come from Pretoria to monitor Mbeki's presence, was conferring with a covey of Security Police on the verandah outside. Furious and disappointed, with a rush of bravado I remarked loudly, 'The whole world will think they're afraid of Mbeki.' A glare from Aucamp and next moment one of the police demanded to see my passport and made a note of my identity. But there was no visible follow-up.

When Terrance Makwabe, a slight, soft-spoken man, gave evidence, the press were not excluded. He was reminded by the prosecutor that the effect of his evidence might well lay him open to renewed prosecution and a longer sentence. He agreed. Why then, asked the prosecutor, was he prepared to give evidence? '*Andi Soyiki*' – I am no longer afraid – Makwabe replied.

In Cradock the courthouse was an impressive granite building on the square, not far from the hotel where I'd stayed in 1961. Before attending the trial there I had morning tea with Calata, now a canon. The location had been demolished and, two miles away, the new township was named Lingelihle. Rather than go to the trouble of applying for the permit which a visitor required, I met him in the home of a white friend. Now seventy, with whitening hair, he was banned from all political activity but nevertheless continued to exert an influence locally.

Afterwards, he drove me to the court. The atmosphere there

was chilly and efficient. A spruce magistrate looked down on a crowded dock occupied by youths bearing cards numbered from 1 to 12. The public gallery as usual was empty. I joined a young man in the press box. As the black-gowned prosecutor, who had a streaming cold, confronted defendant Number 6, I picked up the threads of the case. The youths were accused of having planned to invade a dorp three years earlier. Allegedly they were supporters of the ANC's rival, the Pan Africanist Congress, but the State treated the organizations as one and the same. So extraordinary and disturbing was the cross-examination that I later used it verbatim in a novel and in a radio play.

Number 6, whose name was Gideon, was eighteen years old, thinly clad. His defiant stance was belied by hands which agitatedly kneaded each other. The prosecutor referred to evidence given by State witnesses: Gideon was said to have recruited them, telling them they must fight, they must not let whites own the country. To each question he replied, 'It is not true.' Guns, pangas, axes were to come from Russia and Ghana, the prosecutor accused, blowing his nose like a trumpet. 'No, it was all lies, Your Worship,' the youth reiterated but his voice had begun to flag.

'Everything is lies?' The prosecutor's voice was honeyed.

'Yes, Your Worship.'

'Your name, your address?'

'No! I mean all that is to do with the invasion is not true.'

'Ah! So now you admit some things?' And, in a swirl of fury, 'Listen to me, Gideon! What about Sharpeville, when Saracens were out?'

'1960?'

'Yes! You were a young boy. It impressed you deeply, hey? You saw all the police . . . You were so young,' and the prosecutor squeaked in mimicry of a child's voice. Court officials laughed heartily. The magistrate remained silent, as did defence counsel.

Seriously Gideon protested, 'But I spoke in my same voice then.'

'And you knew of Bantu who burned their passes?'

'I heard. I would never burn mine, I need it to keep my job.'

'You need a pass to get a job?'

'Yes, Your Worship.'

'To get a house?'

'Yes.'

'You need your pass if you go to the bank?'

'Yes.'

'And if you want to go to another town?'

'Yes, Your Worship.'

'So the pass is a burden?'

'No, Your Worship, not for me. It helps me.'

'The white man is baas, is that not so?'

'Yes.'

'And you, as Bantu, can only live in the location?'

'Yes.'

'As Bantu, you cannot go to the bioscope?'

'Yes. No, Your Worship.'

The prosecutor blew his nose several times. 'And you cannot go in the tearooms?'

'No.'

'You Bantu have an inferior education?'

'Yes.'

'What's that? Speak up!'

'Yes, Your Worship.'

'*En jy is dood tevrede*?' The prosecutor quickly corrected himself: 'And you are dead happy with your lot?'

'Dead happy, Your Worship.'

'Dead happy in your job?'

'Dead happy. I get my pay.' Gideon's boyish face was blank but the knuckles gleamed in his clenched fists.

Adjournment for lunch.

After making a request to the clerk of the court, I went in search of a shop to buy cold meat and fruit. It was all I could think of to do. Returning, I asked an official to give the food to the youths. As he accepted the food from me, I could hear the sound of singing. From the barred windows of the cells at the back of the court, song poured out. I knew that in Cradock the spirit of resistance had not been crushed.

Canon Calata died in 1983 at the age of eighty-eight. By then funerals had become the stage for political protest: his coffin was draped in the illegal ANC flag, women wore blouses in those colours and the young men who carried his coffin sang the freedom songs he had composed. The procession accompanying his body to the grave was followed by Security Police.

By March 1985 Cradock had become the 'flashpoint' of the conflict sweeping South Africa like a veldfire. Two young men had inspired the community of Lingelihle with a new sense of self-respect and resistance to oppression. One was a school-master named Matthew Goniwe, the other was Canon Calata's grandson, Fort – so named because he had been born when Calata was imprisoned for treason in the Johannesburg Fort.

Four months later Goniwe and Fort, with two close associates, were assassinated, repeatedly stabbed, then burnt to death. 50,000 people of all races from all parts of the country attended their funeral, a powerful display of outrage but also a celebration of the lives of Goniwe and his friends.

It was in Cradock that Norman Ntshinga was brought to trial in 1965. I had already returned to Johannesburg, and Athol, who spoke eloquently but ineffectually for mitigation of the sentence, reported that Norman had been sent to Robben Island for seven years. And he described the drive back to Port Elizabeth with Norman's wife, Mabel, and Barney Simon. They had stopped to give a lift to an old woman: 'She was fifty and destitute – her husband dead a few days ago; all of her life (it was terribly heavy) on her head, walking along a barren Karoo road under a blazing sun, walking from nothing to nothing, resigned to sleeping in storm water drains; and crying. I'm sure she cried every time she stopped; then went on, and later cried again but went on, and on, and on.

'The enigma of course was the bundle on her head – an old bath, a blanket, a three-legged cast-iron pot, odds and ends – all that was left of her life, but *not* abandoned. Barney said: "The amazing thing is that she still has a use for the things in her life." I said: "Not just the *things* – her life itself. She will feed it tonight, sleep it, and when she finds water, wash it."'

Athol wrote this letter to me at a moment when I had written him a *cri de coeur*. Looking back, I suppose I felt the burden of all I had witnessed in those trials, the inadequacy of the articles I wrote, and although I had returned to the enthralling interludes of my secret meetings with Bram, old friends in Johannesburg suddenly seemed alien. At parties I sought out a lawyer who had conducted a brilliant defence in one case, sitting close beside him as if we were lone survivors of a terrible battle. But also years of suppressing pain and anger undoubtedly contributed to my despairing mood. And there must have been an underlying mid-life loneliness. I had not yet come to think Athol's perception of myself as a 'loner' was rather flattering.

In his reply Athol began by reminding me of Milly in *People Are Living There*. 'You know what you are? You're Milly in the middle of her party. You're making your last fling for something you *won't get*. You want it I know; you need it, but you won't get it. What are we talking about? What is "it"? Put all the impossibles together and I suppose they'll add up to "it" – a new meaning for an old body (I'm old too) – the hunger for love that's been so frustrated in your life. What more is there? What are the other impossibles you want? Children? A home? Youth? I'm Don now – You've had it Mary! When Don forces Milly to see that this is all she gets, she reacts initially, as she must, with a sense of outrage. So do you of course in your more refined accents . . . [Then] she tears down the decorations. She gives up deceptions . . . And she says – with the smallest and tiredest note of affirmation – "This is all I've got. But it's real. It's mine. It's me."

'There are no promises in this life. One moment of happiness is nothing but one moment of happiness. A stone is not a promise of stones. It is itself. And you do not love it, or feel it, or really hold it if you do so because of the promise *you* read into it.'

He went on to describe the old woman on the road from Cradock. 'Using her as a metaphor,' he continued, 'I think Life is asking you, telling you, to take that walk. Like her you are crying. But walk, Mary. Put your life on your head and walk. To do so is not to die. It is to live with the reality of your circumstances. The walk is long, bitter, barren and full of pain, but it is the only way to Live.'

It certainly was, as he noted in his diary, a 'savage' letter, which had me puzzling about what precisely I must put on my head.

'That African woman,' he concluded, 'will be with me to my dying day. She defines a condition we *must* understand.'

The woman provided the irresistible image for Lena when he

came to write a new play. 'Like *The Blood Knot* and *Hello and Goodbye*,' he said, '*Boesman and Lena* is desperately local. God knows if anybody will find the three derelicts in it significant or relevant to anything. It's always the same: "Who could possibly be interested?" But you go on writing.'

Immediately, he and his family had arrived in Johannesburg for the production of *Hello and Goodbye*. Barney Simon had created a theatre in a private house to which he could legally invite mixed audiences. There he directed the play, with Athol an unforgettably poignant and comic Johnnie Smit, his world the back streets of Port Elizabeth which had been such a 'damn good experience' for the young Athol.

We celebrated the play's opening on the night of 11 November. Next morning came news of the capture of Bram Fischer.

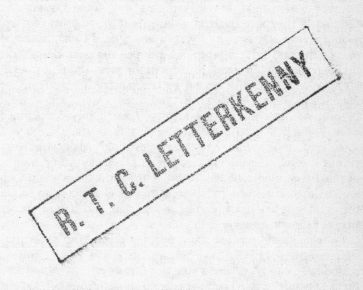

I I

A Threat to the State?

Each day that passed after Bram's arrest, bereavement and fear of being taken into 180 days were strangely mixed with happiness, the happiness of feeling at home. I loved the dilapidated colonial mansion where I was living, with its large, dark rooms, its long corridors and balcony overlooking the garden of tangled grass, pines and jacarandas. I wanted to stay. I did not want to run away.

The police put out a story that Bram had been followed for several months before his capture. If it were true, they would have known about me, they would have known his phone number and would have overheard our last conversation. Obviously they were watching the airport, hoping his contacts would scatter and run. As I waited and waited I imagined that one of the taxi drivers who had dropped me near Bram's car might recognize him from pictures in the press and report a tall woman with a British accent to the police. If I were to be detained in solitary confinement and interrogated, what would become of my courage, my loyalty? I had glibly condemned those who had given evidence against their friends. Now I wondered: who could be sure of resisting? Many had succumbed, some after brief interrogation, others only after months of solitary confinement and torture. During the Inquisition, men and women sustained by their faith had withstood appalling forms of physical torture. But in our age, did honour really matter more than survival?

Bettelheim had written about people held in Nazi concentration camps: if given a real beating, they had taken pride in suffering manfully, whereas constant threats effectively reduced them to helplessness. There was no emotional protection against the humiliation of verbal abuse.

I considered the spectacular bravery of those who had resisted:

Zebia Mpendu and the other women and men brought to trial in the Eastern Cape. However apathetic some appeared, they were the ones who had refused to give in despite beatings or threats. For them, honour did matter.

It was not that I knew any secrets, but what if I were broken to the point of telling lies which could incriminate the innocent?

Bram's heroic attempt to rebuild an opposition against enormous odds reminded Robert Birley of the men who'd plotted against Hitler, honourable men who had little talent for improvising, amateurs. The professionals were all on Hitler's side. Under that tyranny there was no chance of organizing a popular political movement of real revolutionary force. Nor – as was all too true of South Africa – had Western democracies come to their aid. And so, great and noble men were lost to Germany and to the world.

Such thoughts formed the background to a novel I was working on, and now came news that 341 men from the Eastern Cape who were already serving sentences on Robben Island were being retried on identical charges and were likely to be sentenced to several additional years. I wrote urgently to friends in Washington, a Congressman, a Senator's assistant and the editor of the *New Republic*, offering information about events in the Eastern Cape. Their replies to say they would welcome such a report had obviously been opened, adding to my anxieties.

'If you won't leave the country,' said a friend in whom I confided, 'at least leave Johannesburg.' At Christmas I visited Maggie and Anthony Barker at the mission hospital in Nqutu. An accident which necessitated a skin graft to one leg kept me there for several weeks, time in which to correct the proofs of my updated history of the ANC and in which to absorb something of the Barkers' spiritual energy as they ministered to thousands of patients.

Almost recovered, I was packing to leave that safe haven when lightning forked through the dark day-sky and rain curtained the surrounding countryside. As rolling thunder growled on, the liquid notes of frogs sounded. By evening, when I went into the garden, their chorus had grown to a deep baritone rhythm. Suddenly I felt elated. Yes, I might be confused, my motives complex, mean sometimes, sometimes noble, and it was certainly true that I had no rare and wonderful relationship like Maggie's and Anthony's, but I was alive, here and now, a living human being, a marvel of brain, eyes and senses, able to see the stars reappearing through the receding clouds, to hear the frogs and breathe the freshened air – and I had hands and could use them still, however deformed they might be.

Very early on a summer morning in February, arriving in Johannesburg by slow night train, I headed straight for a mailbox to post the preface of the ANC history to Penguin Books. Back in the old house I telephoned friends and as they welcomed me and we chatted, idly I watched the sunlight playing on leaves outside the hall window. A large sedan appeared, circling the drive; from the front seat two men stared directly at me. 'A car's just come, two men . . .' I told Barney, the friend I had just called. 'Jesus!' he said. As the doorbell rang I put down the receiver.

When I opened the door one of them thrust a sheaf of documents at me, asking, 'Dorothy Mary Benson?' while the other announced, 'We are from the Security Police. We have to serve these orders.'

It was very strange. I had been expecting them to arrest me and instead they were asking me to read a document: 'WHEREAS I, BALTHAZAR JOHANNES VORSTER, Minister of Justice, am satisfied that you engage in activities which are furthering or may further the achievement of the objects of communism . . .' My eyes jumped a few lines: 'Prohibit you . . . from absenting yourself from the residential premises' – yes, that was my address – 'at any time except between the hours of six in the forenoon and seven in the afternoon . . .'

'I don't understand,' I said.

'We're only serving the orders. We want you to sign here to say you received them. You must ask the magistrate, or a lawyer.'

Dazed, I signed, and they went down the steps. The telephone rang. It was Barney. They turned to watch me through the window as I told him, 'It seems to be house arrest. I can't understand the detail.'

'Shit, man, that's bad,' he sympathized.

Nine pages of restrictions: house arrest every night, through weekends and public holidays; restriction to the city; weekly reporting to the police; and clause after clause of bans. Banned from schools, courts – I would not be able to attend Bram's trial – factories, newspaper offices and any area for 'Bantu, Coloured or Asiatic persons' – I could not visit Dugmore Boetie, a Coloured writer ill with cancer in hospital. Banned from 'gatherings', which, I knew, was legally interpreted as being with more than one person at a time. Clause 5 banned any writing, even poetry, with sub-clauses (a), (b), (c), (d), then (e) (i) and (ii), and (aa), (bb), (cc) and (dd), which included a ban on 'preparing, compiling, printing, publishing, disseminating and transmitting'. 'Transmitting' – that obviously related to those letters from Washington which had blatantly been opened.

Clause 6 said no visitors to the house apart from a medical practitioner. No sooner had I read it than a friend, a journalist, drove up to the front steps. I hurried out to explain. He was as stunned as I. I quickly handed him notes about the Eastern Cape, which, until half an hour ago, had been a perfectly legal act on my part.

'If somebody is clearly a threat to the State,' Vorster had said on introducing the relevant law, 'if it is at all possible you do not lock him up in jail, but you neutralize him in his own home . . . If he is particularly dangerous you house arrest him for weekends as well.'

Lawyers analysed the bans: even letters or a diary could be illegal. As most of my books had already been banned I was not particularly affected by the overall ban on existing writings, but since it was illegal for anyone to quote a banned person, there was no way of protesting, nor was there any recourse to a court of law. Sentences for breaking a ban ranged from one to ten years.

It was a tremendous relief to realize that the police were ignorant of my meetings with Bram. The least suspicion on their part would have led to immediate interrogation. Yet the shock of the lesser punishment was intense. No reasons were ever given for such banning, but in my case I was convinced the restrictions were aimed at silencing me after the reporting of the Eastern Cape trials.

Nadine Gordimer and Alan Paton, with characteristic generosity, publicly expressed their deep concern, condemning this 'arbitrary curtailment' of basic rights which deprived me of both freedom and livelihood at one blow, 'a terrible "sentence" for one who has never been accused in a court of law of any offence, political or otherwise'. They were supported in their protest by editorials in the Johannesburg *Sunday Times* and the *Rand Daily Mail*.

I was worried that Kurt, the friend who owned the old house, would suffer from my presence. Indeed, he had already done so: on the morning of the Security Police call, his address book had vanished from the hall table. In my dazed state I had not noticed. I offered to leave. The damage had been done, he said wryly – he was always outspoken – but temperamental though he was, I felt genuine warmth in his reassurance that I should remain.

The first Saturday of house arrest was brilliantly hot. Kurt and the other 'lodger', even the servants, were out. The telephone was silent and I could not repress the question: did friends want to protect me or themselves? It reminded me that Helen Joseph had been the first person to be house arrested years ago and I wished that I had telephoned her regularly, but now in any event, since we were both under bans, it would be illegal to speak to each other.

My room was at the back of the house and had barred windows. Outside, a wild thorn tree crammed with red berries attracted a continual traffic of birds – yellow weavers, thrushes, seed-eaters, doves and crested barbets, with their scarlet, yellow, white and black plumage. Bram would have loved to see them. Athol too was a bird-watcher, and my father – *his* father had written a book about Irish songbirds. An ordinary greyish little bird began to sing, its notes at first sweet and tentative, then insistent, almost angry. I wondered why I couldn't express anger, grew sleepy and woke to write letters. I used a sort of code, which doubtless would confuse the recipients more than the Security Police, and then, under the guise of analysing Saul Bellow's *Herzog*, I wrote notes for my novel.

From the nearby police station came the usual Saturday afternoon clatter of Sten gun and rifle fire. Meanwhile, a line of black men in servants' uniforms appeared through the pine trees at the edge of the garden and trotted deliberately towards a clump of acacia, where they would spend the afternoon illicitly drinking. South Africa's laws made for many forms of subversion.

How lively the house had been when the Fugards had stayed there. Every day we'd had lunch on the verandah, looking out on an ancient eucalyptus, and how we had talked. When the heat became unbearable we sat inside on shabby comfortable chairs, listening to Bach's *Preludes* and *Fugues*, the notes cool and clear in the dim room, while outside insects hummed through the bright air. Now, playing that record intensified loneliness.

I applied to the magistrate for permission to visit my sister and her family. It was refused. However, provided I applied in writing each time, stipulating means of transport, reporting at each end to the police, taking the shortest route and returning by 4 p.m., I would be allowed to visit my father in Pretoria once a month. And he would be allowed a monthly visit to me at the house, provided the magistrate approved each time. Rather than submit to these indignities, Pa came once a week from Pretoria, forty miles away by bus and we met in the city. He was indomitable. Now eighty-five, he barely showed his age but for the whiteness of his close-cropped hair and a bad stoop, which he was too vain to relieve by the use of a walking stick. It was a weekly odyssey that must have weighed on him, but he never complained and indeed was touchingly proud of participating. Instead of relaxing at home together, we filled our day in an absurd peregrination from café to restaurant to cinema and again to café. How exhausted he must have been. I felt exhausted myself as I watched him climb stiffly into his bus for the forty-mile return journey.

The pattern of life had changed. Instead of writing by day and visiting friends in the evening and at weekends, I went obsessively to town in the hope of bumping into one of them for coffee or lunch. I say 'bumping into' because lawyers advised that any pre-arranged meeting could be construed as a 'gathering'. Unexpected people contrived to send messages of where they were likely to be and when. And friends joined me in the Outpatients queue at the hospital, where I went regularly for treatment for the skin graft. Tension could evaporate into hilarity – Nadine, Barney, Athol and I performed a ludicrous series of *pas de deux* between tables in a coffee-bar in Hillbrow when we celebrated Athol's departure for London.

But I had become hypersensitive to friends' attitudes, even sulky if disappointed – for instance, when I had to stand in the street with Alan Paton because it had been impressed upon him by a lawyer that having coffee together *might* constitute a 'gathering'. The sulks were dispelled by Tito Gobbi in a movie of *Rigoletto*, which took me back to that thrilling occasion in Rome when his duet with Gilda, '*Si, vendetta tremenda*', brought the house down. Emerging from the cinema in high spirits, I noticed across the street a café where Bram and I had once met and was painfully reminded that in two weeks' time he was due to be sentenced.

And so my mood swung high and low in a kind of banning-syndrome. I felt happy and grateful when Alan, with his grandson, came to the house late in the afternoon of that same day when we had stood so miserably outside the coffee-bar. I had to be in at seven but there was just time to go for a drive, light-heartedly disregarding the lawyer's warning since we three undoubtedly were a gathering. It was natural in the circumstances that people should overreact. Alan said that if he were ever banned from writing and put under house arrest, he would probably leave the country.

It was not only friends overreacting. One Sunday a journalist suspected of links with the Security Police turned up at the house just as I happened to be breaking a ban – I scooted from his presence like a scared rabbit. Such rashness meant constant anxiety, not simply for the risk I was taking but on behalf of those who might be called as witnesses.

I drew encouragement from cables and letters of support – those that were permitted to reach me. For some friends it was difficult to understand the implications of the bans: writing from Oxford, Margery Perham envied me 'the peace and limitless time to write'. One especially moving letter recalled Pretoria in the thirties. It came from the professor who had been tarred and feathered after he'd written a frank novel about the Voortrekkers. 'I had your *African Patriots* in hand,' he wrote, 'when the wireless announced the restriction order served on you. I hope you will be of good cheer.' A cable to say 'THINKING OF MY FAVOURITE PUSSYCAT' transported me to Paris and the day I'd spent there with Clive Donner on the way to South Africa. He was directing *What's New Pussycat?* Now the movie had arrived in Johannesburg and at a matinée I saw a very different Woody Allen from the quiet young man who had dined with us at the

Brasserie Lipp. It was his first movie and his first visit to Europe. 'Don't unpack,' Clive had said on meeting him in London. 'We're going directly to Paris.' 'What about my dirty laundry?' Woody asked – he had arrived with a suitcase full of it. Clive's jolly cable took me even further back, to our early friendship, when we'd both worked for David Lean and then to his editing Michael Scott's documentary film, the manic day of trial and error as we tried to record Michael's elongated commentary so that it fitted the brief sequences. How far away those 'halcyon' days were, and yet I could see a kind of logic in all that had happened since.

Increasingly, family and friends urged me to leave the country, but Guy Clutton-Brock, who had once been imprisoned in Rhodesia and whom I greatly admired, wrote: 'Try to stay and endure to the end. No other weapon than creative suffering can cope with the enormities of the world in which we live.'

If I could not write, at least I had one worthwhile if small job: to compile a survey of the Eastern Cape trials. Until lawyers advised that this too was illegal. 'When does a life become impotent?' Athol wrote from London. 'How much impotence can our need, our struggle for meaning, accommodate? Let me say no more. I'm sure there's enough noise in your life at the moment – even if it's just the clamour of your own emotions.'

Bulbuls had joined the throng in the berry tree. 'For what seems like the first time,' I noted, 'I am actually suffering and not just witnessing others suffer. Real spiritual and intellectual deprivation. Those documents: WHEREAS I, BALTHAZAR JOHANNES VORSTER, Minister of Justice, am satisfied . . . My God, to have accepted Vorster's dictate without protest is a terrible admission of impotence. I can envisage metamorphosis, Kafka's man/beetle, from a label stuck on and all that flows from it.'

'Of course your sister's a Communist,' one of Poppy's friends had declared.

To Athol I expressed a persisting sense that it couldn't matter less whether I decided to go or stay. 'Of course it does, for Christ's sake,' he replied. 'It is *your* life, and the decisions in your life are ultimately all that your life consists of. Decisions are important because more so than any other moment in our lives they are our moments of consciousness. Cherish yours – use it and be aware which God knows you have a capacity for.'

Could I leave the country that finally had become 'home'? I felt just being there had a certain value. When I thought of London, the Sunday papers' gossip columns filled me with gloom – Forster's, 'He could pardon vice, but not triviality' – and our anti-apartheid protests seemed stridently negative rather than supportive of those who tried to create in the face of repression; but of course, much that was creative could not be told about without risking its survival. Yet to stay meant giving up almost all human contact, it meant renunciation, silence. On the other hand, to go could mean 'for ever'. I would not be allowed to return without permission from the Minister of the Interior. As weeks passed and I toiled with these questions, I wondered at what point self-mockery began.

The chorus had grown: 'Go. What use can you be here now?' Agonizing though it was, my father had no doubt that I should go. And somehow Bram managed to get a message to me: 'You can do more overseas.'

It was midnight. Down the corridor from Kurt's room came the wail of his favourite Fada songs. I put on a record of 'Das Lied von der Erde' and listened to the reverberating beauty of Kathleen Ferrier singing 'Der Abschied', the farewell, for ever, 'Ewig . . . ewig . . .'

Weary, but with a curious sense of lightness, I decided to leave.

In the end what made it easier was the knowledge that I was going directly to Washington to testify before a Congressional Committee on Foreign Affairs, recently formed to consider United States–South African relations. I was already planning my statement. I would start by saying that the time to confront the South African Government was now: in five to ten years it would be more powerful, more tyrannical. I would remind the Committee that the Minister of Justice, Vorster, had been detained in the Second World War for pro-Nazi activities. It was important to try to convey what life was like for Mrs Ntlonti and her family and for the 800 men, women and teenagers recently arrested by police raiding servants' quarters in Johannesburg's suburbs. While giving some idea of the psychological effects of bans and house arrest, I wanted to make it clear that most of the 520 people who had been banned were Africans, and that the cruellest restrictions were those imposed on men and women immediately after their release from prison. And of course I would testify about the trials in the Eastern Cape.*

The Chief Magistrate granted a permit enabling me to leave the city of Johannesburg, 'at 10.45 on Saturday, 16 April 1966 for the sole purpose of proceeding to Jan Smuts Airport in order to leave South Africa.'

On my last day I noticed that every red berry had vanished from the tree. At the airport Pa was photographed by the *Sunday Times* mopping up his tears. A large gathering of friends saw me off – watched by the Security Police.

It was not until the plane was high over the stark hills of Asmara that I thought: leaving is betrayal. Even *one* counts. I felt it might be the greatest mistake of my life.

* *African Politics and Society*, ed. I. L. Markovitz, Macmillan Free Press, New York, 1970.

PART IV
Exile

12

Thomas Stubbs

Not until I was back in London did I learn that my great-grandfather, Thomas Stubbs, had written a journal about the family's early experiences in the Eastern Cape, the region which had become so significant for me. Vividly I remembered the train journey from Cradock to Port Elizabeth after I'd left Canon Calata, and the sensation of being wholly involved in the fate of the country, of belonging. Now this enthralling journal revealed an intimate, ancestral connection. Michael Scott's remark about my having a certain responsibility because I was born in South Africa, of my parents, acquired greater depth. I wished that I'd not been bored when Mom and Aunt Annie and Uncle Sonny reminisced about the past; if only I'd listened and questioned them.

Tom Stubbs mentioned that, before emigrating, the family had lived in Kenton Street. Setting off from my small flat on Abbey Road in search of their house in Bloomsbury, I passed Tavistock Square, where I'd first worked with Michael, and discovered that Kenton Street had once been a mere two blocks away, and that the entire street had been bombed during the Second World war; now a Babylonian block of flats dominated the area. But I could imagine the family during the troubled years of the Napoleonic wars, against the background of Georgian houses which still stood in neighbouring streets.

Tom spoke of a comfortable life in London, yet in 1819, when he was a twelve-year-old, his father, John Stubbs, had been seduced by the British government's offer of a free passage to Algoa Bay with £10 in cash and a hundred acres in 'a beautiful, fertile land, the most verdant carpet Nature has planted, with the most healthy and temperate climate in the universe'. 90,000 applied. Forty-one-year-old John Stubbs was among the 4,000 chosen. In December he, his wife and five children sailed for the

Cape Colony. He took two violins along with books, farming implements and mahogany furniture, while his wife, Ann Campbell, travelled with a kist containing linen, satins, laces and family silver.

Clearly they were unaware that the government's euphemistic description of the Suurveld – sour veld – as a 'verdant carpet' hid the real intention. Settlers were the cheapest way of maintaining the frontier which the invading British had defined to ward off the Xhosa inhabitants. And surely the family had not seen George Cruickshank's cartoon of a settler, surrounded by capering savages, crying out, 'Oh Lord, I might as well have stayed in England to be starved to death as come here to be eaten alive!'

Tom Stubbs recalled their arrival, after a four-month journey, at 'a very dreary looking place, nothing but sandhills'. There, on the Indian Ocean, Port Elizabeth would one day be established. Leaving parents and baby sister in a tented camp, he and his brothers took a walk along the beach, where, encountering 'a lot of Hottentots naked' who 'began to jabber', the boys ran and never stopped until they reached the tents – 'we thought it was all up with us!'

Under the guidance of a Dutchman, the family travelled by wagons through brushland speckled with the flaming candelabra of aloes – I could picture them, following a track that became the route along which the young lawyer drove me to Addo. After crossing the Sundays River, then the Bushmans, they reached the rugged land they had been allotted, right at the frontier. 'Where can we buy rations?' John Stubbs asked the Dutchman. 'Bathurst, twenty-six miles by Caffer footpath,' was the reply as the man bade them farewell in a tone of commiseration. The family pitched tents and kindled a fire for their first meal, and to scare away roaming jackals and elephants. Eventually, they built a house out of clay.

At first Tom and his younger brother, William, were 'happy as princes' to become herdsmen, taking their books with them to learn lessons set by their mother. They had not yet realized how dangerous was their location, which verged on clay pits where the Xhosa traditionally collected red clay for ritual and cosmetic purposes. The Stubbs family and their neighbours had amicable relations with these Xhosa, but after eight months the

British authorities ordained that the tribespeople were trespassing illegally. Disastrously, a *landdrost* – a magistrate, whom Tom mocked as 'Pumpkin-guts, alias Humbug' – ruled that the clay must be paid for in goods. Tribesmen who took no notice were shot dead by British soldiers. 'Now commenced our troubles,' wrote Tom, 'the Caffers stole our cattle.' And killed two of their neighbours, one a youth who was studying as he herded cattle. Then, as Tom sombrely recorded, 'Our books were exchanged for guns.'

Meanwhile, year after year rust, blight, drought, swarms of locusts and floods in turn ruined the wheat and oats settlers had planted. Many families drifted to Grahamstown and other newly developed villages. John Stubbs was among those who struggled on. Increasingly, he resorted to illicit trade with the Xhosa, bartering beads, buttons – twenty-five for an ox – and liquor for elephant tusks and cattle.

One night, when Tom was fifteen, his father was brought home dead. 'Murdered by Caffers . . . found with an assegaai in his neck.' Ann Stubbs, heartbroken, died a year later, 'One of the most loving Christian good mothers that ever left England'. The Orphan Chamber sold the family possessions, and the five boys and two girls – the eldest aged seventeen, the youngest, a baby of seven months – were each given £8 3/11 three-farthings before being apprenticed or adopted. Tom was bound to a saddler in Grahamstown for seven years. Looking back half a century on the loss of his parents and their happy home, he poignantly recalled: 'Many nights I sat crying for hours, not having a friend to tell my troubles to.'

In 1838 his elder brother, John, set off by horseback through the Ciskei and the Transkei, 600 miles to Port Natal. Parties of Voortrekkers had been moving steadily northwards into Zulu territory and he found the small settlement in an uproar at the killing of Piet Retief and his party of Boer trekkers by Dingane's warriors. (A massacre commemorated in that poem taught to us children in Afrikaans lessons, which depicted the Zulus creeping like black snakes about the laager.) John Stubbs was among seventeen young whites who rallied a force of 1,500 African levies and a handful of Khoi to avenge those deaths. Crossing the Tugela River, they were ambushed by Zulu impis near

Kranskop. 3,000 warriors, 600 levies and thirteen of the young officers died. According to a survivor, as John Stubbs was stabbed to death by a young Zulu, he cried out in rage, 'Am I to be killed by a boy like you?' Strangely, Tom hardly mentions his brother's epic death, but it has been recorded in histories of the period.

A shrewd and witty raconteur, Tom describes how he himself, 'always ready for a spree', formed a Sporting and Hunting Club. Like most settlers, he was bigoted and he regarded their occupation of the land as a natural right to Englishmen bringing civilization to a savage continent. Only a rare missionary or Thomas Pringle, the Scottish poet, who settled near Cradock, was capable of regarding Xhosa and Khoi as fully human. As for those missionaries, Tom's view was remarkably similar to that of Colonel Rey and Admiral Evans during the thirties; and he would also have understood the disgust which most white South Africans felt for Michael Scott and his activities. He thought they were the 'greatest enemies of the Natives', teaching them to read and write, even to play the piano, but not to work. However, after the citizens of Grahamstown threatened to lynch a Presbyterian minister from Glasgow for teaching the rights of man to rebellious Khoi, it was he who helped the man to escape their wrath.

When what we in history class called the 'Kaffir Wars' broke out, he transformed the Sporting and Hunting Club into Stubbs' Mounted Rangers, guarding an area from Grahamstown to Cradock during sporadic skirmishes, raids, ambushes and minor battles. He has been described as 'a hero of the Frontier Wars of 1846 and 1850', but he found it 'far from pleasant' to command a party waiting to ambush tribesmen. 'You there sit, you hear them coming on, perhaps humming a tune, you see them and almost look into their eyes and you have to give the signal for their death warrant. I have heard people talk very lightly about shooting Caffers, but I believe it is by those who have never experienced it, for I have always felt grieved that my duty compelled me to it.'

When peace came, the Colony had further enlarged its boundaries. Defeated chiefs were exiled to a barren island in the Atlantic Ocean, seven miles from Cape Town: Robben Island.

Having devoted himself to the defence of his fellow-citizens, Tom Stubbs emerged crippled with rheumatism and bankrupt.

222

Obstinate, unconventional and outspoken, he'd been continually at odds with the 'generally conceited' British military. The Colonial Office in Cape Town rejected his application for land or for a pension. His business ventures – running a mail coach, maintaining a toll road – failed. With his wife, Sarah, and their four children, he trekked through desolate country to seek refuge on his younger brother's farm. His only property was 300 goats. It was mid-winter; crossing the mountains, most of the goats perished.

Despite his illness, at the age of sixty-seven, with extraordinary energy, he wrote his journal. '. . . a lively reckoning of one man's life,' the editors called it, 'a man who was very much of his times, but on occasion showed an awkward tendency to swim against the tide.'*

Two portraits of him exist, one as a dark, solidly handsome man in his thirties, the other, white-bearded and humorous. He bore a lively resemblance to Uncle Sonny and also to my mother.

Shortly before his death in 1877, he meditated on the country-side he loved, on the Klipplaats River, flowing down from the distant heights of Gaika's Kop.

'Look on the bright side,' he urges. 'It is the right side. The times may be hard, but it will make them no easier to wear a gloomy and sad countenance. It is the sun shine and not the cloud, that makes the flower. The sky is blue ten times to where it is black once. You have troubles, so have others. None are free from them. Trouble gives sinew and tone to life: fortitude and courage to man . . .' From a man whose difficult and turbulent life must often have brought him to the verge of despair, it is a moving affirmation.

I wished that I could return to search out the far-off patch of scrubland where he and the family struggled to survive. I longed to go 'home'. A longing I've deliberately repressed. But at times I am taken unawares: the cooing of an African dove suddenly heard in some wild-life programme on television never fails to arouse a pang of nostalgia – a primitive essence of sun, heat, summer-dry grass, everywhere buzzing insects hovering above bright flowers, while doves call from a eucalyptus tree.

* Inherited by Jonathan Stubbs, it was published as *The Reminiscences of Thomas Stubbs*, edited by W. A. Maxwell & R. T. McKeogh, Balkema, Cape Town, 1977.

13

Return to Pretoria

'I think my father is dying!' I appealed to Helen Suzman, the Progressive Member of Parliament. At the age of eighty-eight, he had been in hospital in Pretoria for a hernia operation, which for decades he had obstinately refused, and subsequently for an emergency prostrate operation. The whole experience had been psychologically as well as physically traumatic for an ardent Christian Scientist. Since he was alone in South Africa – my sister no longer lived there – I had applied to the Minister of the Interior for permission to be with him, but this had been rejected. After a brief convalescence, Pa had returned to his room in a boarding house, where he again fell ill and it was when his letters abruptly deteriorated into a scrawl of gibberish zigzagging across the pages that I telephoned Mrs Suzman in Johannesburg. Her urgent approach to the Minister succeeded. At last the necessary permit was granted and I flew out in July 1968.

I found him crouched in a chair in his sparsely furnished room. Pa had always seemed much younger than his age but now, eyes dark-rimmed in a white face, he looked tormented, his shoulders pitiful under the shabby dressing-gown, his ankles fearsomely swollen where they emerged from faded pyjamas. I held him as once I'd held my mother and felt relief flow through his scrawny body, until suddenly pain gripped him rigid, then something like terror set his limbs chattering. He had refused to see a doctor, had had his fill of them, but he badly needed sleep and when I suggested pills, he was desperate enough to send me to a chemist he knew in town.

When I returned, a tall bearded young man was with him. Holding out his hand, he introduced himself as 'Sergeant Beukes of the Security Police'. Unwillingly I shook it. 'Why didn't you report your arrival?' he asked. I said I had tried to do so at the airport but the police there had been uninterested. He told me to report to police headquarters next morning, then he departed.

After my father had fallen asleep, I eagerly telephoned friends around the country. Then wearily I dropped into my bed. I was awakened by a banging on the door. 'Come quick, madam!' The African nightwatchman stood outside. 'The old man is troubled!'

Pa was half out of bed, shouting and pleading with phantoms that surrounded him: an old woman in a brown hat, a typist in strange Oriental surroundings who kept shuffling papers. Holding him tight, I assured him it was all right, I was there. 'Am I going mad?' he asked. The nightwatchman hovered, solicitous. I apologized to him for the disturbance. 'No, it is the old man that matters,' he insisted. He was old himself, in worn khaki garments and peaked cap. He helped me move my mattress into Pa's room. The shouting and writhing broke out again, this time more furiously. The hotel manageress came, calm and sensible. 'You've got to see a doctor!' we both pleaded. Pa agreed.

The doctors we knew were not in town and a young Afrikaner responded to the emergency call. During his examination, something Pa said – was it his boast of having once run the hospital, was it his accent, his manner? – triggered off aggression in the young Afrikaner and he began extolling the achievements of the government. Then, 'Nothing serious,' he said curtly. 'Just a matter of relieving the heart by injections. You must go into hospital for a few days.'

An ambulance drove us to 'our' hospital, now imposingly signposted H.F. VERWOERD HOSPITAL. I had to abandon Pa to a ward where everyone, nurses and patients, seemed to speak only Afrikaans.

I caught a bus to town, haunted by images of the crumpled old man groaning at each jolt as he was wheeled through what had once been his domain. He used to explain that the motto of his family crest, and there it was on his signet ring, *Miseris Succurrere*, meant 'to help the wretched'. That it was a tradition inherited from his father, Charles Benson, and that a plaque in Dublin's St Patrick's Cathedral extolled the 'great headmaster', the Doctor of Divinity in the Church of Ireland. How often had I heard it? And how Pa's brothers, after studying at Trinity

College, became clergymen but he, not yet twenty, set off for the Cape in 1899. How he served with the British, commandeering horses in the Boer War, and then, without common ambition, spurned the Chamber of Mines in Johannesburg and chose Pretoria as his home, 'a really nice place'. Once a Boer dorp, now a small colonial town, it had the trappings he'd enjoyed in Dublin: command nights at the Opera House and supper parties – he specified a restaurant with the intriguing name of Cupid Lazarus. And he was rewarded. The Colonial Secretary's office provided him, at the age of twenty-three, with a job fitting the family motto. He was put in charge of hospitals and poor relief.

From the bus terminus in Church Square I paused at the Raadsaal and looked up at the window on the corner where he had worked all those years ago – in the building that President Kruger and his Council had occupied before. Within five years Pa had begun his life-work of administering an ever-expanding teaching hospital, work which he loved. The only shadow on his otherwise happy horizon was the stormcloud of Afrikaner Nationalism. During the 1930s the Union Jack was discarded and Afrikaans was decreed a compulsory language in the Civil Service. He studiously avoided learning it. 'I left one lot of rebels back in Ireland only to find another lot here,' he'd say, adding, 'At least the Irish had a sense of humour!'

And now he was finally, fatally confronted by the very forces that had usurped his world.

I went to police headquarters and reported to the officer on duty. He informed me that I would be restricted to Pretoria but I would not be under house arrest. However, the other bans remained in force: I could not meet more than one person at a time and I could not communicate with other banned people. And finally, he added that I would be permitted to stay for only one month.

The doctors had said that my father would be fit within ten days, but when nurses made him sit in a chair he cried out to God and slumped, keening with pain. I appealed to the sister for a private room. She was a dark, grim woman. She snapped back that private rooms were for far sicker patients. I suggested morphine and explained that my father was begging for relief. 'I won't have you visiting him out of hours!' she barked, and when I protested that I had come thousands of miles, that I had been given special permission, she spat out a venomous, 'I don't care!'

Trying to control angry tears, I wandered through the once familiar corridors to the children's ward and glimpsed the courtyard where on Guy Fawkes night Pa had launched rockets and Catherine wheels, to the delight of small white faces excitedly watching from beds or wheelchairs.

A long passageway led to the nurses' home. At their annual dance, after the first waltz with my mother, he'd fox-trotted and flirted with his favourites. Emerging from a side door I found that a tall new wardblock had obliterated the rose garden he'd planned, which he'd strolled through each morning on the way to his office, pausing – as was his custom at the old hospital – to choose a bud for his buttonhole. Now I could see our house: unchanged, the court where each Wednesday, Saturday and Sunday afternoon he'd had tennis parties. But from the round bed encircled by the drive, where Mom had once grown Iceland poppies, there soared an immense, grossly phallic palm tree.

As for the koppie, it seemed to have shrunk, and my rock, my beautiful rock – of that there was no sign.

Each afternoon during visiting hours, against the din of the ward, I read Christian Science lessons to Pa, but this, and the visits of friends, gave only temporary respite. He pleaded to come away. In those dismal surroundings a faint spark lit his eyes when I reminded him of his youth in Dublin, his personal, his proudest mythology, the Stoker family. His Aunt Susie, 'a blue-eyed beauty', had married Dick Stoker, a doctor in the Indian Army, and been swept off to Tibet, and then pioneering in the forests of British Columbia. Their framed portraits had looked down from our walls. I recalled red-headed Bram Stoker, Henry Irving's manager and author of *Dracula*. But most significant was Sir Thornley, distinguished surgeon, consultant to the Viceroy, who had introduced his young protégé, Pa, to a brilliant society of royal receptions, a world peopled by eccentric intellectuals such as George Moore, Gogarty and Augustine Birrell.

In the bus returning from the hospital the passengers' faces were pasty, sour-mouthed. The faces of 'Poor Whites', the few who could not afford cars.

In the boarding house, which preferred to be known as a 'private hotel', a different breed of whites lodged temporarily; young immigrants, German and Italian, on their way up the ladder towards assured prosperity. On some evenings the Sergeant paced the entrance hall, waiting to check on me. His movements were unpredictable. When friends from Johannesburg took me to restaurants, I caught myself looking over my shoulder, but there was no sign of him.

I moved into my father's room. One night I woke to hear trains shunting back and forth and saw dimly, in the light that filtered through the shrunken cotton curtains, the contours of the washbasin with its visceral pipes – was this the source of the 'funny people' who had animated his hallucinations? Lying there in his bed, memories and reflections invaded me. Oh God, his whole life had been a denial of pain: 'It never happened. Hold the Right Thought!' How often had he bragged that, since he'd 'discovered' Science, there was 'never a day's seediness'? And yet, at tennis, time after time, cackling gleefully as his sliced shots confounded scurrying opponents, suddenly he would bend double, face contorted in agony, hand masking the eyes that 'Knew the Truth'. A heart attack? In Science you must not 'Name'. Might he die? The family waited in dread. Eventually a 'Demonstration' was made and he would give a 'Testimony', expressing gratitude to 'our beloved leader, Mary Baker Eddy'. Long afterwards he explained that it was a ruptured hernia. 'Is that all?' By then I had broken away. 'Then why not have an operation? It's quite simple.' 'No. It's a good thing really, keeps me up to scratch!' His smugness was maddening.

Alone in that room I became painfully aware that when the sister rebuffed me, my feelings had not simply been of fury and revulsion for her and all she represented; I had also felt a strange satisfaction, satisfaction that Pa was being treated like any mortal. My pity for him was tainted by the wish to punish him for the bitter distress he'd caused us for so many years.

Courage! I had urged him. I wanted him to die bravely and tidily. Why the hell shouldn't he shout and rage against the agony, the horrid and ugly indignity? He who'd always had a zest for life. At the age of eighty it was 'Love at first sight!' he said, when he met a woman twenty-five years younger who had been married several times. I was glad his loneliness was ended and relieved at no longer being his main source of interest. More than that, I rather admired his kicking up a whirlwind in his final dervish dance of life. 'He's met his Waterloo now,' Poppy prophesied, and indeed, within a few years the marriage, which had humiliated and impoverished him, was annulled.

He had been at his finest when my mother was dying, nursing her – as she put it – like a baby, day and night, finding enormous red carnations to delight her. Too soon after her death I left him to his loneliness, visiting him when it suited my obsessive concern for 'the Work'.

Suddenly I saw the irony of first my mother and now he himself becoming a patient in 'our' hospital. But for them, after a lifetime of loyalty to their faith, it was a tragedy: by turning to 'Materia Medica' they had betrayed their God.

As dawn brightened to sunrise Pa's two suitcases and the brown wooden wardrobe took shape. Cisterns began to flush, from windows across the courtyard came coughings and hawkings of throats, noises magnified by the enclosing walls. Noises he must have heard every morning. From down the passage came the squeak of a trolley and the rattle of cups. A knock, a key unlocking, a door opening, a pause, a door closing, a key turning. Over and over. A knock on my door – Pa's door. 'Come in,' I called. The door opened, the light was switched on and Philemon said cheerfully, 'Good morning, madam. Two sugars?' Tea spilled into the saucer as he put the cup on the bedside table. 'Last night's tea heated up, madam,' he warned. The beige, lukewarm liquid tasted disgusting but marked the end of the night. And as I drank I recalled tea at the Country Club and one of Mom's golfing friends saying, 'But the natives are better off than ever!' On the table between us a newspaper headline read: NEW 'BLACK SPOT' REMOVALS. This time the families were being dumped at a place called Stinkwater.

And at the hotel Philemon smiled, the nightwatchman smiled, the cleaners smiled.

Pretoria was ugly with symbols of Afrikaner Nationalism's rise to power and prosperity. The massive new Security Police headquarters, the glass-and-concrete banks and office blocks dwarfed the old Boer and Imperial buildings – the Raadsaal and, facing it, the Palace of Justice, where Mandela and Sisulu and the other Rivonia men had been on trial. I crossed Church Square between those relics. Ahead of me strolled a young black couple, the boy in jeans and sneakers, the girl wearing a floral cotton dress. Their laughter, the springing energy of their movements, their appearance of happy confidence at the very heart of Afrikanerdom, signalled, I thought, the future.

As the days went by there was little change in my father's condition. Sergeant Beukes knocked on my door one evening. 'Just passing,' he said. I offered him a chair, and, with a groan, he sat down. He had sprained his knee at rugby. He told me that he'd taken his matric at Afrikaans Boys' High and was now fed up with Pretoria; he loved Johannesburg. I told him that I hoped to visit Bram Fischer in jail and – when he asked about five medals lying on the table among my father's books – I explained that they were my campaign medals from the Second World War. I never asked him how he could bring himself to do that job.

One afternoon as I waited for a bus on a wintry-dry, dusty day, I watched an African deliveryman cycle past. A chill wind tossed scraps of paper about the pavement and rattled pods of the leafless jacarandas. He freewheeled down the steep slope of the street, passing a white schoolgirl pedalling laboriously in the opposite direction. She was wearing a gym-tunic with black stockings and blazer, her schoolbag was strapped to the carrier of her bike. She could have been me thirty and more years ago. It's here I belong, I thought.

The passion that caused spiritual amputation in exile – even while I agonized over my father's slow dying, I felt alive, exhilarated at being back among people I loved, in the country where the dust and brittle air had the power to move me.

Ten days passed and on a Friday morning doctors pronounced my father fit to leave. I had arranged for him to convalesce in a private clinic. But as we were driven there by ambulance his cries of pain were horrifying. The matron said she was quite unable to cope. Back then to the Verwoerd Hospital, to a ward in a hutted extension, where he was wheeled into a room alongside a Rhodesian who stank and cursed dementedly. Pa was beyond caring.

On Sunday morning the Salvation Army's tuba and trombone

accompanied singing in the ward. Pa stirred. I held his hand and assured him it was all a nightmare, it would come to an end. 'I know,' he said. In the evening he slipped into unconsciousness. After four hours a doctor came. One of Pa's lungs had collapsed, he said, but pulse and blood pressure were fine. The nurses advised me to go home for dinner.

Pa died an hour later. They said he had not regained consciousness but I wished desperately that I had been with him. *Miseris Succurrere*. I forgot to ask for his ring.

Back in the hotel the nightwatchman said he was so sorry, he had been wondering how the old man was and he was very sorry for me. I gave him ten shillings and my father's teapot.

The Sergeant came to offer his sympathies and a lift to the funeral. I thanked him and said arrangements had been made.

Sorting Pa's meagre belongings I came across press cuttings of innumerable 'letters to the Editor' written through the years. They had often headed the correspondence columns of the *Pretoria News* or the *Rand Daily Mail*. He wrote under various *noms de plume*: 'A South African Humanitarian', 'Are we whites really Christian?', 'A Friend of the Oppressed' and, most frequently, 'The Golden Rule'. My favourite was signed 'Respector of Human Rights'. In this he asked: 'Have Ministers of Justice and others responsible for oppressive and discriminatory laws against Non-Europeans, laws such as Group Areas, Job Reservation, Pass Laws, separation of families, imprisonment without trial – to mention a few – thought of what kind of reception they can expect when they pass over to the other side?'

Reading them again, an image suddenly filled my consciousness. Wearing white shirt and cream flannels, he was playing tennis, and he was smiling. It was as if, having exposed my dark feelings to the light, I was left with this bright picture of Pa, alive and happy, as he would want to be remembered.

The next day a friend drove me along Potgieter Street, past Defence Headquarters, to the corner next door to the prison. No longer an oasis: our first house still stood, but baldly stripped of jacarandas and flower beds. Where once an orchard of peaches and figs, nectarines and plums had flourished, the ground had been cemented over and a prison warder was washing his car.

Memories crowded: Nanny, starched apron cool and crisp to

231

my cheek. In one deep pocket she kept acid drops. If you were good as gold, she'd give you one. 'Don't bite. Suck!' she'd admonish, her white-powdered face fondly puckering in wrinkles. Hands roughened from all the laundry, her tender hands, which soaped and scrubbed and enveloped me in a towel and rubbed me dry. How old was I – eleven – when she returned to England? Two years later her niece wrote to say she had 'passed on' peacefully: 'Tell Pixie Ah! how she loved her, truly and deeply.'

The verandah where we'd slept, Pumpkin curled in the small of my back, Mom's warm contralto singing my favourite lullaby, 'Go to sleep my little piccaninny, Brer Fox'll catch you if you don't . . .' Her morning practising, 'Coo-coo-coo-coo coooo, ooh-oh-ah . . .' up the scale, then down again, preparing for solos in church.

When I cut my head and ran screaming to Dad, he hugged me tight: 'It never happened! Hold the Right Thought!' as his handkerchief mopped the blood. 'Here's half-a-crown for a cracked crown.' Even with a sore head I laughed at his jokes.

Winter evenings by the fire, gazing at pictures of the latest fashions in English magazines, Mom with her light-brown hair newly shingled and marcelled, Poppy and I standing each side of her at the upright piano to sing, with no thought of its significance:

> Way down upon the Swanee River,
> Far, far away,
> There's where my heart is turning over,
> There's where the old folks stay.
> All the world is sad and dreary
> Everywhere I roam.
> Oh darkies how my heart grows weary . . .

While from the black night moths fluttered to the lamp above our heads, to be trapped in its bowl, their wings darkly beating, until at last they were still.

My pilgrimage took me on to the jail next door. Locked away behind those red-brick turreted walls in a new wing built specifically for white political prisoners was Bram Fischer. My application to visit him had been bluntly rejected; this was the closest I could come.

We drove on past the old façade and, turning to the right, from the hillside we looked down on a huge conglomeration of maximum security buildings and defence establishments which had swallowed up the neighbourhood and soon, no doubt, would devour the red-brick prison and our house. Back in Potgieter Street, I gave a last glance at the small barred windows.

Those faces peering down at Nanny and Poppy and me, those men who were transported from that jail to our house at the new hospital, to hack with their pickaxes at the rockface of our koppie, the power and beauty of their songs, mysterious yet so familiar. Prisoners . . . prisoners . . . and now the political prisoners on Robben Island who with pickaxes laboured in the lime quarry, year after year after year.

Friends from Soweto called to express their sympathy. Athol flew up from the Eastern Cape. In mild winter sunlight we sat talking in Burgers' Park, on a bench where, I told him, Pa and I used to sit. Miniskirted girls with beehive hairdos went by, licking ice cream cones. The only blacks in the park, with its statues of the Boer General Burger and a Highland soldier, were gardeners arranging sprinklers on the dry lawns.

Over dinner in a nearby restaurant we celebrated our reunion and the news that my novel had been accepted by a publisher in Boston. Athol had almost completed his play about the 'trio of derelicts' – Boesman himself, the woman Lena and 'something verminous and dying called Outa'.

'How would you define a touchstone?' I asked.

'Something that helps you deal with, understand, more than just itself. Why?' he replied.

'You and your work are a touchstone for me,' I told him.

'As you have been a sounding-board for me,' he said, and went on to explain: 'We recognize something in each other. I think we love, respond in the same way and that is a powerful and mysterious bond. I can look to you to see if I have, in a new piece of work, affirmed what exists as a common denominator between us. It's to do with complexity, the awesome nature of being a true lover of South Africa. We know how easy it is to hate here, to judge. I think this is why Bram is such a colossally

233

important experience in your life, in my life, and will be for all South Africa when it's finally fully reckoned with and understood that he was an Afrikaner.'

At COMPOL, a cream-painted colonial building, a sign on the outside stated COMMISSIONER OF POLICE. Nothing to indicate what was perpetrated inside but, down the passage, a warning, NO ADMITTANCE EXCEPT . . . Except if you are the interrogator, the torturer, or the victim. In the foyer a Captain of the Security Police added his signature to the permit given by the magistrate, enabling me to leave Pretoria provided I took a single ticket for the train to Botswana, travelled via the shortest available route and did not leave the train at Johannesburg station.

The first dim light filtered through the curtains after a night noisy with the shunting of trains. For the last time I watched the basin take shape, the pipes and taps, and I listened for the tea trolley.

Three of Pa's friends came to see me off. As I leaned from the compartment window and they looked up in smiling conversation, we heard the click of the Security Police photographing us. I apologized to the Christian Scientists, who shrugged off the unpleasantness. A whistle blew – 'Goodbye!'

A last view of the railway yards – those trains, shunting in the night – a last view of the old Boer fort, where, Poppy had once confided, couples 'canoodled'. Then nothing but brown veld. Inside the compartment, firmly stuffed green leather seats and a display of glassed-in vintage photos of rhinos in the game reserve, Zulu warriors and Benoni town hall. Soothing rhythm of wheels over sleepers, and I thought of the people I was leaving behind – Athol without a passport, Bram in prison for life. And Nelson and Walter, after they'd been sentenced, a lawyer had spoken in amazement tinged with dismay of their euphoria, for did it not reveal the besetting defect of the 'liberation movement', evasion of reality? But I recalled Camus' advice that we should say 'in the very midst of the sound and fury of our history: Let us rejoice!'

In Johannesburg station we were shunted from one concrete tunnel to another. Suddenly a young woman friend appeared at the door of the compartment with books and messages from the others who could not come. The whistle blew and, 'Oh Mary,' she said, 'it's so awful here now.' As the train crawled through the entrails of the city I caught a last glimpse of the skyscrapers and yellow mine dumps, and finally wept.

'You must give up all thought of your roots here,' someone had advised. At the funeral, last in the line of family friends uttering conventional phrases, was a woman unknown to me who whispered, 'I just want to say how much I admire the work you are doing.'

The train ground to a halt, spewing out steam; no sign of a dorp, only a platform, a shed and black men loading crates of Coca-Cola on to a lorry. Under a dusty gum tree sparrows scuffled. The train jerked forward, then stopped again. Loading done, the men drove off, leaving a stillness, stifling.

The engine trumpeted and the train set off once more, passing a dorp named Moloney where willows bordered a stream. Green shoots appeared in the black-burnt grass which stretched to the horizon.

Mafeking. The last stop before the border with Botswana. Into the compartment came two men. 'Security Police. We want to search your luggage. Please open everything.' They fumbled through my carefully folded dresses, intently studied gramophone records, then came to an airways bag crammed with books, press cuttings, my father's papers and photos and my coded notebooks. They pulled out a few papers randomly, peered suspiciously at pictures of a robin and a swallow cut from Pa's bird calendar, then gave up.

'Your person must be searched,' said one and, as they left, a girl appeared and apologetically asked me to strip. Amused rather than cross, I undid the zip and began to lower my dress. 'That's all right,' she said. And departed.

The train lurched into action, leaving Mafeking, leaving my country.

Appendix

*Statement by Mary Benson before the Special Committee
on the Policies of Apartheid of the
Government of the Republic of South Africa
at its 28th Meeting on 11th March 1964*

Mr Chairman:

It is almost a year since I had the honour to be the first South African petitioner before your Committee. (Incidentally, I wish you could have the opportunity of hearing from more South Africans now in London, some of whom have experienced imprisonment and house arrest; also church leaders who have been in South Africa.) In that year the situation there has become ever more terrible, but as your excellent reports provide the appalling facts, I propose simply to talk about a few of the men and women there who are on trial for their lives and imprisoned, and some of whom are my friends.

In a world prone to violence where each day as one listens to the news or reads the paper one's heart despairs at new acts of unspeakable cruelty, it has been marvellous to experience the profound humanity in two particular areas: in the African struggle for freedom in South Africa and the Negro struggle in the United States.

The nobility of their chosen method of non-violence should give mankind hope in face of despair, and confidence that we human beings are capable of transforming ourselves.

In South Africa, as you know, for more than fifty years Africans and their allies and friends of all races strove to bring sanity to that country by these methods. Even way back in 1913 and in 1919, and most spectacularly in 1952, hundreds and sometimes thousands went voluntarily to jail as petition and protest gave way to passive resistance and strikes. What bravery and self-sacrifice, what fantastic restraint and civilized conduct. Indeed, looking back at it with hindsight it seems to many an obvious criticism of the conduct of the struggle that it was not ruthless and efficient enough; what an indictment of our world that this criticism should be made at all.

Meanwhile, year upon year the State – all too often sup-pported, even encouraged, by powerful industrialists and mining companies – always with the acquiescence of most of the all-white electorate – tightened the screws of humiliation and oppression. Never once in those fifty years did it respond in a civilized manner – not once! Increasingly, its violence grew more overt.

Despite this it was not until 1961, a year after Sharpeville, when yet one more Stay-at-Home was massively crushed by all the forces the State could command, that African leaders decided a long chapter was closed – as one of them said to me: 'Desperate people will eventually be provoked to acts of retaliation.'

But even in the subsequent sabotage it is clear everything possible is done to avoid harming human beings, though tragically a handful, including a child, have been killed. Indeed, in the sabotage trials taking place all over South Africa, witnesses – among them a policeman – have testified that it is the policy of the Spear of the Nation not to injure people.

An eminent lawyer from Britain, John Arnold, QC, recently visited South Africa on behalf of the International Commission of Jurists to observe the Rivonia Trial . . . [He] told how these men are regarded as heroes and he asked what is the good of a fair trial if, under the 'bestial and brutal' Act of Parliament which provided the framework of the trial, there is no practical possibility but conviction? He concluded: 'The danger is that these men will hang and they must not.'

Mr Chairman, I cannot adequately emphasize how desper-ately, profoundly important it is to South Africa and surely to the continent and the world at large that Mandela, Sisulu, Mbeki – these and other men in the trial – must not be allowed to hang.

Do you remember 1960? In most of Africa it was a year of celebration – Africa Year – when one after another new states were founded and took their place in the United Nations. But in South Africa it was the year of Sharpeville. It was the year when the African National Congress and the Pan Africanist

Congress were outlawed; when day after day the police and army swooped, rounding up more than 20,000 people of all races, who were arbitrarily imprisoned. It seemed then that the movement for liberation must surely be numbed; but it was at this historic time that Nelson Mandela emerged from prison – to call for a national strike and to lead the underground movement. For fifteen months he daringly eluded the State forces. In February 1962 he illegally left South Africa to attend the Addis Ababa conference and to visit many heads of state in Africa, and the leaders of the opposition in London, and then, soon after returning to the Republic, as happens all too often in a police state, he was betrayed by an informer, captured, tried and sentenced to five years in prison. When only a few months of that sentence had run, he was again charged, in the Rivonia trial, along with others, with being a member of the national high command of a revolutionary movement to overthrow the Afrikaner Nationalist Government.

And so, Nelson Mandela is on trial for his life. Yet he – a member of the royal family of the Tembu people – might easily have been one of those chiefs who are puppets of the Government, with a steady income, a shiny motorcar, and sycophantic followers. Or he might simply have remained a lawyer, content to function within the framework of apartheid, living in a comfortable middle-class home, and finding an outlet for humiliation in sport or jazz or religion. He *might* have – but for his strong character, his independence of mind and his responsiveness to people's sufferings and to the imperative need for justice. The London *Observer* has described Mandela as a lawyer 'who in any free country would surely have won the utmost distinction', and has compared him to 'a true leader of the Resistance [to the Nazis] in Occupied France'; in other words, a hero.

I have known Mandela for about ten years and saw a good deal of him during the Treason Trial. In more recent meetings, some of which were in secret when he was underground, he told me something of his life. He spoke of his childhood in the early 1920s as son of a Tembu chief, in a kraal by the banks of the green Mbashe river in the Transkei, of how later, when his cousin the Paramount Chief became his guardian, he found the strict traditional life in the royal kraal dull, of how he was captivated by tales of Xhosa heroes of the past in the battles to preserve their land against the European invaders, and how he enjoyed listening to cases being tried in the tribal courts. In his teens he went to Fort Hare college, with his friend Oliver Tambo took part in a students' strike, and left, determined 'never to rule as chief over an oppressed people'. But he was still politically naïve and it is comic now to think that his first real act of rebellion came when, in 1940, at the age of twenty-two, he fled from a tribal marriage – to Johannesburg, where of all things he became a mine policeman, sitting at the compound gate, clutching his badges of office, a whistle and a knobkerrie!

Then came the transformation, as a new friend, Walter Sisulu, encouraged him in his childhood ambition to study law at the University of the Witwatersrand. And for the first time, in the city and the teeming African townships he learned the bitter facts of life for an African: overcrowding, poverty, constant harassing under the pass laws. He, Sisulu and Tambo were among the intensely nationalist young men who founded the African Youth League, and galvanized the African National Congress into militant action.

Mandela became National-Volunteer-in-Chief of the great Defiance Campaign of 1952, when 8,500 volunteers – including Indians and a few white and Coloured people, went cheerfully to jail. He also devised the M Plan, a scheme of mass organizing through small units. He and other leaders were arrested under the Suppression of Communism Act. It is worth remarking that the Judge said the charge had 'nothing to do with communism as it is commonly known', but under the law he was bound to give them a suspended sentence of nine months. Furthermore he told them: 'I accept the evidence that you have consistently advised your followers to follow a peaceful course of action and to avoid violence in any shape or form.' Eight years later in 1961 this same Judge – Judge Rumpff – was to be the senior Judge in the Treason Trial, when again Mandela and Sisulu were among the accused. Pronouncing sentence, he said: 'You are found not guilty and discharged. You may go.' This, you may remember, was after a trial lasting four and a half years, during which the accused were subject to prolonged strain and great hardship for them and their families. In the case of Mandela and Tambo, it also meant that their legal practice – so much of it concerned with urgent political and human cases – gravely suffered. In the

Treason Trial not only did Mandela, with Duma Nokwe, another ANC leader, take over the defence at one stage, but he was among those chosen to give evidence. Senior lawyers spoke of this being among the most exciting and fearless.

The Government's apprehension of Mandela, or to put it another way, its appreciation of him, was evident as far back as 1953, when he was placed under a fierce triple ban – banned from the ANC, banned from attending meetings, and restricted to the Johannesburg area.

Meanwhile, the exclusive nationalism of Mandela and certain other Youth Leaguers, was transformed through their experience of working with Indians, whites and Coloured people, proving that though white racialism is rampant in South Africa, many Africans refuse to be driven into an equally rabid racialism and have striven for justice and freedom for *all* human beings regardless of race . . .

From my own experience, and from impressions told to me by prominent lawyers and African leaders, I would say Mandela's outstanding characteristic is how he has grown and continues to grow over the years . . . So many men, in face of prolonged persecution and frequent setbacks, shrink into bitter negation or find some excuse to retreat from political action, but Mandela is one of those undeterred, indeed positively stimulated by such obstacles. His natural authority has been greatly enhanced by twenty years of political action. When in 1962 he was sentenced to five years' imprisonment he declared: 'I am prepared to pay the penalty even though I know how bitter and desperate is the situation of an African in the prisons of this country . . . For to men, freedom in their own land is the pinnacle of their ambitions from which nothing can turn men of conviction aside. More powerful than my fear of the dreadful conditions to which I might be subjected is my hatred for the dreadful conditions to which my people are subjected outside prison throughout this country.

'I hate the practice of race discrimination, and in my hatred, I am sustained by the fact that the overwhelming majority of mankind hates it equally.' Before he was led away to jail Mandela concluded: '. . . when my sentence has been completed, I will still be moved, as men are always moved, by their consciences; I will still be moved by my dislike of the race discrimination against my people when I come out from serving my sentence, to take up again, as best I can, the struggle for the removal of those injustices until they are finally abolished once and for all.'

Walter Sisulu, the man who helped Mandela to study law, who was like a brother to him and now sits beside him in the dock, knows probably better than any other leader in South Africa just what it means to be 'a native'. Although tens of thousands of Africans have gone through very similar experiences to his in their lives, like tens of thousands of perfectly good oysters, they have not had in them the grain that would produce a pearl. It may seem incongruous to compare Sisulu to a pearl; he would roar with laughter at the idea, but dogged, determined, from the first he had that grain of rebelliousness, of refusing to lie down and accept injustice, which made him an indomitable fighter. While only a boy of sixteen, brought up traditionally in the Transkei, he had to leave school to take on family responsibilities. He had a variety of the lowly jobs which by law are the only ones most Africans can hold. He was a miner, then a kitchen 'boy' when in spare moments in his white employer's kitchen, he tried to supplement his meagre education by studying an English grammar. His first political lesson came in Johannesburg, where, having picked up a smattering of trade union ideas and – working in a bakery at $6 week – he led a strike, to be quickly outwitted by the boss, and sacked. He was first imprisoned as a result of protesting when a white ticket-collector on a train bullied an African child; the ticket collector assaulted Sisulu, who fought back, and was arrested. He had never been in prison and he told me it was the 'nastiest experience' of his life. Today he can look back on innumerable ugly experiences, as for years he has been the object of odious persecution by the police in attempts to intimidate him. I think the last time I saw him in 1962, he had just been arrested on four or five trumped-up charges, one after another. They picked the wrong man! For one thing his concern for the struggle is selfless, for another he found out early in life that most of the whites Africans encounter are the policemen raiding locations for passes or tax receipts, or officials dealing with queues of so-called 'boys' like cattle, or gaolers who beat up prisoners, and all these things aroused in him not fear, but contempt. For all that, he is

241

no racialist, though as with Mandela, it was his experience of working with Indians organizing the Defiance Campaign in 1952 – when he was Secretary-General of the ANC – that enabled him to outgrow exclusiveness.

Sisulu has seemed to some who have met him to be frustrated and bitter, while others who know him say he is trustworthy and generous. Others again just give him up as an enigma, perhaps influenced by the fact that in 1953 he not only briefly visited Israel and London, but spent five months in Communist countries. China affected him most, for the peasants and their lives and needs reminded him of African peasants, and when he saw the rapid metamorphosis of slums, he thought of the shanties and poverty around Johannesburg.

He returned to South Africa with the knowledge that the greater part of the world was on the side of his people. At the age of forty-one, for the first time in his life he had been consistently treated as a dignified human being instead of as a native. Those whites who had experienced his suspiciousness noticed a change: he had come to realize that an African nationalist's tendency to assert himself – to prove he was not inferior to the white man – was in itself an inferiority complex. (Incidentally, one of the friends who had arranged Sisulu's tour told me they would have liked to send Nelson Mandela to the United States, but unfortunately there were no invitations forthcoming as there had been from the Communist countries.)

There is so much more to tell you about Sisulu, but no time; more about his wife, Albertina, a nurse, the backbone of their stable family life, yet active in women's politics, a woman who generates kindness and hospitality in their home, a bleak little block house which is typical of the kind to which tens of thousands of African families are reduced by the laws of South Africa. About their second son, aged fifteen, who, when he attended the trial of his father the other day, was arrested for not having a pass, despite his mother's protests that he was under the age for passes. He was detained for two hours in the cells before a lawyer was able to demand his release. Can there be more vicious intimidation?

As you know, two Europeans and an Indian are also accused in the Rivonia trial. Lionel (Rusty) Bernstein is one of South Africa's best-known architects, an inventor of mathematical instruments, an intellectual, reserved with a quiet sense of humour. Despite being brought up among all the normal conventions and prejudices of white South Africa and going to an exclusive school, he showed an early awareness of the sickness in that society, but the Labour Party, which he joined, was concerned only about white workers and Bernstein turned to the Communist Party, at that time, in the 1940s, the only party that was not racialist. Then, at the age of twenty-one, he married an Englishwoman, Hilda Watts, also a member of the Party, who during the war years, was elected to the Johannesburg City Council. After war service in Italy, Bernstein returned to his architecture and found himself even more deeply committed in the opposition to the country's racial policies. He is typical of the small group of Europeans who, because of their beliefs, have suffered prejudice to their careers, increasing social isolation, and – above all – regular restriction and imprisonment, along with their non-white allies. Consider only the brief catalogue of the State's attempt to deter him: 1946 arrested and found guilty of assisting the African mine-workers in their strike, suspended sentence. 1954 listed and named under the Suppression of Communism Act, banned from gatherings, restricted to Johannesburg. 1956 arrested and charged with high treason, after nearly five years, declared not guilty. After Sharpeville imprisoned for several months, along with his wife, leaving their four children parentless. Then, restricted from writing. In 1962, among the first to be placed under house arrest. And now, since July 1963, on trial for his life. The character of this man, whom close friends describe as essentially gentle and thoughtful, was never more apparent than during the eighty-eight days in which he, like all the others in the Rivonia trial, was held in solitary confinement. This experience left him – like so many others – the prey to nightmares, unable to concentrate and shaky so that six weeks later he felt proud to find he could write two short letters without having to rest. But even at the worst times of this incarceration, when the police offered him an exit permit to Britain if he would incriminate others, he was resolute, and contemptuous of the offer.

The very considerable role of the Indians in the struggle in South Africa – some drawing their inspiration from Mahatma Gandhi, others from Socialism – can be represented in this short survey only by pointing out that Ahmed Kathrada, another of the Rivonia accused, has been persistently active, imprisoned, restricted, persecuted, but has carried on with a total dedication, ever since as a schoolboy he went to prison in the great Indian passive resistance against the ghetto laws that General Smuts introduced in 1946. Even at that time, there were young South Africans who had a vision of a common society, of what South Africa could and should become, and Kathrada was one of them.

And a man who has a vision of what the Transkei and the long-neglected and overcrowded rural areas of South Africa should become is Govan Mbeki, yet another of the Rivonia accused, who, in this testimony, must represent the many thousands of Xhosa in the Eastern Cape who have provided militant and united resistance and whose leaders have distinctive qualities, a deep sense of being part of the people, and often a passionate religious faith. Mbeki, a distinguished man, has a marked ability to efface himself. A teacher, writer, and an authority on the Transkei, increasingly his political activities led to restrictions on his school teaching and eventually he became Eastern Cape editor for the leftist *New Age*, the now-illegal newspaper that ceaselessly exposed injustice.

Perhaps, if I quote briefly from the prison diary Mbeki kept a few years ago, a vivid document, you will see another side to this disciplined and dedicated man. He wrote with compassion about one old man in the cell, so rheumatic that his limbs swelled, yet never complaining nor using it as an excuse to try for release. Another prisoner who constantly prayed amused Mbeki, who observed that the prayers resembled the demands of workers to their employers for better conditions and higher wages.

Of others again, Mbeki wrote: 'Every afternoon, we heard beatings from prisoners returning from work. Sometimes they would bellow. We heard the splattering of leather belts as they fell on a body. It is intolerable to listen and one shudders to think what effect this type of treatment must have on those who administer it as well as on the recipients. In the long run it is difficult to see how both can escape being turned into beasts.'

And he expressed appreciation of the work of Welfare Committees – for instance, warm underwear was distributed. 'The state of emergency,' he said, 'has sealed bonds of friendship between the Africans and that section of the white population which realizes that the narrow racial nationalism of the Nationalist party cannot work in the world today.'

And if anyone in the outside world doubts whether boycotts have any effect, they should read what it meant to the prisoners – forty of them cooped up in the cell – when they heard that dockers in Trinidad had refused to handle South African goods . . .

Mr Chairman, your Report of 27 February is a long catalogue of horror: of mass trials, almost daily arrests, of torture both physical and mental. Yet there is more that could be added. The case of Alfred Nzo, for instance, detained in Johannesburg in solitary confinement for 238 days. The Geneva Convention on the treatment of prisoners of war states that no one should be held in solitary for more than thirty days. Mr Nzo was never charged and, when released, he was a mental wreck . . . 'Torture by mind-breaking' is the dreadfully apt description of the Ninety Day detention law given by J. Hamilton Russell, a former Member of Parliament who is now compaigning splendidly in South Africa for the revoke of this cruel law.

I have spoken of how the South African authorities try to intimidate political suspects by the despicable device of attacking members of their families. Even the unborn suffer: Lettie Sibeko, a thirty-year-old woman, was arrested eight months ago. The authorities were trying to find her husband, Archie, a vital young man, active both in the former ANC and as a trade unionist. One might say that Lettie was held as a hostage. She was a few weeks pregnant when arrested but she was held in solitary confinement for the first five months of her detention. South African psychiatric specialists stated that this treatment could have the most serious consequences, not only for the mother but also for the baby. Mrs Sibeko was finally released one week before the baby was due to be born.

I ought to mention the pass laws and the poverty and malnutrition that continues to cause human misery to tens of thousands of African families. All this against a fantastic wave of prosperity for white South Africa with increasing investment especially from Britain and America. According to the South African Foundation the average dividend in South Africa is 12.6

per cent compared with 6.6 per cent in Western Europe, while American companies are averaging profits of up to 27 per cent on capital invested in South Africa.

To tell the truth, my heart is so sick at the endless churning out of the horrible facts, which we all know all too well, and have known for years, when all the time the iniquities we tell each other about, ceaselessly and so unnecessarily are hurting human beings – and this is their only life. Therefore, I beg that we stop cataloguing facts, and plan action and then *act*. Economic sanctions are surely the obvious civilized form of action when diplomatic and moral pressures long ago failed to make any impact on the South African Government.

I feel my voice is not powerful enough to make my last desperate appeal to you, so I quote Bishop Ambrose Reeves, former Bishop of Johannesburg. He says of the men facing the possibility of being sentenced to death at the Rivonia trial: 'Let us see that such a cry goes up that this does not happen. It is up to us to see that they do not die. Let us act at once!'

Index

FOR THE BEST IN PAPERBACKS, LOOK FOR THE 🐧

In every corner of the world, on every subject under the sun, Penguin represents quality and variety – the very best in publishing today.

For complete information about books available from Penguin – including Puffins, Penguin Classics and Arkana – and how to order them, write to us at the appropriate address below. Please note that for copyright reasons the selection of books varies from country to country.

In the United Kingdom: Please write to *Dept E.P., Penguin Books Ltd, Harmondsworth, Middlesex, UB7 0DA.*

If you have any difficulty in obtaining a title, please send your order with the correct money, plus ten per cent for postage and packaging, to *PO Box No 11, West Drayton, Middlesex*

In the United States: Please write to *Dept BA, Penguin, 299 Murray Hill Parkway, East Rutherford, New Jersey 07073*

In Canada: Please write to *Penguin Books Canada Ltd, 2801 John Street, Markham, Ontario L3R 1B4*

In Australia: Please write to the *Marketing Department, Penguin Books Australia Ltd, P.O. Box 257, Ringwood, Victoria 3134*

In New Zealand: Please write to the *Marketing Department, Penguin Books (NZ) Ltd, Private Bag, Takapuna, Auckland 9*

In India: Please write to *Penguin Overseas Ltd, 706 Eros Apartments, 56 Nehru Place, New Delhi, 110019*

In the Netherlands: Please write to *Penguin Books Nederland B.V., Postbus 195, NL–1380AD Weesp*

In West Germany: Please write to *Penguin Books Ltd, Friedrichstrasse 10–12, D–6000 Frankfurt/Main 1*

In Spain: Please write to *Longman Penguin España, Calle San Nicolas 15, E–28013 Madrid*

In Italy: Please write to *Penguin Italia s.r.l., Via Como 4, I-20096 Pioltello (Milano)*

In France: Please write to *Penguin Books Ltd, 39 Rue de Montmorency, F-75003 Paris*

In Japan: Please write to *Longman Penguin Japan Co Ltd, Yamaguchi Building, 2–12–9 Kanda Jimbocho, Chiyoda-Ku, Tokyo 101*

Riding the Iron Rooster Paul Theroux

An eye-opening and entertaining account of travels in old and new China, from the author of *The Great Railway Bazaar*. 'Mr Theroux cannot write badly ... in the course of a year there was almost no train in the vast Chinese rail network on which he did not travel' – Ludovic Kennedy

The Markets of London Alex Forshaw and Theo Bergstrom

From Camden Lock and Columbia Road to Petticoat Lane and Portobello Road, from the world-famous to the well-kept secrets, here is the ultimate guide to London's markets: as old, as entertaining and as diverse as the capital itself.

The Chinese David Bonavia

'I can think of no other work which so urbanely and entertainingly succeeds in introducing the general Western reader to China' – *Sunday Telegraph*. 'Strongly recommended' – *The Times Literary Supplement*

The Diary of Virginia Woolf
Five volumes edited by Quentin Bell and Anne Olivier Bell

'As an account of intellectual and cultural life of our century, Virginia Woolf's diaries are invaluable; as the record of one bruised and unquiet mind, they are unique' – Peter Ackroyd in the *Sunday Times*

Voices of the Old Sea Norman Lewis

'I will wager that *Voices of the Old Sea* will be a classic in the literature about Spain' – *Mail on Sunday*. 'Limpidly and lovingly, Norman Lewis has caught the helpless, unwitting, often foolish, but always hopeful village in its dying summers, and saved the tragedy with sublime comedy' – *Observer*

Ninety-Two Days Evelyn Waugh

With characteristic honesty, Evelyn Waugh here debunks the romantic notions attached to rough travelling. His journey in Guiana and Brazil is difficult, dangerous and extremely uncomfortable, and his account of it is witty and unquestionably compelling.

A CHOICE OF PENGUINS

The Assassination of Federico García Lorca   Ian Gibson

Lorca's 'crime' was his antipathy to pomposity, conformity and intolerance. His punishment was murder. Ian Gibson – author of the acclaimed new biography of Lorca – reveals the truth about his death and the atmosphere in Spain that allowed it to happen.

Between the Woods and the Water   Patrick Leigh Fermor

Patrick Leigh Fermor continues his celebrated account – begun in *A Time of Gifts* – of his journey on foot from the Hook of Holland to Constantinople. 'Even better than everyone says it is' – Peter Levi. 'Indescribably rich and beautiful' – *Guardian*

The Hunting of the Whale   Jeremy Cherfas

'*The Hunting of the Whale* is a story of declining profits and mounting pigheadedness ... it involves a catalogue of crass carelessness ... Jeremy Cherfas brings a fresh eye to [his] material ... for anyone wanting a whale in a nutshell this must be the book to choose' – *The Times Literary Supplement*

Metamagical Themas   Douglas R. Hofstadter

This astonishing sequel to the bestselling, Pulitzer Prize-winning *Gödel, Escher, Bach* swarms with 'extraordinary ideas, brilliant fables, deep philosophical questions and Carrollian word play' – Martin Gardner

Into the Heart of Borneo   Redmond O'Hanlon

'Perceptive, hilarious and at the same time a serious natural-history journey into one of the last remaining unspoilt paradises' – *New Statesman*. 'Consistently exciting, often funny and erudite without ever being overwhelming' – *Punch*

When the Wind Blows   Raymond Briggs

'A visual parable against nuclear war: all the more chilling for being in the form of a strip cartoon' – *Sunday Times*. 'The most eloquent anti-Bomb statement you are likely to read' – *Daily Mail*

FOR THE BEST IN PAPERBACKS, LOOK FOR THE

A CHOICE OF PENGUINS

Better Together Christian Partnership in a Hurt City
David Sheppard and Derek Warlock

The Anglican and Roman Catholic Bishops of Liverpool tell the uplifting and heartening story of their alliance in the fight for their city – an alliance that has again and again reached out to heal a community torn by sectarian loyalties and bitter deprivation.

Fantastic Invasion Patrick Marnham

Explored and exploited, Africa has carried a different meaning for each wave of foreign invaders – from ivory traders to aid workers. Now, in the crisis that has followed Independence, which way should Africa turn? 'A courageous and brilliant effort' – Paul Theroux

Jean Rhys: Letters 1931–66
Edited by Francis Wyndham and Diana Melly

'Eloquent and invaluable … her life emerges, and with it a portrait of an unexpectedly indomitable figure' – Marina Warner in the *Sunday Times*

Among the Russians Colin Thubron

One man's solitary journey by car across Russia provides an enthralling and revealing account of the habits and idiosyncrasies of a fascinating people. 'He sees things with the freshness of an innocent and the erudition of a scholar' – *Daily Telegraph*

They Went to Portugal Rose Macaulay

An exotic and entertaining account of travellers to Portugal from the pirate-crusaders, through poets, aesthetes and ambassadors, to the new wave of romantic travellers. A wonderful mixture of literature, history and adventure, by one of our most stylish and seductive writers.

The Separation Survival Handbook Helen Garlick

Separation and divorce almost inevitably entail a long journey through a morass of legal, financial, custodial and emotional problems. Stripping the experience of both jargon and guilt, marital lawyer Helen Garlick maps clearly the various routes that can be taken.

A CHOICE OF PENGUINS

Trail of Havoc Patrick Marnham

In this brilliant piece of detective work, Patrick Marnham has traced the steps of Lord Lucan from the fateful night of 7 November 1974 when he murdered his children's nanny and attempted to kill his ex-wife. As well as being a fascinating investigation, the book is also a brilliant portrayal of a privileged section of society living under great stress.

Light Years Gary Kinder

Eduard Meier, an uneducated Swiss farmer, claims since 1975 to have had over 100 UFO sightings and encounters with 'beamships' from the Pleiades. His evidence is such that even the most die-hard sceptics have been unable to explain away the phenomenon.

And the Band Played On Politics, People and the AIDS Epidemic
Randy Shilts

Written after years of extensive research by the only American journalist to cover the epidemic full-time, *And the Band Played On* is a masterpiece of reportage and a tragic record of mismanaged institutions and scientific vendettas, of sexual politics and personal suffering.

The Return of a Native Reporter Robert Chesshyre

Robert Chesshyre returned to Britain in 1985 from the United States, where he had spent four years as the *Observer*'s correspondent. This is his devastating account of the country he came home to: intolerant, brutal, grasping and politically and economically divided. It is a nation, he asserts, struggling to find a role.

Women and Love Shere Hite

In this culmination of *The Hite Report* trilogy, 4,500 women provide an eloquent testimony to the disturbingly unsatisfying nature of their emotional relationships and point to what they see as the causes. *Women and Love* reveals a new cultural perspective in formation: as women change the emotional structure of their lives, they are defining a fundamental debate over the future of our society.

A SELECTION OF BOOKS ON SOUTH AFRICA

I Write What I Like   Steve Biko

More than a decade after Biko's death in detention in 1977, this book continues to cry out against the continuing tyranny of white South Africa. 'Like Nelson Mandela's *No Easy Walk to Freedom*, Biko's selfless pieces of thought, resilience and longer-term faith in a humanely shared planet will influence South Africa's transition to majority rule' – *Tribune*

Cry Freedom   John Briley

Written by award-winning scriptwriter John Briley, the book of Richard Attenborough's powerful film. Beginning with Donald Woods's first encounter with Steve Biko, it follows their friendship, their political activism and their determination to fight minority rule to Steve Biko's death and Donald Woods's dramatic escape. It is both a thrilling adventure and a bold political statement.

The Apartheid Handbook   Roger Omond

A guide to South Africa's everyday racist policies.
'Should be required reading in schools and colleges as well as legislatures all over the world . . . a revealing study' – *BBC World Service*

A SELECTION OF BOOKS ON SOUTH AFRICA

Two major books by banned journalist Donald Woods

Biko   Revised Edition

The life and brutal death of the founder of the Black Consciousness Movement. 'Courageous and passionate . . . Mr Woods's brave attack on the shabby and ultimately murderous expedients of society dominated by fear and greed should serve as both an inspiration and a warning' – *Sunday Times*

Asking for Trouble

By 1977 Donald Woods, editor of the *Daily Dispatch* in South Africa, had made his disdain of apartheid very clear. He was banned from editing his newspaper. The growth of personal attacks on him and his family, along with the death of Steve Biko, political activist and close friend of Woods, compelled him to flee the country. This book is an inspiring portrait of a courageous and uncompromising man at war with justice.

Biko and *Asking for Trouble* formed the basis of Richard Attenborough's film *Cry Freedom*.